CREATURES *of* HABITAT

The Changing Nature of Wildlife and Wild Places
in Utah and the Intermountain West

T0308744

© MARK PARCHMAN

Black-footed ferret cubs.

CREATURES *of* HABITAT

The Changing Nature of Wildlife and Wild Places

in Utah and the Intermountain West

by Mark Gerard Hengesbaugh

Dan Miller, Photo Editor
Foreword by Barry Scholl

Utah State University Press
Logan, Utah

Copyright © 2001 Mark Gerard Hengesbaugh
All rights reserved

Utah State University Press
Logan, Utah 84322-7800

Manufactured in the United States of America
Printed on acid-free paper

Cover photo—Ron Stewart
Back cover photos—Black bear, Mark Parchman
                Kit fox pups, Bob Sutton
Pen-and-ink illustrations—Karen Riddell / *Sports Guide*
Maps—Dan Miller
Cover design—Dan Miller
Book design—Mark Hengesbaugh

Chapters in this book were previously published in the same or similar form in the following places: Gila Monster, *Sports Guide*, Mar. 2000; Spotted Frog, *Sports Guide*, July 1998; Loggerhead Shrike, *Sports Guide*, Nov. 1999; Mexican Spotted Owl, *Sports Guide*, Jan. 2000; Pika, *Sports Guide*, Dec. 1999; Moss Campion, *Sports Guide*, June 1999; Desert Tortoise, *Sports Guide*, Mar. 1999; East Shore Great Salt Lake, *Sports Guide*, Aug./Sept. 1999; Flying Squirrels, *Sports Guide*, July 1999; Bison, *Sports Guide*, Nov. 1998; Pronghorn, *Sports Guide*, Feb. 1999; Peccary, *Sports Guide*, Jan. 1999; Burke's Mustard, *Sports Guide*, Dec. 1998; Whooping Crane, *Sports Guide*, Aug./Sept. 1998; Black-footed Ferret, *Sports Guide*, Apr. 1998; Utah Prairie Dog, *Sports Guide*, May 1998; Bighorn Sheep, *Sports Guide*, May 1997; Burrowing Owl, *Sports Guide*, June 1998; Utah's Island Syndrome Extinctions, *Sports Guide*, Nov. 1996; Weeds, *Sports Guide*, May 1999; Jordan River Restoration, *Sports Guide*, Apr. 1999; Treasure Buried Beneath Lake Powell, *Mountain Times*, Oct. 1996; Skier Numbers Dwindle, But Ski Areas Expand, *Mountain Times*, Jan. 1997; What Harm Can a Ski Run Do? *Mountain Times*, Jan. 1997; Destination Resorts: Can They Ski a Flat Market, *Utah Business*, Dec./Jan. 1998; Golf Courses, *Sports Guide*, June 1997; Who's Calling the Shots? *Mountain Times*, Mar. 1997; The Decline of Hunting and Habitat, *Mountain Times*, Oct. 1997; Tough Times for Adolescent Predators, *Mountain Times*, Mar. 1997; Desert Lore in St. George, *Salt Lake* magazine, Mar./Apr. 2000; The Nature Conservancy of Utah, Racing Against Extinction, *Sports Guide*, Dec. 1996; Birding the Beehive State, *Salt Lake* magazine, Mar./Apr. 1999; Nevada's Desert National Wildlife Range, *Sports Guide*, Feb. 1997; Cabeza Prieta, *Sports Guide*, Feb. 1998.

Library of Congress Cataloging-in-Publication Data

Hengesbaugh, Mark Gerard.
   Creatures of habitat : the changing nature of wildlife and wild places
in Utah and the intermountain West / by Mark Gerard Hengesbaugh ; Dan
Miller, photo editor ; foreword by Barry Scholl.
      p. cm.
   ISBN 0-87421-417-3 (pbk.)
   1. Zoology—Utah. 2. Habitat (Ecology)—Utah. 3. Zoology—Great
Basin. 4. Habitat (Ecology)—Great Basin. I. Title.
   QL208 .H46 2001
   591.9792—dc21
                                    2001000415

In memory of

Bernard L. Hengesbaugh, 1918–1999
William G. Henige, 1928–1999
Larry Baughan, 1937–1999

Mojave Desert, desert tortoise habitat.

© DAN MILLER

Acknowledgments

Thanks to everyone who lent their support for this book or who encouraged me to write it, especially my wife, Jean. Thanks to Dan Miller for his tireless work in gathering photos for the book and his uncompromisingly high standards for judging them. Thanks to Barry Scholl for writing the foreword, which includes compliments I don't deserve—but am leaving in. Thanks to Drew Ross, who, when he was editor of *Sports Guide* magazine, asked me to write a monthly column on endangered, or just interesting, native plants and animals. Thanks to Karen Riddell who took great care and applied her considerable skill in creating the pen-and-ink illustrations in this book as part of her work for *Sports Guide*. Thanks, too, to all the wildlife biologists and other scientists who patiently answered my questions and reviewed my manuscripts. Although I write often about natural history, I am not a scientist. The scientific facts and theories in this book were gleaned from published sources or from scientists themselves.

© DAN MILLER

Utah's San Rafael Swell.

Contents

PART THREE—WHAT DOES THE FUTURE HOLD?

Foreword
Lessons from song dogs

Barry Scholl

A few years ago, while camping in a remote canyon (I forget exactly where), I was shocked from sleep by a sound that has stayed with me ever since.

I've been sleeping on the ground for more years than I care to remember and have squandered countless nights entombed in a sleeping bag futilely trying to dislodge the pebbles that had somehow lodged under my back during the night. But I had never been so violently dragged from a deep sleep. Undiminished by a city's glare, stars soared overhead, big as dinner plates, and a satellite blinked in its ongoing orbit around the Earth like a blue nightlight, the only sign that another human construct existed in the entire universe. Wrapped to my chin in a mummy bag against the bite of early spring air, I decided the sound that had awakened me came from a dream.

Then the coyote howled again. First one, then a second, and, I thought, a third, they sang a ragged, undulating chorus that was neither nearby nor far away. In the close canyon, the howls seemed to originate from the top of each butte and beyond each boulder, like a troupe of ventriloquist song dogs. Spurred by a deep racial memory, the hairs on the back of my neck were suddenly stiff as quills. I unzipped my bag, reached for the dim shapes of my boots, and decided to spend the remainder of the night in my truck.

Then something happened, something that didn't seem too significant at the time but in the intervening years has gone on to assume greater meaning. Consciously wrestling against every image perpetuated by popular culture, I took a deep breath, then another, and lay back down in my bag, hands crossed behind my head, intent on remaining where I was. Intellectually, I understood that the trio of coyote musicians (at least I

Barry Scholl is editor-in-chief of *Utah Outdoors* and author of *Utah, a Guide to the State.*

thought there were three; as they were in Trickster mode, there could easily have been as many as six or as few as two) presented me absolutely no threat. But it took a while to convince my slamming heart of that fact. Just think of them as dogs, I reminded myself—not as the opportunistic heirs to a mantle abdicated when Big Bad Wolf went out for lunch and never came back.

That worked, sort of, though if I dozed off, it was only fitfully. Ignoring my presence, the coyotes continued their on-and-off practice session (one animal in particular seemed to be having trouble mastering his part and repeated the same three-note figure over and over until his compatriots were satisfied and once again began howling lustily). When the sky at last began to perceptibly brighten, the coyotes grew silent, padding off to their dens to do whatever coyotes do with their days. But I could swear one of them paused partway up the trail, turned around, and aimed a farewell yip my way.

As outdoor drama, it may not have rivaled Ed Abbey's encounter with the bullsnakes in *Desert Solitaire* or Peter Matthiessen's pursuit of the elusive (and possibly illusory) snow leopard in that same-titled book, but my Coyote Concert, as I later dubbed it, affected me in ways my direct encounters with wildlife haven't. Maybe because it was an unexpected encounter, something that could never be replicated, I took it as a kind of reminder of what a remarkable place the world can be if only we open our senses to experience its wonders.

As I read this marvelous book, I found myself recalling that experience. It goes without saying that Hengesbaugh's a gifted writer—evocative, passionate, at turns dismayed by how much damage has been done to our planet's fellow inhabitants and guardedly optimistic about what can be done to mitigate future damage. Like the naturalist author David Quammen, who once confided to me that he was "hopeful but not optimistic" about the future of the planet's open spaces and endangered species, Hengesbaugh is, at the core, a pragmatist with a heart.

And, it must be added, a finely developed sense of the absurd. Hengesbaugh delights in the unlikely facts of wild creatures and happily shares them with us, his readers. Thus, we are introduced to butt-kicking pikas, bison wrestle-mania, and (my personal favorite) owls that ward off predators by perfectly imitating a rattlesnake's buzz. Who ever would have guessed that nature's denizens represented such a menagerie? So overjoyed was I with the creatures that inhabit these vividly alive pages that I wanted nothing more than to put the book momentarily aside and wrestle my way to the top of the nearest tree, in search of a flying squirrel.

But once I came down to resume my reading, there would be no shortage of sobering information awaiting me, as Hengesbaugh points out: Glen Canyon, for the time being at least, is gone—sacrificed to provide Las Vegas casinos with overflowing fountains and Los Angeles with sparkling swimming pools. The state's few remaining black bear and cougar are pursued in the name of "sport," and amphibians (a barometer species of the planet's environmental health) are disappearing at an alarming rate. Meanwhile, mankind, despite increasingly desperate insistence to the contrary, does not exist apart from the health of the planet.

In fact, one of the most remarkable elements of this remarkable book is Hengesbaugh's ability to vividly link cause and effect, thereby illustrating the interconnectedness of life. Thus, as we eradicate wolves, coyotes flow into their empty niche. And when we respond to a burgeoning coyote population by poisoning, trapping, shooting, and otherwise attempting to exterminate them, the coyotes react quite sensibly by bearing more pups at a younger age.

In the end, Hengesbaugh's achievement is that this work is neither a blank indictment of human development nor a justification for reckless forms of it. Like the coyotes I witnessed that night, nature can be—frequently is—unpredictable. And in spite of our sheath of civilization, we humans are nature. Like the cow parsnip, loggerhead shrike, and black-footed ferret, we are all "creatures of habitat."

And for reminding us of that fact, we should applaud Mark Hengesbaugh for this book. 🦎

Kit fox pups.

© BOB SUTTON

Introduction
How well do you know your neighbors?

From seep-watered hanging gardens in redrock canyons to flying squirrels on wooded plateaus, the Intermountain West is a celebration of unique plants, animals, and places. With contrasting geographical regions—Rocky Mountains, Great Basin, Colorado Plateau—we're blessed with a natural heritage that includes some of the world's rarest and most fascinating plants and animals.

This is no exaggeration. Approximately one in ten of Utah's native plant species grow nowhere else in the world. Another example: black-footed ferrets, recently reintroduced into eastern Utah, are considered the rarest mammal on earth. The talents of the native plants and animals with whom we share these landscapes are remarkable as well. A brine shrimp-powered shorebird named Wilson's phalarope flies nonstop from the Great Salt Lake to Argentina each year on an equivalent energy expenditure of the fat grams in three Snickers bars. The hardy moss campion plant flowers on rocky Wasatch peaks hammered by Arctic-caliber weather.

By enduring things we can't bear, by going places we can't fit, and by seeing things we can't see, native plants and animals link us to a world beyond our direct experience. Yet, we know so little about them. Like most Americans, an ordinary citizen in the Intermountain West can instantly recognize a hundred international corporate logos but can name fewer than a dozen native plants. This is a result of our increasingly urban lifestyles. In 1940, nine of ten Utahns lived in rural areas, such as ranches, farms, and small towns that are near natural landscapes; today, nine of ten Utahns live in urban areas.

This disconnect with the natural world works against us as citizens who are heirs to an irreplaceable natural legacy. We wonder, "Why *not* build a highway through this swamp land? Why *not* dam this river?" If we continue with this same lack of understanding, much of our inherited natural wealth—many of these native plants and animals—will continue to dwindle in number and disappear.

1

After all, the extinction of native species is not caused by overhunting in today's Intermountain West; it's driven by habitat destruction. As open spaces such as ranches, farms, and native landscapes are converted to highways, strip malls, subdivisions, mountain cabins, and ski runs for the convenience of our growing urban population, native plants and animals in their path are destroyed or driven out. Often we laypeople think displaced wildlife simply move elsewhere when a new subdivision is built. Not so, biologists tell us. Any other suitable habitat for them is already occupied by animals defending that territory for themselves. Instead, displaced animals usually die without successfully reproducing and rearing young; it's a death sentence for their lineage.

Death by habitat loss is simple to understand when you take a fish out of water. It's more complicated—but just as certain—when we deprive an avocet of its Great Salt Lake marsh during the migratory season or a Burke's mustard wildflower of its specialized niche on Mt. Allen or a cougar of the large territory it needs to roam. Then, losing one native species of plant or animal in an area changes the habitat, and this has a cascading effect; when one species dies out, so may five or six others that depended upon it. Our native landscapes are a complex weave of plant and animal interactions. We don't get to choose to keep what we believe are the most beneficial species and let others go. A rare native bee you don't especially care about may be the only thing that can pollinate a brilliant wildflower you'd really like to keep.

It's a big problem—literally. Big, valuable spaces coveted by humans are occupied by unique native plants and animals that need these landscapes left in a natural condition in order to survive over the long haul. Our historical momentum and cultural drift is to consider native landscapes as either expendable or inexhaustible. The wastefulness of this perspective is stunning, like burning one-of-a-kind books. In the same way libraries preserve our cultural heritage in manuscripts, so do these natural landscapes safeguard our biological legacy of native species.

In one sense, it is a simple problem. We humans can choose which landscapes to use, native plants and animals cannot. So the question is, will we choose to preserve these remaining natural spaces and allow our wealth of native wildlife to continue? I believe that if we know what needs to be done to conserve native wildlife and habitat—and why—we're likely to do it.

It's your natural heritage, so read on. 🌿

© BRENT R. PAULL

Burrowing owl.

Canyonlands National Park, Mexican spotted owl habitat.

PART I
What's Happening to Wildlife?

© DAN MILLER

Mexican spotted owls.

© STEVE HOWE / THIRD PLANET

CHAPTER ONE

Animal life on the edge
Does it take a special breed?

Does it take a special breed to live on the edge? Or does living on the edge create a special breed? Small groups of animals who live on the outer limits of their species' range—such as Utah's Mexican spotted owls, desert tortoises, and Gila monsters and Arizona's peccaries—encounter a tougher environment than individuals of the same species who live in the optimal conditions of their core habitat. But far from being sideshows, these small populations that survive the challenging conditions on the fringe of their habitat make a critical contribution to the evolution and survival of their entire species, scientists say.

MEXICAN SPOTTED OWL

Utah's Mexican spotted owls live on the edge—literally. These one-pound feathered hunting machines perch and pounce on woodrats and bats from the ledges of towering cliffs in southern Utah's steep-walled canyons. On the edge figuratively, they live at the extreme northwestern fringe of Mexican spotted owl habitat, which stretches south from Utah's Colorado Plateau to central Mexico.

In the sheer, narrow sandstone canyons of places such as Zion National Park and Canyonlands National Park, the Utah group of Mexican spotted owls meets especially challenging conditions. For example, they lack old-growth forests that spotted owls usually require for nesting. In addition, they must adjust to temperatures that are alternately scorching and freezing. Here on the rugged northern border of the Colorado Plateau, Utah's isolated Mexican spotted owl population demonstrates an adaptability and hardiness that one day may prove crucial to preserving the declining spotted owl species as a whole, scientists say. Or this small population on the edge of its range may just wink out of existence.

AS A GROUP, OWLS have survived a long time, at least 38 million years. And among all birds of prey, they own the franchise on night hunting. Eagles and hawks use daylight and speed to nab prey, but owls have another strategy.

With oversized pupils in eyes that are surrounded by light-gathering feathered facial disks, an owl's stereoscopic vision is three to four times better at night than human eyesight. But most people figure that. What's less well known is that an owl's facial disks also collect and direct sound into two large ear openings concealed on the disks' periphery. This enables the owl to hear prey that's quiet as a mouse. In addition, one of the owl's ear openings is higher on the head than the other, allowing an owl to pinpoint the location of concealed prey by comparing the timing and intensity of faint sounds funneled into the offset ears. These facial disks allow an owl's eyes and ears to work together. For this reason, their eyeballs don't rotate in sockets; their entire head swivels three-quarters of a turn in either direction.

Camouflage is a tactic owls have perfected. Owls are difficult enough to spot behind chicken wire in a zoo, even when a nameplate tells you an owl's in there. It's no wonder that we seldom sight motionless, perched owls in the wild. An owl will roost on a tree branch near its trunk, and when it does, it blends perfectly with the tree bark and the shadows.

While eagles and hawks make a whooshing noise in flight, the owl's ultra-soft feathers and broad, rounded wings are designed to muffle sound. Silent flight allows an owl to listen while cruising and to surprise its prey, which typically has keen hearing as well.

Spotted owls, one of 20 owl species in North America, are medium-size. A foot and a half tall, their plumage is dark brown with white spots on the

MEXICAN SPOTTED OWL

Status: State Threatened.

Estimated Number Remaining: 2,200 throughout their range. Utah has 120 breeding sites.

Tips for Viewing: Dusk is the best time. Look in steep walled canyons, they may be roosting on tree branches.

head and shoulder and a lighter brown breast and belly. The facial disks are light brown and the eyes are black. Though a spotted owl has a wingspan of three-and-one-half feet, with wings folded it will fit into a shoebox.

Mexican spotted owls, like the ones living in southern Utah, are one of three subspecies of spotted owl. The California spotted owl is considered uncommon, while the northern spotted owl of Oregon and Washington is rare. The northern spotted owl got lots of ink a few years back when it was listed by the federal government as threatened. In the Northwest, spotted owls prefer to live in the multi-layered canopy of mature—old-growth—forests but will live in a younger forest if it has dense canopy and protected nest areas. Preserving these increasingly rare woodlands for spotted owls clashes with loggers' desire to continue cutting them for timber.

Where you can see Mexican spotted owls

★ Boise

★ Carson City

★ Salt Lake City

o

A lighter color and more spotty than the other two kinds of spotted owls, Mexican spotted owls range from southern Colorado and Utah through New Mexico, west Texas, and Arizona and into central Mexico. They are the only spotted owls that live in Utah.

★ Phoenix

Here on the northwestern edge of the Colorado Plateau, Mexican spotted owls live in narrow sandstone canyons. "In Utah, Mexican spotted owls are canyon specialists," says Frank Howe, Utah Division of Wildlife Resources (DWR) non-game avian coordinator. "In other places they are mature forest specialists."

The caves and cavities in cliffs they inhabit keep daytime temperatures cool for the birds. Dr. David Willey, a professor of biology at the University of Alaska-Fairbanks who has studied owls on the Colorado Plateau since 1988, says he believes the "steep-walled canyons provide them with protection from heat, from predators, and act as a nursery for the young." Woodrats, the Mexican spotted owl's favorite meal, also live in the canyons, as do bats, which the owls snatch in midflight, according to Willey. "Bats make up about 9 percent of their diet."

In difficult years when their prey is scarce, Mexican spotted owls can forego breeding. "They are a long-lived species," notes Howe, "so they can afford to hold off raising young when necessary."

Spotted owl pairs mate for life and begin to breed at two to three years old. The female incubates a clutch of two or three eggs while the male delivers food to the nest. The female is larger than the male, "maybe to keep her mate in line or to protect the nest from predators," speculates Willey. The eggs hatch in May. Young owls can fly, weakly, at about six weeks and can capture insects at about ten weeks. Juveniles hang out with their parents until late summer or fall, then they split to find their own territories and mates.

That first year is risky for young Mexican spotted owls. "We've recorded 90 percent mortality in juveniles," reports Willey. Juveniles usually die from starvation and predation, which go hand-in-hand. "Lack of food makes them weak and more susceptible to disease and predators, such as great horned owls, golden eagles, and red tail hawks."

Utah has about 120 Mexican spotted owl breeding sites. In their entire range, the Mexican spotted owl population is estimated at approximately 2,200 and they appear to be declining at a rate of 7 percent per year. They are federally listed as a threatened species. (A threatened species is one that soon is likely to become endangered. A species listed as endangered is considered in danger of extinction in all of, or in a significant portion of, its range).

To survive over time, scientists believe an animal species like the spotted owl needs to maintain a diverse gene pool. This allows the species the potential to weather natural disasters, such as a virus that wipes out all genetically similar birds, or an unnatural disaster, such as loss of suitable nesting sites to logging in old-growth forests. Small subpopulations, like the northern Colorado Plateau's Mexican spotted owls, that adapt and reproduce despite the intense conditions on the edge of their habitat range represent a robust genetic mix for the spotted owl species as a whole.

At the same time, these "small subpopulations on the periphery of their habitat can wink right out," Willey says. All animal populations fluctuate in size from year to year in response to favorable or unfavorable conditions. Small groups can disappear quickly because for them, a population of zero is not far away.

"It's this loss of genetic signal that we need to avoid," Willey notes. "Otherwise, just by chance, as the population declines, we might end up with a group of owls that's not very adaptable to coming changes. For example, maybe we'd end up with a variety of Mexican spotted owls that can't handle extreme heat or cold."

In that sense, Utah's small group of Mexican spotted owls is not just a sideshow in a larger conservation problem, Willey says. "Given trends like global warming and the current conversion of habitat to more open, hot environments," Utah's Mexican spotted owl population may prove key to the long-term adaptation and survival of the spotted owl species as a whole.

DESERT TORTOISE

To survive in southwestern Utah's Mojave Desert, it helps if you look like a rock, store water like a camel, and tunnel like a gopher. In addition, if your cruising speed in open country is three hours per mile, you need armor, like a knight.

The desert tortoise—Utah's only native turtle—has all these qualities. As a reptile, it belongs to the order of backboned animals that first adapted to arid turf hundreds of millions of years ago. The turtle's hard-shelled design is so successful that it remains nearly unchanged since the dinosaur era. Nature, however, did not prepare these armored reptiles to live in contemporary southern Utah's golf courses, strip malls, and subdivisions—or to survive infections carried by abandoned pet turtles.

WITH SOLEMN, AMBER EYES, leathery neck, and a plodding gait, the desert tortoise is easily recognized as a member of the turtle family. An adult desert tortoise is more than a foot long and weighs in at fifteen pounds. Its oblong black-to-tan shell serves as part of its bone structure; spine and ribs are fused to it. The tortoise has four stout legs and the hind two are shaped like shovels.

It's these built-in trowels that allow the desert tortoise to thrive despite the Mojave's wild temperature swings. Here, the mercury soars to 115 degrees in summer, then plunges to freezing in winter. Because turtles have no internal mechanism for controlling their body temperature, you'd think they would never survive in such a place. Just a few feet underground, however, the temperature

---

DESERT TORTOISE

Status: State Endangered.

Estimated Number Remaining: Red Cliff Desert Preserve near St. George has approximately 5,000 according to 1999 count.

Tips for Viewing: In the Mojave Desert, look for them in washes or on rock ledges in the morning hours during May and early June.

The Mojave, desert tortoise habitat.

© DAN MILLER

of the Earth remains around 55 degrees year-round, varying only by a few degrees. Desert tortoises take advantage of this and dig burrows in which to hole-up when the temperatures are extreme. In the winter they hibernate in tunnels that may be thirty feet deep, while in summer they shelter in shallower dens.

The Mojave sunlight is scorching and rain is scarce, so the desert tortoise is a water miser. Its skin and shell are waterproof and won't dry out easily. The tortoise's bladder is a reservoir in which it can store and reclaim water for months. It depends on the grass and plants it eats for most of its water but will tank up on standing water when available, increasing its weight by 40 percent in the process. In addition, desert tortoises sometimes collect rainwater by digging shallow, pan-like depressions in the ground.

Like humans, desert tortoises have a life expectancy of about 80 years; but they don't reach sexual maturity until their late teens. Courtship begins in spring for these reptiles. An amorous male will stick out its neck and bob his head up and down or will even bite or ram a female to get her attention.

A female, once her eggs are fertilized, digs a shallow nest and buries a clutch of about a half-dozen eggs. In the late summer or fall, tortoise hatchlings dig themselves out. About the size of a silver dollar, the hatchlings' color and shape make them nearly invisible among the desert stones. But because it takes seven years for their shells to harden, young tortoises are nearly defenseless against ravens and other predators; only about three in a hundred make it to maturity.

If lucky enough to survive, the armored shell serves an adult desert tortoise well. When caught in the open by a predator, it will retract its head and fold in its legs, making it difficult for an animal to maim or kill it. "A mountain lion is the only predator that can crack an adult's shell," says Ann McLuckie, a wildlife biologist with Utah's Division of Wildlife Resources who studies desert tortoises. A coyote can only gnaw off a tortoise's limb if it can fasten onto it, she notes. Once in its burrow, a desert tortoise can brace itself with its legs and resist mighty attempts to remove it.

Where you can see desert tortoises

★ Boise

★ Salt Lake City

★ Carson City

★ Phoenix

More than a match for predators, the desert tortoise has been successful in the Mojave. The first white settlers in the area estimated there were a thousand desert tortoises per square mile. Today, in many areas of their range—western Arizona, southern Nevada, southeastern California, as well as southwestern Utah—there are fewer than 25 per square mile. A century of overgrazing, road building, and water diversion projects in the Mojave have taken a toll.

Worse, a killer upper respiratory infection has spread from desert tortoises first captured as pets and then released into the wild. "When Californians have a captive tortoise that's sick, they release it into the wild where they think it will heal itself in nature—or some such pipe-dream," says Jerry Freilich, an ecologist who studied desert tortoises at Joshua Tree National Park for six years. "What happens is that the disease is spread into wild populations." At remote Joshua Tree he saw only a few infected tortoises, but close to population centers sick tortoises are numerous, he points out.

The upper respiratory infection is associated with major tortoise declines in California, McLuckie reports. In Utah, the disease symptoms

13

© RICK A. FRIDELL

Desert tortoise.

have been observed in desert tortoises, but the number infected is not yet known. The main threat to Utah's desert tortoises is that they're sharing their home with one of the fastest growing human populations in the United States. Washington County's golf courses, subdivisions, and strip malls are transforming the Mojave in ways to which the desert tortoise cannot adapt.

Because of alarming population declines, Utah's desert tortoise is listed as an endangered species. A habitat conservation plan in Washington County did spare 60,000 acres for a desert tortoise refuge. However, the human population growth is unrelenting here. In 1980 there were 26,000 people in the county and by 1990 the population nearly doubled; it is expected to hit 125,000 by 2010.

We can take the health of desert tortoise populations as an indicator of the well-being of the entire Mojave Desert, Freilich says. "Desert tortoises respond badly to all those things that also decline with human impacts. They don't like to be shot at with guns. They do poorly when run over . . .

Parking lots and city sprawl have bad effects on them . . . But they're not so rare that they're completely gone. Maybe we can attract human attention to their plight before it's too late."

GILA MONSTER

It has an armored hide like a dinosaur. It has venom like a rattlesnake. It has a bite like a pit bull. And it can thrive on just a few meals each year. The Gila monster is overequipped for desert survival. It's no wonder this unique reptile—the largest lizard in the U.S.—has been flicking its forked tongue into the North American breeze since the age of dinosaurs.

Gila monsters are native to southwestern Utah and to the Arizona, southern Nevada, and northern Mexico deserts. Though well known in Western folklore, few hikers see Gila monsters in the wild today. In past decades they were overcollected for exotic pets, and now, roads, subdivisions, and strip malls are taming large parts of their harsh desert turf.

Experts say Gila monsters may be the next unlucky candidate for the federal endangered species list.

"Last year we saw five Gila monsters while traveling back and forth over about 180 square miles of desert" recalls wildlife biologist McLuckie. At the time, McLuckie and her crew were traversing Washington County's Mojave counting desert tortoises. "Some of the Gila monsters were walking in washes, a few were digging at burrows," she says.

If you're lucky enough to see a Gila monster, you'll know what it is instantly. No other creature looks like a Halloween-colored sausage that's sprouted legs. Typically one-and-a-half feet long and weighing one-and-a-half to two pounds, a Gila monster has a heavy flattened head, elongated body, and stubby legs bristling with five, clawed toes. Its normally plump tail is half as long as its body. A Gila monster's color scheme is bright, like a highway construction warning sign—black stripes and marbling over an orange background that may sometimes appear yellow or salmon pink.

> **GILA MONSTER**
>
> **Status:** State Endangered.
>
> **Estimated Number Remaining:** Most recent estimate, 1985, was 450-800 in Utah.
>
> **Tips for Viewing:** In the Mojave look for wispy feet and tail tracks in sand washes during May and early June.

15

Gila monster.

© BRENT R. PAULL

The colorful hide looks beaded, or pebbled. It's actually armor in a form that was common on dinosaurs but which today is only found on the Gila monster and its cousin, the Mexican beaded lizard. This skin is made of tightly woven scales, each of which encloses a particle of rounded bone. The protective covering is woven so tightly that only the sharpest, strongest teeth can puncture it.

Despite this eye-catching coat of armor, Gila monsters are seldom seen. They have keen hearing and the ability to detect subtle ground vibrations, so it's nearly impossible to sneak up on them. In addition, their lifestyle is reclusive. When scientists put radio collars on Gila monsters in the 1970s, they discovered Gila monsters spend 95 percent of their time dormant, underground.

A Gila monster may be active only two weeks in a year, coming out in the spring to eat and to mate, then emerging irregularly after that. "All of our Gila monsters sightings last year were in May and early June," McLuckie says. It's no coincidence that spring is when their normal prey—juvenile rodents, small birds, and eggs—are most abundant.

In spring, a Gila monster hunts for food and for a mate by working washes and rocky slopes, "tasting" the air with frequent flicks of its forked tongue. Each fork of the tongue gathers separate chemical cues, creating a kind of stereo receiver arrangement. This helps a Gila monster lock in the location of odors. When it reaches a prey's nest, it digs into it with powerful claws.

As a cold-blooded creature with a low metabolism, a Gila monster requires many fewer calories than a warm-blooded animal of comparable size. And when a Gila monster eats, it gorges, consuming up to half its body weight in a single feast. One expert estimates that the eggs from three Gamble's quail nests provide all the food an adult Gila monster needs for a year. It stores extra calories as fat in its tail, so a chubby tail on a Gila monster means it is well fed, a skinny derriere means it's starving.

A healthy booty full of fat is important to both male and female Gila monsters in spring. Females must store enough food to produce eggs. Males need the calories to tussle with other males for mating privileges. These brawls are brutal, World Wrestling Federation Smackdown-like endurance contests that include everything but hurling folding chairs at each other: lateral head shoves, head bites, body rolls, and tail thrashes. They finish with a dorsal straddle of the inferior male by the winner. But afterwards, the males are all sweetness with the females, stroking them with tongue caresses, chin rubbing, and nose nudging. Female Gila monsters deliver a clutch of five to six leathery eggs that, when hatched, look like small adults, complete with choppers and venom.

Gila monsters are not aggressive toward humans. An individual will try to retreat from an encounter, and if it can't, it will hiss and may lunge at its tormentor. A Gila monster's backup defensive weapon is a bite that probably won't kill you but will make you wish you were dead. Its curved teeth are quarter-inch daggers with grooves running from base to point. The creases in each tooth help channel a toxin—which is created by modified spit glands—into puncture wounds. A Gila monster will bite and clamp down like a bulldog, grinding its powerful jaws to chew the venom into its victim.

The effect is stunning. "I worked with a herpetologist who was showing a live Gila monster's teeth during a demonstration," McLuckie remembers. "He was distracted and the Gila monster clamped down on his finger and held on. He said it was the worst pain he'd ever felt. In order to pry the Gila monster's jaws loose, he kept asking for a pencil, but it took a while for the audience to understand this bite wasn't part of the show. He said the pain was so bad that he passed out."

A Gila monster's venom inflicts immediate, severe pain and causes its victim's blood pressure to drop. Still, it's rarely fatal to anything as large as a cat, and it is considered a milder toxin than a rattlesnake's venom, a scorpion's sting, or a black widow spider's bite. But venom is an unusual weapon for a lizard. Of more than 3,000 species of lizards in the world, only two are poisonous: the Gila monster and the Mexican beaded lizard. These two are the only known creatures—living or extinct—with both venom and grooved teeth as a toxin delivery system.

A powerful digger, the Gila monster excavates its own winter den site by enlarging crevices under rocks. In summer, it may use the shaded shelter of a desert tortoise burrow or a pack rat nest as a motel in which to rest and cool down. No one knows how long a typical Gila monster lives in the wild. In captivity, they have lived to be 27. Natural mortality for them may be low. Being at the top of the food chain, adult Gila monsters appear to have no primary predator. Badgers and desert tortoises have been observed driving prowling Gila monsters away from their nests, McLuckie says, but not eating them.

However, road kill and overcollecting of Gila monsters for exotic pets in the 1950s, '60s, and '70s reduced the population. In many places where they were regularly spotted in the 1960s, they were rarely seen by 1975. State laws were passed to protect them. In 1985, the estimated population of Gila monsters in Utah was between 450 and 800, McLuckie reports. "No current estimates of their population exist. We don't know if their numbers have increased or decreased."

Scientists are interested in using Gila monster venom as a new blood pressure drug or perhaps as a diabetes medication. However, the venom is so rare that one round of experiments uses up the entire U.S. supply, according to a recent *New York Times* article.

Habitat loss hits Gila monsters especially hard. Recent research shows that individuals need their hereditary home base and won't survive transplant of more than a half mile. Utah's Gila monsters benefit from the recent Desert Tortoise Habitat Conservation Plan agreed upon in Washington County. They live in the same range as Utah's only native turtle, so by protecting tortoises, the Gila monster gets a break too.

Still, notes McLuckie, "People in our Division of Wildlife Resources office are concerned about Gila monsters. We think they may be the next endangered species listed by the federal government."

PECCARY

She busted in like a Hell's Angel at a Sunday picnic. I'd been wandering in the utter silence of southern Arizona's Sonoran desert when a nearby palo verde bush erupted. With a grunt and the papery rustle of leaves, a hairy, pig-like animal the size of a pit bull stalked into my path.

I had trespassed on a javalina's turf. And while I didn't argue territory with her then, I can point out now that the northern Sonora desert hasn't been home to her kind for all that long. Although there are about 50,000 javalinas—more correctly called collared peccaries—in the southwestern U.S. today, archaeologists say no peccary bones show up in digs in the area earlier than the 1700s. The first report of peccaries in what is now the southwestern United States came from trappers in the early 1800s.

Peccaries are a tropical species of animal whose core population inhabits South America and Mexico. Southern Arizona's collared peccaries—like the one I met—arrived here after migrating north for generations along river bottoms. These individuals are pioneering life for their kind on the extreme northern fringe of their range—Arizona, New Mexico, Texas. For any creature, life on the edge of its habitat is especially challenging. A peccary for example, unlike a desert-adapted mammal, can neither store water nor recycle it; the cactus in its diet can give it kidney disease; and, because it's tropically adapted, it has no underfur or fat

PECCARY

Status: Abundant.

Estimated Number: Approximately 50,000 in southwestern U.S.

Tips for Viewing: Walk up Sonoran washes any time of year.

© RICK A. FRIDELL

Cabeza Prieta National Wildlife Refuge, Arizona,
peccary habitat.

layer to keep it warm on frosty winter nights in a desert where dry air allows temps to drop to freezing.

ALTHOUGH PECCARIES LOOK AND ACT much like pigs, they are a distant relation. Pigs are native to Europe and Asia, brought here as domestic livestock. Peccaries are the only pig-like species naturally occurring in North or South America.

A peccary has tiny ears and weak eyes set in an oversized wedge-shaped head. Its disk-shaped snout is both strong and very sensitive—it can lift logs as well as sniff out roots several inches underground. Its mouth has two tusk-like canine teeth useful for self-defense and for cutting roots. Its rump is small and terminates in a short tail. Collared peccaries—the ones commonly called javalinas—have long bristly charcoal fur, stand over a foot and a half high, are three feet long and may weigh up to 60 pounds. The "collar" is a pale stripe of fur that rings its shoulders.

Peccaries are the only wild, hoofed mammal of the Western Hemisphere with a year-round breeding season; consequently litters—usually pairs—may be born any time of year. Pregnancy is five months long and young reach sexual maturity in less than a year. Peccaries live in parties of up to two dozen individuals with a strict pecking order, and they practice group self-defense. They don't appear to be built for speed, but can sprint 20 miles per hour for short distances.

Where you can see peccaries

★ Boise

★ Carson City

★ Salt Lake City

★ Phoenix

Though there are no documented cases of a collared peccary injuring a human, they do have a reputation for being ornery. Encounters between peccaries and untrained dogs usually end in a dead or crippled pooch; however, in fights with dogs, peccaries are not the aggressors. In the wild, peccaries are known to chase off bobcats and coyotes, their primary predators other than humans.

Peccaries aren't adapted to endure many days without drinking water. They drink from cattle tanks and springs, but when it gets dry in the northern Sonora desert, they pass up their preferred food—acorns, palo verde beans, and roots—to eat mostly prickly pear cactus for its high water

Peccary, also known as javalina.

© EDDIE COCKING / ARIZONA GAME AND FISH DEPARTMENT

content. However, this prickly pear diet is low in nutrients and high in an acid that can cause them kidney disease.

Because they are tropical animals, collared peccaries have no built-in insulation to keep them warm during the chilly Sonoran winters. So, they change their behavior to adapt. Rather than nap during the day, which is their natural schedule in their core tropical habitat, collared peccaries in Arizona forage during the warmth of the day in the winter. At night, they huddle together for warmth. Still, on this northern end of their habitat, peccaries sometimes die of lung infections brought on from the stress of enduring cold temperatures.

These extreme conditions that peripheral populations of javalinas encounter—those that may cause kidney disease and lung infections in individuals—are what biologists call "intense selection pressures." Individuals who don't survive the challenge don't pass on their genes as frequently as those who do. It's evolution speeded up. "On the periphery of their habitat, individuals of a species encounter challenging conditions. Because their gene flow is often somewhat isolated (little mating with members of the core population), evolution may occur faster here," notes Eric A. Rickart, curator of mammals for the Utah Natural History Museum. A core population of a species lives in optimal conditions, and the sheer number of individuals dilutes their genetic differences, Rickart says. A group on the edge that has a different gene pool may evolve over time into a whole new species if it becomes completely isolated. But the evidence is theoretical, he adds.

As the only individuals left alive when a massive epidemic occurs in the main population, groups on the edge are vital to the survival of a species, points out Bob Walters, Watchable Wildlife coordinator for the Utah Division of Wildlife Resources. This recently happened when tens of thousands of eared grebes died of cholera on the Great Salt Lake. The surviving fringe populations of eared grebes "now become especially important for repopulating after this die-off," he observes.

Global warming, which promises to shift the habitat range of all plants and animals, may make the diverse gene pools that edge populations contribute even more important to the long-term survival of each species. Unless we preserve the diversity that these groups living on the edge of their habitat bring to their own species, we may cause, if not the end of that species, perhaps a major limitation on the way it can evolve and survive. ❧

© BRENT R. PAULL

Burrowing owl.

CHAPTER TWO

Endangered animal communities
The keystone concept.

Prairie dogs are a keystone species. A keystone is a particular block of stone in the central position of an arched entranceway; all the other blocks lean on it for support. The keystone locks the stones of the arch in place and, if you remove it, the arch collapses. Like a keystone, prairie dogs are the central species in a natural community that supports a large complement of other kinds of creatures, such as black-footed ferrets and burrowing owls. Biologists have identified more than 170 species that rely on prairie dog towns in some way. Each of these species is like a block of stone in the archway, and if we exterminate prairie dogs, we lose these other species as well. "The listing of animals that rely on prairie dogs reads like a catalog of rare, endangered, or threatened species," says Bill Stroh, a wildlife biologist for the U.S. Bureau of Land Management (BLM). Burrowing owls, kit foxes, sage grouse, Swainson's hawks—all species whose long-term survival is questionable today—depend on prairie dogs for food, shelter, or both.

UTAH PRAIRIE DOG

When you drive south on I-15 through Cedar City, scan the median strip between the north and southbound lanes near the 200 North interchange. Here you'll see—sandwiched between four lanes of roaring interstate traffic— a thriving colony of rare Utah prairie dogs.

25

There may be only 5,000 individuals of this species of ground-dwelling squirrel remaining on Earth, mainly because humans don't want prairie dogs on their ranches and farms. Massive poisoning campaigns decimated the colonies on private land. Now, the Utah prairie dog—one of three species of prairie dog that live in the state—survives only in seven southwestern Utah counties.

These squirrels-without-trees are fun to watch. They're energetic in the daytime and they don't store food in their burrows, so you can observe them eat and play in daylight. Also, prairie dogs clip the tall vegetation around their burrows, which makes them easier to spot.

Individually, Utah prairie dogs are unimposing. They are about a foot long, stocky, and have short legs, ears, and tails. Their fur is buff or light brown with a paler underbelly. They weigh about two pounds and have sharp claws for tunneling. Like the four species of prairie dogs that survive in other places, Utah prairie dogs live in burrows in small family groups adjacent to other prairie dog households.

When on the surface feeding, several individuals stand guard on hind legs and watch for approaching trouble while their relatives eat. The warning barks, squeaks, and yips that serve as alarms—delivered with a tail flip, head snap, outstretched paws—are elements of the world's most sophisticated animal language. "Specific prairie dog vocalizations seem to be tied to aerial predators, terrestrial predators, or humans, and they vary with the level of danger," notes Keith Day, native species biologist with the Utah Division of Wildlife Resources. The more enthusiastically a watchdog delivers the alarm, the more immediate the threat. When the warning is sounded, all dogs within earshot disappear into burrows.

Prairie dog burrows are elaborate underground condos. What we see on

Where you can see Utah prairie dogs

★ Boise

★ Carson City

★ Salt Lake City

★ Phoenix

UTAH PRAIRIE DOG

Status: State Threatened.

Estimated Number: 5,000.

Tips for Viewing: In open country in southwestern Utah, look for small mounds with heads peering out or adults standing watch.

Utah prairie dog colony next to I-15 outside of Cedar City.

© DAN MILLER

the surface are small volcano-shaped mounds drilled with six-inch diameter holes. Prairie dogs work hard to maintain those mounds because they prevent their homes from flooding during a hard rain.

The burrows twist down into the earth for 10 to 15 feet. Then they branch into several horizontal tunnels that hold grass nests. Down there, prairie dogs are safe from temperature extremes and from most predators.

A typical Utah prairie dog family includes one adult male, several females, and pups from the past year. Each family defends its territory from other prairie dogs. Within families, prairie dogs kiss, nuzzle, groom, and touch teeth to reinforce their kinship. In the spring, boundaries between families relax to allow interbreeding. Pups come in litters of three to five, and emerge from their burrows to forage at six weeks.

Though prairie dogs are known as vegetarians and prefer to munch on grasses and broad-leafed weeds, they also eat insects, particularly grasshoppers and crickets. They don't drink water but instead get all the moisture they need from the food they eat.

Utah prairie dog.

© RICK A. FRIDELL

Because Utah prairie dogs are digging, spawning, and fertilizing machines, their colonies support a vast array of local plants and animals, from burrowing owls, kit foxes, sage grouse, and Swainson's hawks to many kinds of toads, spiders, salamanders, ants, and beetles. "The trouble is that Utah prairie dogs prefer the same land that is most productive for humans," Day says. "And the main problem now is that most of them are on private land."

Next to humans, plague is the Utah prairie dog's worst enemy. They have no immunity to it, and a colony can go from 1,000 individuals to zero very quickly.

Iron County, where the Cedar City colony thrives, has a habitat conservation plan for the Utah prairie dog. The goal of wildlife officials is to establish three self-sustaining populations on public land. The plan is supported by the Utah Division of Wildlife Resources and by Iron County, said Marilet Zablan, a U.S. Fish and Wildlife Service biologist who has worked on it for the past two years. The plan will protect some existing habitat and care for Utah prairie dogs displaced from private property, she says.

Just as importantly, it will have an educational component, which may include an area for animal watchers to view a prairie dog town. "We want to turn around negative public opinion about Utah prairie dogs," Zablan says. "We want to show that they are unique and an indicator of a healthy ecosystem. We want people to know that the Utah prairie dog can coexist with man."

BURROWING OWL

What bird borrows a rodent's nest, a cow's smell, and a rattlesnake's warning sound? Here's a hint: you can see them most times of the year in a small park in suburban Salt Lake City.

Imitation is the most effective form of self-defense for the stubby-tailed, long-legged, ground-dwelling burrowing owl. And, thanks to biologist Bob

Walters of the Utah Division of Wildlife Resources, you don't need to travel to a remote wilderness area to watch this rare and resourceful bird in its natural habitat.

Common in the Salt Lake Valley when the Mormon pioneers arrived, the number of local burrowing owls plummeted when plows furrowed the valley into farm fields. Today, those burrowing owls remaining are threatened when bulldozers blade over farm fields for subdivisions and strip malls.

Adapted to treeless plains, you'll see this vigilant small owl perched on the mound of abandoned rock squirrel or prairie dog burrows. Because they hunt and stand watch during most of the day, they're easy to spot. About the size of a prairie dog—slightly less than a foot tall—burrowing owls have a round head without ear tufts, and plumage that is checkered light and dark brown. They have oversize yellow eyes, and above each is a stroke of white feathers that looks like an eyebrow.

Where you can see burrowing owls

★ Boise

★ Salt Lake City

★ Carson City

★ Phoenix

"Burrowing owls migrate into the Salt Lake Valley in mid-March, probably from Arizona," Walters states. "The same nests are used each year, but we don't know if it's the same pairs that are nesting in them." Walters, director of DWR's Watchable Wildlife program, observed pairs of burrowing owls nest each year in an open lot, near 6700 South and 4800 West in West Valley City, Utah, that had been an informal neighborhood dumping ground. In 1994, as the rapidly growing human population closed in on them, Walters lobbied Salt Lake County to set aside a small open area for the owls as a nature preserve. Then, with the help of friends, he built a surrounding fence that protects the owl nests from the thumping that off-road vehicles had been giving them. Burrowing owls are remarkably

BURROWING OWL

Status: State Species of Special Concern.

Estimated Number: 1999 estimate is 80 to 100 pairs in Utah.

Tips for Viewing: In open landscapes, look for a small owl with a rounded head and long legs standing watch on a low mound or sitting on a fence post.

Cougar Park, burrowing owl habitat in Murray, Utah.

© DAN MILLER

tolerant of human intrusion, he notes, but four-wheelers catching air over their homes is too much.

The owls depend on finding abandoned nests of ground-dwelling mammals—in West Valley City, it's rock squirrels; other places it's prairie dog towns—to incubate their eggs and to raise their young.

Burrowing owls seem to live in permanent pairs. When they find a suitable burrow, they move in and renovate it. Digging with beak and claws, they kick loose dirt backwards and out of their new home. The male owl scouts the area and collects dried horse or cow dung to leave at the burrow entrance. The female shreds the droppings and lines the nest inches deep with it. The pungent aroma is so effective in concealing their smell that biologists have reported watching badgers sniff the entrance to burrowing owl nests and trot away, apparently confused. Scientists believe that the dung lining provides insulation and regulates humidity in the nests as well.

A female burrowing owl incubates her six to nine eggs for a month. During that time, her male partner does all the hunting and delivers meals to her. Three weeks after her eggs hatch, the young birds can hop and flap. Eventually, both mom and dad go out to hunt. The young birds wait at the burrow entrance for their parents to deliver food. If threatened, the fledg-lings retreat into their nest and make a chattering sound that perfectly imitates a rattlesnake. After eight weeks, the fledglings can practice hunting by chasing and mugging disabled bugs their parents bring them.

Unlike most owls, burrowing owls hunt during the day and at dusk. They spot prey by perching on observation points such as fence posts or prominent rocks. They have a rising and falling flight pattern, can hover, and snag meals with their talons. They chow on insects such as grasshoppers, beetles, and crickets and can snatch—on the wing—moths and dragonflies. Their diet is var-ied though: they also eat mice, lizards, snakes, small birds, and the young, unprotected pups of rock squirrels and prairie dogs.

As the young family grows and the burrow gets crowded, the owls improve their nest by enlarging it. They shov-el it out—along with the dung lining. The male stands guard day and night—except in the midday heat when no predators hunt—alert for approaching trouble. For a five-ounce animal, the burrowing owl is big-hearted: it will frighten trespassers by bobbing up and down and fluffing its feathers and will chase and strike intruders. In November when daylight is brief and temperatures dive, burrowing owls head south for the winter.

As clever and courageous as these small owls are, it remains to be seen if they can survive constant human encroachment. "The burrowing owl is a Utah Species of Special Concern because its population is declining," observes Walters. "Urban and rural expansion is squeezing them out." Campaigns to eradicate ground-dwelling mammals, such as the prairie dog, also limit the burrowing owls' nesting and food choices. "It goes to show that if we treat one animal—like the prairie dog—as vermin, it endangers other species as well," Walters notes.

But the reverse is also true. By saving a small piece of natural area for burrowing owls, Walters has provided a home and a way to make a living for other native Salt Lake Valley animals. On a recent visit to this seven-acre, postage stamp wilderness, we listened to a yellow-throated mead-owlark singing its *chirtly-chir* melody with zippity-do-dah-like optimism.

Burrowing owls.

© MARK PARCHMAN

We watched a blue-winged American kestrel—a type of falcon—hovering and swooping for bugs. A rock squirrel bolted in and out of stone crevices, then suddenly froze, eyes like black buttons and tail arched. Walters said he'd seen a red fox nearby that morning.

"These burrowing owl pairs have successfully hatched and raised young" in an area surrounded by subdivisions, Walters says. "It's one of only a half-dozen locations in the Salt Lake Valley in which they're known to exist." His only question is, will humans allow them to continue here?

BLACK-FOOTED FERRET

With any luck, alert hikers and bikers in the Uintah Basin may see the rarest mammal in North America. The U.S. Fish and Wildlife Service has released captive-bred black-footed ferrets—a squirrel-size member of the weasel family—into several healthy white-tailed prairie dog towns west of Vernal, Utah.

Black-footed ferrets are difficult to spot, but easy to identify. They have a slender, torpedo-like body and short legs. They are often seen with their long backs arched gracefully, both when walking and standing still. A black-footed ferret's coat is buff with paler buff on the underside, but its most distinctive coloration is its black mask, feet, and last quarter of its tail. Its throat, its muzzle, and a band across its forehead are white, while the top of its head is brown and it has a brown stripe down its back. The black-footed ferret is North America's only native ferret.

Though measuring just two feet long and weighing only two and a half pounds, the black-footed ferret is remarkable for its ability to snatch and kill—single-handedly—prairie dogs that are nearly its own size. One swift bite to the back of the neck nails its meal, which it then drags back to its own burrow. Prairie dogs are feisty, however, and ferrets endure cuts and scratches to the muzzle and head from their struggle.

Black-footed ferrets depend on prairie dogs for both food and shelter.

BLACK-FOOTED FERRET

Status: State Endangered.

Estimated Number: World population was 18 in 1986. Seventy-two captive-bred black-footed ferrets were reintroduced into Utah's Coyote Basin in 1999, and they are reproducing in the wild.

Tips for Viewing: They are primarily nocturnal; look for them in prairie dog towns.

Ferrets live in prairie dog burrows and dine on these rodents almost exclusively. A female black-footed ferret with young will eat a prairie dog about every other day.

It was this dependence on prairie dogs that nearly led to the black-footed ferrets' extinction. When the first European settlers came to eastern Utah, they found large white-tailed prairie dog colonies on the high deserts and plateaus. As the pioneers settled in, they began a massive effort to shoot and poison prairie dogs, thinking that it wasn't safe for cattle to step around their burrows.

Black-footed ferret sightings, which were rare even when their population was healthy, shrank to almost none in the late 1970s. By 1986, the worldwide population was 18. Since then, the U.S. Fish and Wildlife Service has operated a successful captive-breeding program and reintroduced the black-footed ferret into several other states. Now the plan is to bring them back into the healthy white-tailed prairie dog towns of Coyote Basin—25 miles east of Vernal and a few miles south of U.S. Highway 40—or to other nearby colonies.

Where you can see black-footed ferrets

★ Boise

★ Salt Lake City

★ Carson City

★ Phoenix

Scientists are still learning about this polecat-like carnivore. Black-footed ferrets are nocturnal and move primarily underground, so they're difficult to observe. They're thought to be solitary, but they're not isolated. One prairie dog complex in Wyoming had over 60 ferrets, "which is at least a visiting density," says BLM biologist Stroh. "We're learning more about them all the time."

Females have litters of one to six pups. Offspring leave mom's den within a few months after birth. Young females remain close by, but males must range long distances to find their own territory. Life expectancy in the wild is about four years.

Despite increased scientific knowledge about it, the black-footed ferret will reenter an environment that's changed from the one to which it was adapted before it disappeared. The ferrets' survival on the high desert of today's eastern Utah is not a sure bet. For one thing, coyotes are top dog in Utah now. Coyotes eat black-footed ferrets and compete with them for prairie dogs. Before European-Americans settled the area, wolf packs kept coyote populations down. Now that wolves themselves have been driven out, coyotes are here in greater numbers. Also, black-footed ferrets are vulnerable

© RICK EGAN / SALT LAKE TRIBUNE

Black-footed ferret.

to the canine distemper virus carried by domestic dogs, and the ferrets' essential food supply, prairie dogs, can be wiped out by plague.

It takes 100 to 150 acres of white-tail prairie dog town to support one adult ferret. The colonies in eastern Utah are large, so that's not a problem. Eastern Utah still has 60 to 65 percent of the white-tailed prairie dog colonies that it had when European-American settlers arrived, reports Stroh.

The reintroduced population of black-footed ferrets in the Coyote Basin area will have the special legal designation "experimental" and "nonessential," which exempts them from full Endangered Species Act protection. This was supposed to reduce opposition from local human residents to regulations that accompany endangered animals. "But there's been a lot of local resistance and I think it's based on misinformation," Stroh says. Black-footed ferrets are no threat to grazing animals and aren't bothered by oil wells or mining operations. "If any endangered species is compatible with multiple use of the land, it's the black-footed ferret."

Stroh is optimistic: "If the reintroduction is successful, we fully expect it to become a popular pastime for the public to come out to eastern Utah and watch the black-footed ferrets and the prairie dog towns." 🐾

© DAN MILLER

Bison, often inaccurately referred to as buffalo.

CHAPTER THREE

Historic herds
Reintroducing native large animals into today's limited space.

At one time, bison, antelope, and bighorn sheep were abundant in the Intermountain West. By 1900, however, most of the herds had disappeared from overhunting. When wildlife biologists attempt to reintroduce these native grazing animals into our transformed modern environment, they aren't sure how many will live—or for how long.

BISON

The stout, white buffalo bones littering a ravine bottom near Woodruff, Utah, look five, rather than fifteen hundred, years old. But on closer inspection you can see that many of the hefty vertebrae and femurs have fine grooves cut across tendon attachment points—a sure sign these bison were butchered with flint blades.

Hidden among the convoluted grassy buttes near the Wyoming border, Woodruff is Utah's only known buffalo jump. Here, around A.D. 500, a gutsy band of Fremont Indians stampeded 350 bison off a 30-foot cliff, launching bulls, cows, and calves headfirst into a steep draw. The skeletal remains of this herd of grass-powered locomotives—identical to modern bison—are now eroding from the remote hillside in mint condition.

Bison were once common in this part of Utah, arriving long before the first humans. Ancestors of modern bison lived here more than a million years ago, during a time when mammoths, giant bears, and saber-toothed cats prowled what is now the Beehive State.

A living relic of the Ice Age, bison are the only surviving large mammals from that era. Though smaller than their Pleistocene ancestors, a modern bison bull may grow to seven feet tall and twelve feet long and weigh one ton. These North American bison, usually mistakenly called buffalo, are a different species than the water buffalo and Cape buffalo of Asia and Africa.

The bison's silhouette has not changed from that of its Ice Age forebears. A massive, shaggy-maned head and heavy forequarters are surmounted by a hump, which then tapers down to narrow hips. The bushy, dark hair in front and the contrasting short, light brown hair on its rear half exaggerate the narrowing effect of its profile. Bison have short, curved horns above brown-button eyes and they hold their heads low, at grass-top height.

In the same family as domestic cattle, bison are grass eaters, and their reddish-brown calves are nearly indistinguishable from the calves of domestic cows. Bison cows are smaller than bison bulls, averaging about seven feet long and one thousand pounds. A bison cow produces her first calf at the age of three or four after a nine-and-a-half month pregnancy.

Because bison are large enough to stand in groups and defend themselves against packs of wolves, yet swift enough to outrun human hunters on foot, they are superbly adapted to life on open grasslands. For protection, they graze in herds composed of cows, calves, and young bulls. Mature bulls keep to the outside of the herd—or go off to graze with other bulls—except during the summer breeding season. The summer rut is *Bigtime Wrestle-mania*, as bulls impress cows by showing off their long shaggy hair and compete with other suitors by snorting, pawing, rolling in the dust, charging, and colliding head on.

In Utah and in most of North America, human history is tightly linked with bison. Human hunters first arrived on this continent over 40,000 years ago by following herds of bison

BISON IN UTAH

Status: Once extinct in Utah, the state now has two free-roaming herds.

Estimated Number: Antelope Island herd numbers between 550 and 700, the Henry Mountain herd numbers between 300 and 400.

Tips for Viewing: In open country, look for the dark silhouette of a huge, shaggy head and shoulders tapering to narrow hips. Keep a safe distance away.

across a bridge of land that once connected Siberia with Alaska. The early, giant-sized species of bison died out in North America at the end of the Ice Age. This left the grassy range open for a smaller species of bison that spread northward—from what is now Mexico—into the Great Plains east of the Rockies.

These modern bison eventually migrated into the Intermountain West from passes in the upper Missouri River drainage, traveling into southeastern Idaho. There, halted by desert to the west, they spread south and filled the valley of the Bear River and the Salt Lake Valley. At the time, they were the most widely distributed mammals on earth, aside from humans.

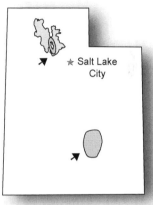

Where you can see Utah bison

Archeological discoveries show that Utah's prehistoric inhabitants used bison parts for everything from clothing and armament to tools. For example, a stash of over two hundred pairs of bison- and deer-hide moccasins, 1,000 years old, was found near Promontory Point, west of Salt Lake City. Three shields made of bison leather—the oldest ever discovered in North America—were found near what is now Capitol Reef National Park. A hollowed-out bison horn, still full of rust-red paint, was unearthed in Hogup Cave on the Great Salt Lake. Utah's prehistoric artists decorated cliff walls with bison images in both Nine Mile Canyon, near Price, and in Horseshoe Canyon, further south.

The bison's range in the state may have been limited mostly to the northern half. "In prehistoric sites in northern Utah, like the Bear River marshes, we find a substantial number of bison bones," observes Duncan Metcalfe, curator of archaeology for the Utah Natural History Museum at the University of Utah. "Around Utah Lake, we do find some bison bones, but in southern Utah, we find only an occasional bison bone."

Mountain man Jim Bridger reported seeing herds of bison when he first explored the Salt Lake Valley in 1824. But by the time Mormon pioneers arrived here, the bison were gone.

Elsewhere, in the Great Plains, the U.S. Army began exterminating bison herds as a strategy to cut off the economic lifeline of the Indian nations blocking westward expansion of European-Americans. By the beginning of the twentieth century, bison were nearly extinct in North America. But small groups survived, and today, Utah has herds that have been transplanted on both Antelope Island and in southern Utah's Henry Mountains.

"Summer is the best time to catch a glimpse of the Henry Mountain bison," says Rod Hodson, wildlife biologist for Utah's Division of Wildlife Resources, who works with the herd. But you won't get too close. After a million years of coevolution, when an open-country bison catches a whiff of a human, it usually turns and runs, and it may not stop for miles. "Bison are built for walking and you'll wear out a good pair of hiking boots if you try to follow them," Hodson notes. And bison can go almost anywhere. "They use all of the habitat in the Henrys," Hodson says. "They range from the canyon bottoms all the way up the extremely steep mountain slopes that domestic cattle are too lazy to get to."

Some ranchers are switching from raising domestic cattle to raising bison for this and other reasons. Unlike cattle, bison can take care of themselves in extreme weather, such as deep snow and subzero temperatures. They are not prone to overgraze pasture, and bison meat packs a nutritional wallop. It's three times as nutritious as beef and leaner than skinless chicken. The drawbacks to raising them, though, will make even a seasoned cowboy pause. Fences and handling facilities for bison need to be stout and high. A bison bull can top a standing six-foot fence without a running start. Also, if a rancher needs to capture an individual bison, he will find they're wild and fast. Imagine trying to tackle an angry linebacker who weighs 2,000 pounds and has horns.

It makes you appreciate the task a small band of Fremont Indians accomplished 1,500 years ago at the Woodruff buffalo jump. The ledge over which the Woodruff bison were spooked is not broad. In order to get them to go over the cliff, several people had to risk being trampled while keeping the hysterical, charging beasts within a 100-foot wide path over the last 100 yards. Otherwise, that bison herd would have avoided the precipice, thundered down an adjacent hillside, and never looked back.

SONORAN PRONGHORN

It must be thirsty work, being the fastest land animal on Earth in any race longer than a sprint. But so little is known of the fleet pronghorn antelope that live in the desert no-man's-land where southwestern Arizona meets Mexico that, until recently, scientists were not sure if Sonoran pronghorn drink standing water—ever.

Sonoran pronghorn are a subgroup of the unique and adaptable North American pronghorn. And the possibility that they could metabolize all of the water they need from the plants they munch—a well-documented talent of such desert-adapted neighbors as the kangaroo rat—was not out of the question.

Pronghorn are singular animals. Though we call them antelope, they are as closely related to goats; antelope occur naturally only in Africa and Asia. Pronghorns are the sole members of their own biological classification—neither goat nor antelope—and are native only to North America.

Shaped like a torpedo with long skinny legs attached, a pronghorn has a supercharged cardiovascular system—oversized windpipe, lungs, and heart—allowing it to consume oxygen three times better than animals of comparable size. Pronghorn can explode into a mile-a-minute run for short distances, then cruise for longer periods at 40 miles per hour. They take fluid, 20-foot leaps over rugged terrain.

Where you can see pronghorns

Boise

Salt Lake City

Carson City

Phoenix

Compared to elk or to deer, pronghorn are not large. A mature pronghorn buck stands slightly over three-and-a-half feet high at the shoulder and weighs about 100 pounds. But while elk are at home in the forest, and deer adapt to farmland, pronghorns are built to run in open range. Because they can outrace anything on four legs, pronghorn don't rely on blending in with their surroundings. Consequently, their colors are dazzling. They have rusty brown and tan body hair with splashes of white at the throat, underbelly, and neck. Their faces are a vigorous black and white.

PRONGHORN

Status: Sonoran subspecies of pronghorn is Endangered in U.S.

Estimated Number: 172.

Tips for Viewing: Usually seen in small groups in open country; look for white patches on rumps and two short horns on head.

© DAN MILLER

Pronghorn.

But pronghorn have more than quickness going for them; their vision is exceptionally keen. They have eyes the size of golf balls that scientists believe are the equivalent of a human looking through a pair of eight-power binoculars. These oversized peepers are set on either side of their head for superb peripheral vision.

Pronghorn get their name from their inward curved horns, which, on bucks, have a stubby branch, or prong. Unlike the antlers of elk or deer, pronghorn have true horns—bones covered with sheaths of fused hair. Antlers, on the other hand, are all bone. Pronghorn are the only animals in the world that shed horns each year. Both sexes have them, but the female's horns are seldom longer than her ears while a male's may grow to a foot and a half long.

Active in morning and evening, pronghorns graze leafy plants, shrubs, and grass—in that order of preference. They don't compete for the same forage as cattle.

In the fall, while female pronghorns load up on the leafy forage that is critical to a successful pregnancy, males joust with each other for mating privileges. The most aggressive buck breeds with a group of females, who then give birth in the spring, usually to twins. Pronghorn moms eat the afterbirth and then tongue-bathe their newborn fawns until they are odorless. Fawns instinctively lie motionless and are nearly invisible to predators.

No western desert is too parched and few places are too frigid for the adaptable pronghorn. Their bristly hair is hollow for insulation during cold weather yet can be erected in patches to cool down. The pronghorn's historic range stretched from what is now Mexico City to present Alberta, Canada—more than a million square miles of grassy prairie, sagebrush scrub, and rocky desert.

Like the bison, tens of millions of pronghorns once roamed the American West. And like the bison, pronghorn were nearly snuffed out by large numbers of migrating European-Americans in the nineteenth century. By the 1920s only about 30,000 pronghorn survived. Since then, their numbers have rebounded to about a million, most of which are the type of pronghorn frequently seen in Wyoming, Montana, and parts of Utah.

While these common pronghorn are not in danger of extinction, the number of the Sonoran subspecies is low, and it has been listed as endangered since 1967. "Our latest aerial survey, in 1998, counted 172 individuals," reports Laura Thompson-Olais, the U.S. Fish and Wildlife Service ecologist who wrote the Endangered Species Recovery Plan for the Sonoran pronghorn. "That includes 12 fawns from last year."

It's a modest increase in numbers. Most of the Sonoran pronghorn on the U.S. side of the border live in the rugged Cabeza Prieta National Wildlife Refuge. Across the border in Mexico live about 300 more, Thompson-Olais believes.

The Sonoran subspecies is visibly different from the pronghorn we see further north. "Sonoran pronghorn are smaller, lighter colored, and have smaller horns" than common pronghorn, Thompson-Olais says, but little specific research has been done on them. "Sonoran pronghorn have not gotten the attention that better-known species, like the Mexican wolf, have, so funding for research and recovery efforts has been difficult to come by." However, she adds, "We did just discover that they do drink standing water." Thirteen Sonoran pronghorn were recently videotaped drinking from a well on Luke Air Force Range, which is adjacent to the Cabeza Prieta Wildlife Refuge.

BIGHORN SHEEP

Two dusty livestock trailers—call them "Ewe-Hauls"—towed by Ford Broncos from the Utah Division of Wildlife Resources, rolled to a stop beneath Antelope Island's Frary Peak. One trailer gate dropped open and nineteen bighorn sheep ewes pounded down the ramp. In a dead run, the wild sheep zigzagged up the mountain in a tight, fluid pack like a school of fish. Out from the second trailer, four rams squirted up the hillside, their tan and buff rumps flashing. Within minutes, all twenty-four bighorn sheep had melted into the mountainside, invisible against the rocky cliffs.

With the addition of bighorn sheep, Antelope Island has become a sanctuary and showcase for all of the Great Basin's native, large prey mammals. Bison, pronghorn antelope, mule deer, and one cow elk live on the treeless, windswept Great Salt Lake island.

If all goes well with the bighorn sheep reintroduction, wildlife watchers will get a close look at one of the rarest large mammals in North America.

Natural resource officials and wild sheep hunters hope the herd will thrive so that, over time, extra bighorns can be moved to start new herds elsewhere. All 19 of the released ewes appeared pregnant.

Bighorn sheep lived on Antelope Island in prehistoric times—DWR and state park officials are guessing—so their reintroduction here is fitting. Archaeologists have found the bones of desert bighorn sheep on neighboring Stansbury Island; but little is known of Antelope Island's prehistory. Serious archaeological work didn't begin there until 1995.

Because they have stomachs tougher than trash compactors, superbly camouflaged coats, and agility on cliffs, bighorn sheep thrived in the Great Basin from the last Ice Age until about 1900. Then their populations plummeted as they were overhunted, caught domestic sheep diseases, and lost their water sources to mining operations.

Reintroducing and transplanting wild animals is tricky. Only four years earlier, wildlife officials released 18 elk on Antelope Island. Once out of their trailers, the elk spotted the distant, snow-capped Wasatch peaks and raced straight for them, plunging into the Great Salt Lake. All but one drowned. However, the transplanted bighorn sheep headed for high ground—a relief to the project's organizers.

BIGHORN SHEEP

Status: Desert bighorn are a U.S. Subspecies of Special Concern.

Estimated Number: In 1960, Utah had only a remnant population of desert bighorn sheep; by 1993, there were approximately 2,200.

Tips for Viewing: Near cliffs in steep canyons, listen for rocks falling as they climb. They're tough to spot because the color of their coats blends perfectly with the surrounding rock, but look for a light-colored rump patch.

"We think this is good habitat for bighorn sheep," says Tim Smith, Antelope Island State Park manager. "It's high elevation [up to 6,300 feet], rocky cliffs, and has good—mostly native—grass. There aren't as many exotic plants up here as there are at lower elevations where there's been more cattle and sheep grazing in the past." The steep range of the newly placed bighorns is rarely used by antelope or mule deer. The island has good water sources as well, noted Smith. Though it seems parched, Antelope Island has over 40 freshwater springs.

"The two major problems with bighorn sheep reintroductions are predators and domestic sheep diseases," Lou

Antelope Island, bighorn sheep habitat.

© DAN MILLER

Cornicelli, wildlife supervisor for DWR, points out. "On Antelope Island, we think we have both of those under control." No sheep or cattle graze on Antelope Island. Also, the bighorn's most avid predator—the cougar—does not live here. And don't expect DWR trailers to chauffeur a couple of them over.

"We want this to be a nursery for bighorn sheep," one DWR official states. "The island already has coyotes and bobcats; we're not interested in more predators." A cougar could still cross to Antelope Island from the Oquirrh Mountains during a low water year. "The problem with cougars is that one may set up house right where the bighorns live and wipe them out," Cornicelli worries. But does prey behavior change permanently in areas where large carnivores are absent? Growing up without cougars, how will the bighorns learn to escape them when they are later transplanted to riskier locations? Cornicelli says a bighorn's predator evasion behavior is genetic.

That's one theory. Biologists from the University of Nevada are testing another. The researchers played wolf calls near moose in Wyoming, where wolves are rare and not a common predator of moose. They did the same to moose in southeast Alaska, where wolves often prey upon them. The Wyoming moose failed to respond to this cue of a predator's presence, but the Alaska moose reacted by cutting their feeding time in half. Because many remaining natural areas are losing or have lost their large carnivore populations, scientists say it's important to find out how prey behavior changes in response. A report on the wolf-moose study is in the February 1997 *Scientific American*.

Bighorns prefer habitat that gives them a clear field of vision, allowing them to spot and escape predators, so Antelope Island works well for them. The lack of cover is helpful for wildlife watchers too; humans will be able to get a relatively close look at these elusive ovines. "But we have an important rule for bighorn sheep watchers on Antelope Island," Smith continues. "Stay on the trails. A vital part of the habituation of bighorns to humans is that they expect to see people on the trails and not in other places." Island hiking trails will close briefly each year during the sheep's critical lambing season.

"If you look at it from a historical perspective," Smith notes, "the most limited large native mammals from the scene today are bison and bighorn sheep"; now Antelope Island has both. The island is famous for its bison, which were absent from the island when European-Americans arrived. Bison were reintroduced in 1893 after they were nearly exterminated everywhere else in the United States. The Antelope Island herd, numbering 550 to 700 individuals, is the largest publicly owned herd in the U.S. and one of the oldest in the country.

Pronghorn antelope were reintroduced successfully onto Antelope Island in 1993 after a failed transplant 65 years earlier. Mule deer also live on the island. After the unsuccessful transplant in 1993, Smith says the idea of bringing elk onto the island was reconsidered. "The elk's summer range here is not that great. In addition, we have the problem of what to do with excess animals." Most remaining areas of elk habitat have as many elk as they can support. Hunting elk to reduce the herd is not a practical option on Antelope Island. Only bison are hunted there. Six licenses are sold for

Where you can see bighorn sheep

Boise

Carson City

Salt Lake City

Phoenix

Bighorn sheep.

© DAN MILLER

the once-a-year bison hunt. Proceeds from the sale of the licenses go to pay part of the state park's wildlife expenses.

Bighorns will not be hunted here; the island will act as a rookery. Excess bighorns produced will be relocated to other places, such as the Stansbury Mountains to the southwest or the Newfoundland Mountains to the northwest. Transplants may be ten years down the road, however.

State officials chose the intermediate-sized variety called California bighorn sheep to introduce on Antelope Island. California bighorns are larger than desert bighorns but smaller than the Rocky Mountain variety. Desert bighorns once lived on Stansbury Island to the west and Rocky Mountain bighorns lived in the Wasatch Mountains on the east, so wildlife scientists believe the medium-sized California type will adapt to Antelope Island well. Genetically, all three kinds of wild sheep are closely related. Most of the size difference results from harsh desert environments yielding smaller sheep, and better feed in the Rocky Mountains growing larger ones.

Herd size matters. Transplanted wild sheep herds often flourish for a few years, then their populations crash and stabilize at very low levels, experts find. Researchers say groups of less than 50 bighorn sheep rarely last 50 years. "Anything can happen," Cornicelli notes. "But these Antelope Island bighorns came from two different groups, and so they have some hybrid vigor." Because one dominant ram impregnates all the ewes in a herd, genetic variation may always be a problem in small groups of wild sheep. A group of scientists from Weber State University, led by Sue Fairbanks, will monitor the island's population of bighorns for genetic changes over time.

"A herd of 100 to 150 wild sheep is a prime group and may be the minimum" viable size, says Lee Howard of the Utah Foundation for North American Wild Sheep (UFNAWS), which funded part of the bighorn transplant. "But in Montana they're having success keeping groups of bighorns smaller and transplanting the excess animals." A group of conservationist-hunters, the UFNAWS auctioned bighorn hunting licenses given to them by Utah's wildlife board. In return, the nonprofit foundation pledged to spend the proceeds on promoting the well-being and habitat of wild bighorn sheep. Utah State Parks Division and DWR employees took on the paperwork and transportation tasks of moving the bighorns from their former home in western Canada to Antelope Island. This year, UFNAWS's parent organization sold one desert bighorn hunting license for $47,000 and a Rocky Mountain bighorn permit for $39,000.

Wild bighorn sheep tend to catch a fatal pneumonia-lungworm complex from their domestic cousins, Howard said, so UFNAWS works with sheep ranchers operating near wild sheep herds, helping them convert from raising domestic sheep to cattle. The Forest Service asked UFNAWS to study the possibility of reintroducing Rocky Mountain bighorns onto Mount Timpanogos. Howard said the existing Timpanogos herd of mountain goats can live alongside wild sheep, but a domestic-sheep grazing allotment would need to be moved.

Not long after the "Ewe-Hauls" discharged their precious cargo, DWR's Cornicelli made an airplane overflight to check on them. He reported that Antelope Island's new bighorns seemed to be doing well. ❧

© DAN MILLER

The alpine zone of a Wasatch peak.

CHAPTER FOUR

Alpine plants and animals
Hardy inhabitants of Utah's high country.

Hiking to the top of a high peak in Utah is like traveling to the Arctic. As you ascend, the mountain-adapted plants and trees become more dwarf-like and hug the ground because they must survive hammering by harsh weather. The summer growing season is a blink of an eye, then winter roars back with hurricane-force winds and subzero temperatures. The robust native plants and animals up here have a strategy that centers on endurance. They are often specialists, requiring very specific habitats in a rare environment surrounded by a sea of lowlands.

ALPINE ISLAND IN THE SKY

From a hundred miles west you can see Snowbird ski resort's home—it's that massive wall of mountains towering 5,000 feet above Salt Lake Valley, the Wasatch Front. The western storm track doesn't miss this sheer rampart either; these mountains are hammered by storm after Pacific storm. The steep vertical exposure creates its own climate, snagging four times as much rain and snow, and staying thirty degrees cooler, than the surrounding valleys.

Isolated by altitude and climate, the Wasatch Range is an island in the sky, home to different communities of plants and animals than you'll find at lower elevations. All are hardy, many are specialized, and some—like the wildflower Garret's fleabane—you'll see nowhere else on Earth.

For a brief window of time between the snow melt in June and the snowfall in early September, the Wasatch is all roaring creeks, nodding wildflowers, and buzzing bees. The mountainsides come alive for this fleeting growing season, then winter returns, bringing subzero temperatures, hurricane force winds, and blizzards that try to blast away every limb or stem foolish enough to poke above the deep cloak of snow.

Every rise of 1,000 feet in elevation is the same as traveling 300 miles north at sea level, so a walk up a Wasatch mountainside will take you from one climatic neighborhood into another. For example, you'll see the same type of ground-hugging plants that grow in Lapland on Snowbird's 11,000-foot Hidden Peak.

At Snowbird's lower elevations, however, because there's plenty of moisture and warmer average temperatures, fir and aspen trees take root and grow tall almost anywhere. Beneath the trees is an understory of bushy plants such as elderberry and mountain ash and on the edges are wildflowers and grasses. Small furry mammals and birds are abundant at this altitude.

Fireweed, a striking magenta wildflower, is easy to spot in open areas. So named because it is the first plant to return to an area scorched by wildfire, fireweed stands on a sturdy five-foot tall stalk topped by a spearhead of many small, four-pedaled flowers. You'll find fireweed growing wherever trees have been cleared, places such as avalanche paths and ski runs. At one time, Native Americans used the tough fibers of the fireweed stalk to make twine and nets. Today, people still use the young fireweed shoots as an herb.

Also at Snowbird's lower elevations, you'll find a Herculean member of the carrot family—the cow parsnip—which stands up to nine feet tall. This hearty wildflower is shaped like an umbrella, with many stems radiating from a central point on the stalk. The stems are covered with tiny, white, lacy blooms. According to folk tradition, the roots of the cow parsnip, which taste like rutabaga when boiled, cures rheumatism.

If you hear a high-pitched bleating sound as you round a corner, you've been spotted by a pika. These miniature members of the rabbit family look like guinea pigs because of their tiny ears. Short ears, tails, and legs reduce heat loss and are a characteristic of mammals living with low average temperatures. Another Snowbird resident, the brassy Clark's nutcracker, may come find you—especially if you're eating lunch on the trail. You'll hear a hoarse *kraw! kraw!* as it approaches. It's a large-bodied gray bird with black wings and tail. When not begging Ding-Dongs from your picnic basket, this bird has a diet of evergreen tree seeds. To gather food, they smash pine cones and grab the nuts with their toes, cracking them with their beaks. After stowing a hundred or so seeds in their throat, a Clark's nutcracker will soar off and bury caches of the seeds an inch deep, the perfect depth for sprouting. The many stashes of seeds the Clark's nutcrackers forget to recover become patches of tree seedlings the following summer.

As you climb higher up the mountainside, the trees appear stunted and shrub-like, hammered by the weather and by the short growing season. At the edge of evergreens and in open areas, you'll see varieties of lupine, also known as bluebonnet. These wildflowers have small blue-to-purple, pea-shaped flowers growing in whorls on stalks that stand a foot high. Lupine are members of the pea family; you can tell by their hairy seedpods. Those striking flowers that look like brushes dipped in crimson paint are Indian paintbrush. Note that the showy scarlet color comes from the leaves, not the flower. The flower is just a narrow green tube surrounded by colorful leaves.

At higher elevations, on the fringe of trees and near seeps, you may encounter the crown jewel of mountain wildflowers—the delicate, graceful, showy columbine. It's a five-petal flower with flamboyant spurs that project backward for one or two inches. Most of the columbines here are yellow, but you also may see the Colorado blue columbine—the state flower of Colorado—which are white to pale blue.

Watch for the native Wasatch wildflower Garret's fleabane at these higher elevations. Six inches tall, it has a daisy-like flower with a yellow disk at the center surrounded by a fringe of slender white petals. Though Garret's fleabane is locally abundant, it grows only on the twenty miles of the Wasatch Mountains from Guardsman Pass to Mt. Timpanogos.

When you've passed the last tree at the 10,000-foot elevation, you've reached the equivalent of Utah's arctic—the alpine zone. On these wind-lashed summits and ridges, plants hug the ground in mats and produce Lilliputian flowers without stems, to stay out of the cold. Some may take ten years to flower the first time and twenty-five years to grow to six inches wide.

Observant walkers may sight a hawk up here, kiting along Little Cottonwood Canyon's ridgeline. These heavy-bodied birds of prey migrate on ridge updrafts in spring and fall. Along the way, they patrol the mountainsides for pikas, mice, and small birds. If you're lucky, you may spot an increasingly rare raptor, the northern goshawk. This hawk is distinguished by its large size—it's heftier than a crow—and has blue-gray coloring on top and bars of white and gray on its underparts. Unfortunately, northern goshawk numbers are shrinking, and soon it may be listed as an endangered species. This is worrisome because the harsh alpine world does not rebound quickly from loss. Because the food chain here is so short—grass-pika-goshawk, for example—the loss of one link in the chain can cause prompt and drastic changes. For this reason too, tread lightly up here. When the alpine tundra is trampled, it will remain bare for years.

But enjoy the view. If you look west long enough, you may spot the next winter storm rolling in.

PIKA

Ever get the unsettling feeling that someone—or something—is watching you when you're on a high mountainside? Most likely a pika has you under close surveillance to make sure you don't go near its food pile. And if you do, he or she will offer to kick your butt, scolding you with a piercing, high-pitched *bleat!*

Go ahead, laugh. Pikas do look like cuddly guinea pigs—fuzzy brown eggs with tiny soup-spoon ears, short legs, no tail—but if you try to touch a pika's carefully accumulated haystack of dried vegetation, it'll be ready to rumble. And it doesn't matter if you're a 150-pound scientist or a 6-ounce next-door neighbor. "Pikas are like little dogs who think they're big dogs," observes Chris Ray, a University of Nevada-Reno biologist who's been studying these high-altitude vegetarians for more than a decade. "Once I was out in the field with six assistants, one of whom was my father. My father sat down at the base of a talus slope and leaned against a rock. Up at the top of the slope, a pika stood on its lookout and gave out a *bleat!* Then it bounded down a few yards towards my father, stopped, and bleated again. It bounded down a few more yards, and let out another bleat. Finally the pika ran down to where my father was sitting and bit him on the finger—with seven huge people standing there!"

> **PIKA**
>
> **Status:** State Species of Special Concern Due to Limited Distribution.
>
> **Tips for Viewing:** On talus slopes in alpine areas, look for tiny "haystacks" of dried grasses. It is smaller than a marmot, but fatter than a chipmunk, with no tail.

Pika.

© DICK SPENCER / PIKA STREET PHOTOGRAPHY

Pikas are fiercely territorial by necessity. They live only on high-altitude scree slopes and are active all winter, so each pika depends almost entirely on the plants it clips, dries, and stores during the brief alpine summer to feed it through the winter. As any skier who has paid $8.50 for a ski resort hamburger can confirm—a winter food supply in the mountains is dear and worth defending.

Both North American species of pika (there are a dozen species in Eurasia) are talus slope specialists; they live only in the scree of Western mountains above 8,500 feet. It's an extreme environment, and a pika's chunky shape—short ears, abbreviated legs, and lack of tail—reduce its heat loss and help it thrive in the low alpine temperatures.

Because its gray-brown fur blends with the surrounding rock so well, it can be tough to spot a pika if you don't hear it first. "With the right conditions in winter, skiers can sometimes hear pikas under the snowpack," Ray comments. Once you see one, a pika's easy to identify. About eight inches long and three inches high and weighing in at six ounces, picas are fatter than chipmunks but much smaller than marmots. Any small, furry animal on a talus slope with no visible tail is probably a pika.

Scientists once thought pikas were rodents but now know they are only distantly related, separated by 50 million years of evolution; pikas are closely related to hares and rabbits. But pikas can't jump like rabbits and they aren't fast runners, so they stick close to rocky shelter, often staking out territory where a high meadow meets a talus slope.

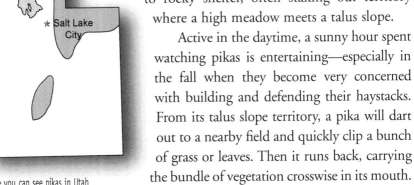
Where you can see pikas in Utah

Active in the daytime, a sunny hour spent watching pikas is entertaining—especially in the fall when they become very concerned with building and defending their haystacks. From its talus slope territory, a pika will dart out to a nearby field and quickly clip a bunch of grass or leaves. Then it runs back, carrying the bundle of vegetation crosswise in its mouth.

Once in its own territory again, it will fussily arrange the fresh clippings to dry in the sun. After drying these plant clippings, it stacks them in a sheltered place in the rocks. These miniature haystacks may be piled three feet wide and two feet high and may contain 20 species of vegetation.

As a pika works, it continuously calls to the other pikas in adjacent territories. "Probably the reason they constantly call is to let other pikas know to stay out of their territory. Pikas are individually territorial—both males and females—and they will chase each other out," Ray notes. "We know that soon after a pika stops calling, its neighbors will move in and start stealing from its haystack." In addition to letting neighbors know they're present by constantly calling out, pikas also mark their turf by rubbing a scent gland against rocks and by spraying them with urine.

Adult pikas ease up on this zealous turf defense long enough to mate with their neighbors in the spring. Gestation of babies lasts one month, then a litter of two to five young are born, naked and blind. Pika babies develop quickly. After a week they can crawl and peep; by day 10 they have grown choppers and fur. Within a couple of months, the young are booted out of mom's territory to find new turf and to begin building a winter haystack of their own.

Hawks, eagles, martins, and coyotes snatch up pikas—especially juveniles—but their primary predator is the weasel. "Weasels use the element of surprise when they hunt, they don't lurk," Ray says, "and weasels can get anywhere a pika can." However, adult pikas are skilled at ditching these sausage-shaped carnivores. "When an adult pika spies a weasel, it gets up into full view and bleats. If the weasel comes after it, the adult will continue to call as it runs into the rocks," she says. So how does the pika get away? "Here's what I think happens. Inside the talus slopes, the broken rock creates many different corridors, and within an adult pika's territory, all the rocks smell like that pika. So, once a weasel is down in the rocks, it must make a choice about which way the pika went at each passageway—left or right. Chances are the weasel will choose correctly 50 percent of the time. After two turns, there's a 25 percent chance it's chosen correctly, and after four turns, there's virtually no chance the weasel has guessed correctly each time. I've seen lots of predation in the field and in almost all instances it is juveniles, not adults" that are nabbed, Ray observes.

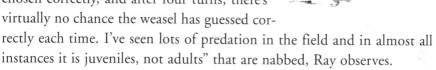

Though pikas expertly evade predators and are well adapted to their cold environment, it's a curious fact that they are extinct in some places that have excellent habitat for them. For example, certain mountain ranges, like the Snake Range in Nevada (home of Great Basin National Park) have excellent pika habitat but no pikas, Ray reports, although the fossil evidence—pika scat in pack rat middens—shows that they lived in the Snake Range within the last 10,000 years.

One reason researchers like Ray are studying pikas is that, because of the specialized nature of pika habitat, individual populations are small and scattered. As animal habitats everywhere become fragmented by human intrusions, scientists can learn how small pika populations go extinct within larger regional populations. From pikas, they hope to discover what reproduction rates, survival rates, and genetic diversity may be necessary to conserve fragmented populations of other species of animals.

Ray's research reveals more interesting pika behavior: "It's not in the literature, but I'm collecting evidence that an adult male pika may begin building a haystack in nearby unclaimed territory in order to lure a juvenile female pika into moving in next door. It's kind of like a hope chest. My evidence is only anecdotal so far, but for a juvenile female it makes sense to locate in an unclaimed territory where a haystack is already jump-started for her." By luring a female to live nearby, the male is assured of mating possibilities next spring. And as long as she keeps her paws off the haystack in *his* territory, they should get along fine.

MOSS CAMPION

To check out arctic tundra plants like those that grow in Lapland and northern Alaska, take a hike up to the highest Wasatch peaks in the summer. Weather, especially temperature, dictates what grows where, so climbing a Wasatch mountainside or traveling far to the north produces a remarkably similar sequence of changes in the surrounding vegetation.

At trailhead altitude, the Wasatch experiences relatively warmer average temperatures than higher up, so evergreens grow abundantly with an understory of bushy plants. However, after climbing a few thousand feet in elevation, the landscape opens up because trees are fewer and the ones that do grow are stunted and wind trained. At this altitude, violent wind gusts and battering storms keep limbs pruned off the windward side of exposed trees. In addition, frigid conditions most of the year ensure trees and shrubs remain small—just like those in places like Canada's southern Yukon, for example. "Plants in Utah's alpine zone are ground huggers because it's too cold and too windy up there to survive winter above the insulating layer of snow," says Michael Windham, curator of the Utah Museum of Natural History's Garrett Herbarium. Grasses and sedges carpet Utah's alpine zone while lichen and cushion plants dot the rocky areas.

An example of a cushion plant that grows above the Arctic Circle as well as in the high Wasatch is moss campion. It is a tight mat of tiny, stiff green leaves

---

MOSS CAMPION

Status: Relatively abundant.

Estimated Number: Well distributed in alpine zones.

Tips for Viewing: Look in Utah's highest alpine areas, around 10,000 feet, for tiny pink flowers and slender, needle-like leaves growing in a ground-hugging mat.

Moss campion.

© WILLIAM H. KING / UTAH NATIVE PLANT SOCIETY

covered with miniature pink flowers. The slender, needle-like leaves make it look like a moss and give the plant its common name.

Like most alpine plants, moss campion is a perennial, allowing it to resprout, bloom, and seed during a brief growing season and to survive occasional freezes—even during flowering season. "Moss campion's scientific name, *acaulis* means 'no stem,'" Windham explains. It's a description of the way the plant's Lilliputian flowers hug its leafy mat rather than rising on stalks from which the wind would rip them apart. The air is in constant motion at high altitude, but the low-growing, matted shape of moss campion allows it to spread out in the sun without catching the breeze. This creates a microclimate in which the inside of the plant is several degrees warmer than the outside. The relentless alpine wind whisks out the sparse soil from every crack in mountain peaks, but moss campion's bristly leaves catch dirt and windblown debris, building up soil around the plant.

Rugged weather conditions mean a slow life cycle for alpine and arctic plants. The energy of moss campion's first years is spent drilling a deep taproot for an anchor. The plant will grow only a half inch in five years, and by the time it's the size of a salad plate—25 years—that tap root will have penetrated four or five feet deep. For this reason, it may be ten years before moss campion flowers for the first time, 20 years before it flowers abundantly.

Pollination is a struggle at high altitudes because the cool summer temperatures restrict insect activity to the sunniest, warmest times. Flies are important pollinators in these conditions because they have lower energy requirements than bees, which are grounded in temperatures below 50 degrees. Moss campions' blossoms "taper into a very slender nectar-holding tube that can be pollinated only by butterflies whose mouth parts have been specially adapted into coiled sucking tubes to siphon nectar," report Ann Zwinger and Beatrice Willard in their book, *Land Above the Trees*. The authors also observe that moss campion's leaves are sticky in order to discourage the foot traffic of ants and beetles. Asked to confirm that a butterfly is moss campion's pollinator, Windham said that Zwinger and Willard are probably correct, but noted that most high-altitude pollinators haven't been positively identified yet.

So when you hike up to the high Wasatch in summer, kneel down and check out the miniature world of these hardy tundra plants—you may as well be in the Arctic. Watch to see what insect is pollinating which plant; your observations can add to a slim body of knowledge on the subject.

BURKE'S MUSTARD

For a few days in 2002, the world's wildest skiers will lunge off the peak of Mt. Allen, accelerating downslope more quickly than a Formula One race car. The Olympic downhill skiing competition—a blur of 45-second runs—is coming to Snowbasin Ski Resort on Mt. Allen and Mt. Ogden when Salt Lake City hosts the Winter Olympics.

Directly in the path of this international extravaganza—on an ancient ridge smack in the heart of the future men's downhill run—grew a patch of unique alpine flowers that live only on Mt. Allen and on a few other nearby peaks. Snowbasin dynamited about 500 of these plants along with the ridge. Conservation collided with the Olympic industry up here, and

Utahns—citizens of one of the few states in the nation without laws protecting its rare plants—had no voice in the matter.

The plant in question, Burke's mustard, is a high-altitude member of the 3,000-species mustard family. Its more famous lowland relations include broccoli, cabbage, and Brussels sprouts as well as the mustard spice, to which Burke's is not closely related. Burke's mustard has silver-green leaves and a dwarfish yellow flower and grows in alpine crags and crevices.

It's a tough place to make home. Here, plants are hammered by harsh weather and stunted by poor soil. To survive, they develop unique features. For example, some alpine flowers have evolved the ability to generate enough heat to melt out pockets from snowdrifts in the spring. This allows a plant to leaf and flower quickly during a fleeting, 60-day growing season.

Mt. Ogden's caretakers, the U.S. Forest Service, launched a biological inventory of the Snowbasin area because they knew a rare species of mustard lives there. They believed it was a plant named Maguire mustard, possibly endangered. "The survey intended to find out how rare Maguire mustard is, and to identify other locations in which it grows," Garrett Herbarium's Michael Windham recalls. The mustard named Maguire was thought to live only in the Wasatch, Wellsville, and Bear River Mountains.

However, Windham ran chromosome, enzyme, and DNA tests on the rare mustard samples throughout this range. His investigation proved that the Mt. Ogden plant—to be designated Burke's mustard—is a different species than the Maguire mustard found in the Bear River Mountains.

"Burke's and Maguire are like horses and donkeys," Windham explains, they can't successfully breed with each other, which is the primary definition of a species. In fact, Burke's is more closely related to several other kinds of mustard than it is to Maguire, Windham found.

As separate species, the two mountain mustards are scarce. The total population of Burke's mustard is about 10,000, with the largest concentration of them on Mt. Allen and Mt. Ogden. According to biologists, these small,

---

BURKE'S MUSTARD

Status: Utah has no state laws to protect its native plants.

Estimated Number: Less than 10,000.

Tips for Viewing: In alpine crags and crannies, look for silver-green leaves and a small yellow flower.

© MARK HENGESBAUGH

Snow Basin preparing new ski run for 2002 Winter Olympics.

isolated populations of rare plants are especially vulnerable to extinction during naturally harsh climatic cycles and during man-made disturbances.

The identification of a new, rare plant on Mt. Allen didn't faze Snowbasin's construction crews. However, the possible extinction of a plant like Burke's mustard—dynamiting the men's downhill run took out nearly ten percent of the Mt. Allen-Mt. Ogden population—concerns scientists such as Windham. The consequences may be both short- and long-term. In the near term, does Burke's contain a compound that cures cancer? Do farmers need genes from it to improve domestic mustard strains?

As a temporary measure, there is not much hope for transplanting Burke's or for replanting it from seed. "We collect the seeds," Windham explains, "but we don't know the appropriate conditions to store and germinate them. It's very difficult. We've done germination experiments for years on the dwarf bearclaw poppy [another rare Utah plant] and haven't gotten them to work." It's doubtful that many Burke's mustard plants would recover from the trauma of transplant, he notes. "They live in cracks, ledges, and crevices. It's tough getting the whole plant out, you lose much of the underground biomass (roots)."

Another major worry: in the long run, would the extinction of Burke's mustard unravel the biology of Mt. Allen's plant and animal community? We may lose other plants, insects, or animals if Burke's mustard goes extinct, and these losses will ripple through the alpine biology with unforeseeable results, Windham worries. "It's almost impossible to predict what will happen. We don't know how Burke's fits in. For example, if Burke's mustard goes extinct, it may take out a pollinator, such as a bee, that's solely or primarily dependent upon it," Windham notes.

Because plants and their pollinators have evolved together over millions of years, a species of flower like Burke's often depends on one species of bee for pollination; likewise, that species of bee may be able to pollinate only that one kind of flower. The plant species and the insect species don't survive without each other. A prime example of this dilemma is Utah's endangered dwarf bearclaw poppy flower, which is only pollinated by a rare species of native Utah bee named perdita. Their survival is interdependent. "It's a chicken-and-egg question with the dwarf bearclaw poppy and perdita," Windham says. Which one became endangered first? Did pesticides in southern Utah kill off the bee, which caused the poppy to become rare? Or did habitat destruction kill off the dwarf bearclaw poppy, decimating the perdita population?

Where you can see Burke's mustard

★ Boise

★ Carson City

0

★ Salt Lake City

★ Phoenix

If Burke's disappears and takes out a species of bee, how would that affect other plants and animals dependent on the insect? It may make no noticeable difference. Or, as a species, Burke's may be functioning like a keystone. No one knows.

In the meantime, Snowbasin continues to carve up Burke's only stronghold, blasting out a platform for a race starthouse and trenching the alpine slopes for snowmaking pipelines and powerlines. A mountaintop restaurant is in the works.

Because we have no state laws to protect rare native plants, Utah is especially vulnerable to losing them. About one in ten of our state's plant species live nowhere else in the world. In addition, the number of native Utah plants considered for listing by the U.S. Fish and Wildlife Service as threatened or endangered is among the highest in the continental U.S. Seven scientists from the University of Utah and from Brigham Young University documented these state conservation troubles in their landmark paper, "Selecting Wilderness Areas to Conserve Utah's Biological Diversity" published in the April 1996 *Great Basin Naturalist.*

No one knows the final price Utahns will pay for hosting the 2002 Winter Olympics. But in terms of the state's natural heritage, blasting this one downhill ski run may prove to be recklessly extravagant.

SPOTTED FROG

It's not easy being green on the Wasatch Front. Just ask a spotted frog—if you can find one. These mountain-adapted amphibians were common in Salt Lake creeks and ponds when the valley was settled. In fact, Mormon pioneers depended on the presence of frogs in water to indicate it was fit for humans to drink.

A century and a half later, Wasatch spotted frogs are disappearing by leaps and bounds, so the amphibians you *don't* see in your city water supply may be an ominous sign. Whatever is killing off frogs, one thing is sure: where frogs *do* live, the water is uncontaminated.

As amphibians, frogs are cold-blooded, moist-skinned creatures that spend part of their lives in water, part on land. Amphibians are a tough kind of animal. As a class, they lived through whatever cataclysm killed off the dinosaurs. Whether they will survive the age of man, however, is unclear. One-third of North America's 86 species of frogs and toads are in trouble, and amphibians are the most threatened class of animal on Earth today.

Three primary populations of spotted frogs survive in Utah. Only one group lives in the Wasatch; it's on the Provo River in Heber Valley between Deer Creek and the Jordanelle Dam. For at least 10,000 years, and perhaps as long as a million years prior, spotted frogs thrived in the Heber Valley, having survived Lake Bonneville and its disappearance.

Spotted frogs are difficult to see today, not only because they've become rare, but also because they spend most of their time in water and they're well

Upper Provo River, spotted frog habitat.

© DAN MILLER

camouflaged. Their backs are dark—from black to dark brown—and spotted. The spots are lighter at the center and fuzzy on the edges. Their legs are dotted and irregularly striped with brown. This coloration on their topsides makes them very difficult to see in the dappled light of wetland reeds. A spotted frog's concealed hind-leg surfaces and lower abdomen are brightly colored from salmon to orange-yellow, and they sport cream-colored blotches as well. Males are two to three inches long, while females are three to four inches. Their heads are round and broader than long, with slightly bugged-out eyes.

You may see a spotted frog in the daytime sitting at a marsh's edge near permanent, cold streams and pools, but not in warm stagnant ponds grown to cattails. If disturbed, they'll jump in the water and burrow into the muck. If floating, they may simply sink into the water.

Like most frogs, spotted frogs swim by kicking out their powerful hind legs and alternately spreading and folding the large webs on their feet. A spotted frog's foot webs are enormous for its body size: they may spread an inch-and-a-half wide on a frog only two-and-a-half inches long.

In the Wasatch, spotted fogs come out in March or April to mate. The males croak a series of a half-dozen short bass notes. Females lay as many as 1,500 eggs in a pint-size mass. The mass is a transparent jelly-like glob left in a marshy area rather than deep in a lake. Frogs don't nest and females abandon their eggs. Tadpoles hatch from these frog eggs in a couple of weeks. A tadpole—basically a long muscular tail attached to a tiny globe of sense organs and guts—develops slowly. It may not become a frog until the end of summer, then it takes four or five years for a spotted frog to reach adult size.

The Wasatch's spotted frogs may feed on bugs or small fish, but Salt Lake biologist Peter Hovingh says they haven't been studied enough to know for certain. In the fall, local spotted frogs may bury themselves in the bottom ooze or in embankments by the water, again the data are incomplete.

A lack of biological data was the reason the U.S. Fish and Wildlife Service gave for taking years longer than it promised to determine whether the spotted frog should be designated as an endangered species. The Fish and Wildlife Service didn't make its decision until after Utah's Jordanelle Reservoir began to fill, drowning many acres of prime spotted frog habitat.

Dams are not the only things killing off spotted frogs in the Wasatch, other human projects take a toll as well. "The small ponds and streams spotted frogs live in are part of the adjacent

SPOTTED FROG

Status: State Conservation Species.

Estimated Number: DWR monitors 14 populations in Utah. Eight in the west desert are doing well with at least 1,000 frogs per unit. Five populations on the Wasatch Front and one on the Sevier River are not doing as well. A 1999 estimate is that there are approximately 11,000 in Utah.

Tips for Viewing: Look for them on the edge of the Provo River between Deer Creek and Jordanelle Dam.

Where you can see spotted frogs

Spotted frog.

© RICK A. FRIDELL

land. If you manage that land for just one thing—such as a golf course—it's bad for everything else," Hovingh observes. Another example: "At lakes in the Sierra Nevadas that are managed for rainbow trout, this nonnative sport fish wipes out all the frogs.

"One thing we know is that urban development is not good for frogs. In the 1960s, several populations of spotted frogs lived in the water by the Van Winkle Expressway. Today, the water is still there, but the spotted frogs are gone." The culprits may be kids, dogs, cats, pesticides, fertilizer, or any number of things; we can only guess, he says.

Silty water caused by construction and livestock overgrazing also wipes out frog populations. Because the presence of frogs indicates healthy water, what these industries are doing to the purity of our drinking water is a serious unanswered question.

Until 1996, the spotted frog was listed by the federal government as a conservation species, which is a species that deserves to be classified as endangered or threatened under the Endangered Species Act but instead is left to the tender mercies of a conservation plan organized by a state government.

Unfortunately, Utah's record is not good when it comes to amphibians. The Division of Wildlife Resources eliminated its herpetologist position in 1993, shortly after State Herpetologist Dave Ross reported that the Wasatch Front population of spotted frogs is on its way to extinction. At the time, Utah's members of congress were worried that acknowledging the rarity of the spotted frog would delay construction and filling of the Jordanelle Reservoir.

Our local politicians depend on the notion that voters won't warm up to cold-blooded critters like frogs. Hey, being green is not easy for either scientists *or* spotted frogs on the Wasatch Front.

FLYING SQUIRRELS

Flying squirrels catch big air, soaring hundreds of feet from tree to tree in Utah's mountain forests. They don't fly by flapping wings, but their flight—like that of clever hang glider pilots—isn't necessarily passive either. "Flying squirrels have a remarkable ability to work with air currents. I've seen one launch as low as four or five feet off the ground, then zoom up forty or fifty feet in the air," remarks George Oliver, a zoologist with Utah's Division of Wildlife Resources. If you add a leather helmet and goggles, that's a familiar picture for Rocky and Bullwinkle fans. But the future of these furry aviators is clouded by logging and other deforestation of Utah's high timberland.

Living in the evergreen forests at mid-elevations of Utah's mountains and plateaus, flying squirrels are seldom seen by those who are not specifically looking for them. Although they are relatively

> **NORTHERN FLYING SQUIRREL**
>
> **Status:** State Species of Special Concern Due to Limited Distribution.
>
> **Estimated Number:** Believed to be well distributed through the major mountain ranges of central and eastern Utah, primarily in the dense, closed forests of riparian zones.
>
> **Tips for Viewing:** Nocturnal, secretive, and small, flying squirrels are difficult to spot. They are active approximately one-half to one hour after sunset; look for gliding shadows in deep forest.

Book Cliffs, northern flying squirrel habitat.

© DAN MILLER

abundant in places such as the Uinta Mountains, they usually go unnoticed because they are active only at night.

Flying squirrels are members of a family of rodents that have evolved a remarkable array of body styles and behavior. For example, their close relatives include marmots, prairie dogs, and chipmunks as well as ground and tree squirrels. Because they are adaptable, members of the squirrel family are native to every continent except Australia and Antarctica. The northern flying squirrel is the only flying squirrel native to Utah and is one of only two species in North America.

Smaller than the more familiar tree squirrel, flying squirrels nonetheless have a similar cylindrical body shape, a pair of chisel-like front teeth, short forepaws with four toes and an abbreviated thumb, two strong hind legs with five toes, and a tail. As with tree squirrels, each toe ends in a sharp claw. Northern flying squirrels have exceptionally plush fur, gray-white on the underbody and mahogany brown on top.

What makes a flying squirrel obviously different from other species of squirrels, aside from larger eyes and ears, are furry flaps of skin that stretch from the front legs to the back legs. In flight, they spread all four legs and flatten out like a pancake. Cord-like muscles hold the outer edge of the furry flap taut. "When flying, the whole body becomes an air foil," notes Utah Museum of Natural History's Eric Rickart. Like hang gliders, flying squirrels have a descent ratio of about three feet forward for each foot of decline.

A flying squirrel usually takes off from a horizontal surface, like a limb, or while hanging head-down from a tree trunk, but researchers have reported that they launch from backflips as well. When a preflight check of its intended glide path is necessary, a flying squirrel will bob and weave its head or skitter sideways on a branch in order to get several perspectives of the position and distance of its targeted landing zone. Once in the air, it may instantly spread its flaps, or it may plummet a short distance, then open like a parachute and glide. Immediately before touching down, it goes into a sharp upward turn and puts all four legs out in front. Often it will land and dart to the far side of the trunk in one predator-evading motion.

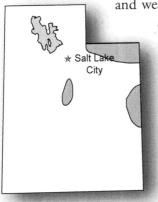

Where you can see flying squirrels in Utah

When a flying squirrel isn't gliding, a second set of muscles holds its flaps against its flanks. Gliding from tree to tree is an energy efficient way to travel in the forest, scientists say, and a quick escape technique from tree-climbing predators such as martens. The folded flaps, however, make flying squirrels slightly less agile on the ground than other squirrels. It's no accident then, that flying squirrels are active only at night, when darkness shields them from most sharp-eyed birds of prey on the lookout for a furry appetizer.

Like other squirrel species, flying squirrels do not hibernate but depend on food storage to get them through winter. They have a brief, frantic mating season in early spring, and after a 40-day gestation period, females give birth to litters that average three pups. Females rear and wean the young and don't allow males near them. A female can carry a baby when gliding by holding it gently in her teeth.

Unlike other squirrel species, flying squirrels are not fussy about what they eat. "Most other squirrels eat only plant material, flying squirrels are omnivorous," Rickart says. They eat insects—a family may consume a quart of June bugs at one meal—and they'll steal bird eggs or chow on nuts, berries, and fungus.

But flying squirrels do need deep timberland to fly and forage. The northern flying squirrel is listed by the Utah Division of Wildlife Resources as a species of special concern because of its limited distribution in the state. Flying squirrels are found only in dense forests, and Utah's timberlands are often completely stripped of trees by large-scale industrial logging techniques.

How much danger Utah's northern flying squirrels face from the current rate of deforestation is uncertain. Because they nest high in trees and only come out at night, flying squirrels are difficult to observe in the wild, so scientists know less about them than other kinds of squirrels. "We don't know for certain—no one's done adequate studies on the northern flying squirrel in Utah—but the two biggest threats appear to be timber harvest and forest fires," zoologist Oliver observes.

Rickart believes Utah's flying squirrels should remain relatively abundant as long as the state's timberland is protected. "If a forest is clear-cut, that's very harmful; they need a closed forest." U.S. Forest Service policy in the past has been to compensate timber companies for bulldozing roads into western forests to clear-cut trees, but current Forest Service chief Michael Dombeck has called for a moratorium on new logging routes in roadless areas, including several in Utah.

However, not everyone agrees with the ban on new logging roads; Utah Representative James V. Hansen (Republican, First District) opposes it because, according to a *Deseret News* article, it will hurt Americans: "by decreasing recreational opportunities, the cost of homes goes even higher and, most importantly, our forests die." Like Boris and Natasha, he's ready to fire up the chainsaws. 🌿

© BRENT R. PAULL

Bear River Migratory Bird Refuge.

CHAPTER FIVE

Great Basin birds
Frequent flyers at Utah's busiest airport.

Millions of birds depend on the east shore of the Great Salt Lake and other water sources in the Great Basin to provide their resting, nesting, breeding, and feeding needs. Migrating birds need specific habitats in seasonal sequence, so at certain times of year, the abundance of wildlife in places such as the Great Salt Lake's Bear River Migratory Bird Refuge is unmatched nearly anywhere else in the world but the Serengeti Plains of east Africa.

MIGRATORY BIRDS ON THE GREAT SALT LAKE

Utah's busiest airport is north of Salt Lake International's runways. It's the east shore of the Great Salt Lake—where the Bear, Weber, and Jordan rivers pour fresh water into briny marshland—that witnesses the arrival and departure of millions of frequent flyers each year. This east shore is an oasis for more than two hundred species of birds, including huge flocks that rest and refuel here on their annual migratory marathons.

For 10,000 years, a significant portion of the Western Hemisphere's shorebirds and waterfowl have depended on this complex of wetlands to rest, nest, breed, or feed. Although the Great Salt Lake is enormous, 1,500 square miles, the overwhelming majority of birds visit the east shore because it is flushed by runoff from the Wasatch Front. Unfortunately, the east shore is where, in the past 100 years, humans have begun to congregate in huge numbers too. With only a narrow strip of land between the Wasatch Mountains and the lake, human sprawl is poised to change forever one of the most important wildlife habitats in the Western Hemisphere.

Staggering numbers of birds have been counted by scientists on the Great Salt Lake's east shore—congregations of a half-million Wilson's phalaropes, a quarter-million American avocets, and a million northern pintail ducks, for example. And it hosts the world's largest concentrations of several species of birds that spend half their year migrating between breeding grounds in North America and wintering areas in South America.

Location of Bear River Migratory Bird Refuge.

But whopping bird counts are just figures on a page. To get a sense of the wealth of wildlife Utah hosts, take a trip to the east shore's Bear River Migratory Bird Refuge. Here, you drive out onto the Great Salt Lake's freshwater marshes on 12 miles of narrow dikes. On either side, you see hundreds of floating birds, such as tundra swans and grebes. In the shallow water, you see scores of spindly-legged shorebirds, like herons and ibis, feeding and fussing with each other. Roll down your car windows and the racket is a PBS nature show in Surround Sound.

Blackbirds screech, stilts weep, avocets peep—and when hundreds of ducks take off together, the beating of wings on water rumbles like a passing freight train. Overhead, squadrons of pelicans glide wingtip-to-wingtip in aerial t'ai chi, their wide bodies a snowy white and their bucket-beaks traffic-cone orange.

In a patch of refuge mud flat no larger than a living room, you can watch a half-dozen birds of different species feeding side by side. An avocet will sweep its upcurved bill like a sickle through the shallow water; a dowitcher probes the muck with a knitting-needle beak while a Wilson's phalarope spins in circles on the water, stirring up grub then stabbing at it. Each type of bird works this Great Salt Lake buffet with different tools. The wide variety of food here—everything from minnows, water bugs, and larvae to clouds of midges—is one reason why the east shore draws such a wide variety of wildlife. Wetlands such as these are second only to rainforests in the number and variety of species they support.

Today, a string of preserves like the Bear River Migratory Bird Refuge dot the Great Salt Lake's east shore, protecting fragments of its wetlands. But these are not enough to support the profusion of wildlife that depends on it. The birds need marshes, mud flats, and fields in continuous open space, uncut by roads. These wide-open spaces support huge breeding flocks, and it's this wide genetic base—a deep gene pool—that will keep these types of birds off the endangered species list for the foreseeable future.

In addition, the Great Salt Lake's birds need uninterrupted water flows from Wasatch rivers and creeks. But nongame wildlife needs are a low priority to local politicians. The state of Utah plans to dam the Bear River, essentially so Salt Lakers can water their thirsty, nonnative bluegrass lawns through the next millennium. Additionally, Utah governor Mike Leavitt intends to pave a four-lane highway through prime east shore wetlands—though less damaging routes are available—so car commuters won't have slowdowns during rush hour in Davis County.

But these kinds of habitat loss are a death sentence for wildlife. "This is the last of the best habitat for these birds," says Al Trout, manager of the Bear River Migratory Bird Refuge. "There are no other places of this size and quality for them to go. Some will attempt to go other places, but whenever they go to new places, that's when they suffer their highest mortality. A lot don't survive." Competing birds are already using all other available habitat that displaced birds may find, say biologists, and they defend their territory against newcomers.

A natural water flow is critical to Great Salt Lake birds as well. "Our main concern with the Bear River dam is the amount of water reduction that will occur," Trout comments. "The natural cycle we need is lots of runoff in May and June. This flushes the salt out of the wetlands and makes them productive for the ducks and the shorebirds that depend on them." Altering the natural water cycle and reducing wetlands on the Great Salt Lake's east shore spell trouble for its migratory birds. These epic avian journeys are only possible if all the links—stopovers—in the chain are available. Migrating birds won't survive without each link in place.

For Davis County commuters, 15 miles of slow auto traffic during rush hour is annoying, but compare it to the trek of a migrating Wilson's phalarope. Most of the world's population of Wilson's phalaropes depends on doubling their weight at the Great Salt Lake's brine shrimp buffet each June and July in order to fly nearly 2,000 miles—60 hours nonstop—to Argentina, Chile, or Peru. The effort, researchers say, may be comparable to a human running four-minute miles for 60 hours.

Now that's a commute.

WHOOPING CRANES AND SANDHILL CRANES

Cranes must enjoy standing in ice water. At Grays Lake, Idaho—where a soaker numbs your foot like a shot of Novocaine—hundreds of sandhill cranes come to wade, mate, eat, and loaf around each year. Grays "Lake" is actually a broad, shallow marsh cradled in a high mountain bowl 60 miles north of the Utah border. It's brimming with crystal runoff streaming down from the snow-draped shoulders of 9,800-foot Caribou Mountain and from the grassy foothills that surround it.

A national wildlife refuge, Grays Lake hosts the world's largest population of nesting sandhill cranes. For a time, biologists thought this remote mountain wetlands would be a perfect home for North America's tallest and rarest bird—the whooping crane.

Cranes, remember, are those tall, stately birds with spindly legs, long necks, and straight bills. They're often noted for their wild and graceful courtship dance and because they pair up for life. If you're lucky enough to see a sandhill crane and a whooping crane together, the difference will be readily apparent. Whoopers stand about a foot taller and are a luminous white except for black wing tips and a black moustache-like stripe near the bill. Sandhills are smaller bodied and gray. Both cranes have a striking patch of bare red skin like a scarlet skullcap on top of their heads.

Everything about whooping cranes is big, from their voices to the stretch of their wings. They are by far the largest of the three crane species in North America. Whoopers may stand five-feet tall and have a wingspan of nearly eight feet, and they trumpet a shrill *ker-loo, ker-lee-oo,* which can be heard for two miles. The bugle of a call resonates from the whooper's five-foot long windpipe, which is looped like a French horn within their breast-bone. On the ground, the call is a commanding alarm. While traveling, it keeps whoopers together.

And they do travel. The last remaining migra-tory group of whoopers journeys south 2,400 miles from summer nests near the Arctic Circle to the Gulf of Mexico each year. They can cruise at 35 to 45 miles an hour and log 175 miles a day.

Like other cranes, whoopers hang out in wet-lands and estuaries scarfing up whatever wiggles: bugs, clams, small fish, and tiny rodents. Until Europeans col-onized North America and relentlessly drained its prairie marshes, whooping cranes ranged from coast to coast. The wholesale conversion of wetlands to farmland reduced the population of whooping cranes to about 600 individuals by the late nineteenth century. By 1941, only 22 whooping cranes were left in the world.

The largest group of those remain-ing—15 that wintered on the Gulf of Mexico—could have been wiped out easily by one natural disaster, such as a hurricane. So, in 1975, U.S. Fish and Wildlife biologists tried an urgent experiment in the hope of starting a new population of migrating whooping cranes that would nest at Grays Lake. It went like this: whooping cranes lay two eggs, but usually raise only one chick,

Where you can see sandhill cranes

★ Boise

★ Salt Lake City

★ Carson City

★ Phoenix

CRANES

Status: Whooping cranes are U.S. Endangered, sandhill cranes are relatively abundant.

Estimated Number: Less than 300 whooping cranes exist in the world.

Tips for Viewing: Cranes are tall stately birds, white to rust to gray. Sandhills have a scarlet cap. Look for them in wetlands and in grassy upland areas.

© DICK SPENCER / PIKA STREET PHOTOGRAPHY

Grays Lake, sandhill crane habitat.

unlike sandhills. So, biologists pinched one egg each from the nests of wild whoopers and slipped them into sandhill crane nests at Grays Lake. Scientists hoped the sandhills would foster parent the whoopers.

This part of the experiment worked. By the 1980s, the Grays Lake population of whoopers grew to three dozen. The immature whoopers migrated with their sandhill foster parents 750 miles to New Mexico each winter. But trouble came in unpredictable ways. Whooping crane chicks didn't recognize the warning calls of their sandhill crane parents. Instead of running for cover when a sandhill sounded the alarm, the young whoopers wandered around confused. Worse, when the surviving cross-parented whoopers did reach adult age—four years old—they showed no interest in pairing up with their own kind. When it came to mating with other whoopers, these Grays Lake cranes had cold feet.

Scientists now believe that sandhill crane parents can't teach adopted whooping cranes the correct courtship dance for their species. And without proper role models, cranes don't mate. All cranes pair up by an elaborate dance, and each crane species has unique variations of it. For example,

Sandhill crane.

© BRENT R. PAULL

whoopers dance silently. One lowers its head and flaps its wings, then leaps into the air with its head stretched back. Its mate runs forward a few steps, pumping its head up and down and flapping its wings. Both birds then spring up and down like they're on Pogo sticks. Without that specific dance, whooping cranes just don't get in the mood. Ever.

Attempting to create a new migrating group of whooping cranes was a heroic—and expensive—effort by scientists. It ended in 1988 and the number of cross-parented whooping cranes has dwindled to two. "The last time a whooping crane was spotted at Grays Lake was several years ago," said Steve Bouffard, a biologist at the U.S. Fish and Wildlife Service's Southeast Idaho complex. "And we really don't expect to see them here again. Of the two left, one summers at Red Rock Lakes National Wildlife Refuge in Montana, the other stays in Yellowstone."

It goes to show that all the expensive science we care to pay for with taxes will not, in itself, save a species. Only preserving habitat gives whooping cranes—or any type of creature—the opportunity to survive. Because so much avian habitat is disappearing, bird species are currently going extinct at a rate of 100 species per year per million bird species, according to Stuart Pimm, an ecologist at the University of Tennessee. Birds commonly seen just 15 years ago are nearly impossible to spot now, he points out.

So, a visit to Grays Lake is like a step into the past, back to a time when North America had a wealth of bird species because it had many kinds of habitat. The Grays Lake area has marshy wetlands, grassy foothills, and wooded alpine slopes; two hundred species of birds have been identified there.

But spotting a whooping crane standing in the cold water at Grays Lake would be too sad a sight today: solitary, celibate, and still one of the rarest birds in the world.

LOGGERHEAD SHRIKE

A songbird that hunts like a hawk and skewers prey on a thorn or barbed wire—like a butcher hanging meat—is not an uncommon sight in Utah. The robin-size loggerhead shrike is famous in North America for making grasshopper, mouse, or sparrow shish kebab, though no one is certain exactly why it impales dinner on sharp objects. And while naturalists debate the reasons for this skewering behavior, the "butcher bird" is disappearing from large sections of its traditional range in the northeastern states.

With its black Lone Ranger mask and powerful, falcon-like beak, the loggerhead shrike looks like a songbird with attitude. While its overall size is unremarkable for a perching bird, its head is larger than most, which gives it the first part of its name, loggerhead, a Scottish term for large, or thick, head. It has a gray back, a white chest and belly, black wings, and a longish black tail that's striped with white. A bit smaller than a robin, it is 8 to 10 inches long.

The loggerhead is an aggressive predator that hunts large insects such as Mormon crickets (grasshoppers) and bumblebees in the summer when they are plentiful and nabs small birds and mice when the weather turns cold. It perches on a post, bush, or wire with a wide view of the surrounding area and with keen vision spots small prey more than 100 feet away. The loggerhead may pounce from its low perch or it may hover, then dive. It kills prey with a hard blow from a sharply curved beak. Lacking the strong talons of a raptor, the loggerhead then transports dinner in its bill.

Its relatively weak claw grip is what leads some naturalists to believe the loggerhead impales prey so that it can hold the carcass stationary while tearing it apart with its bill. Unlike a hawk, which holds its prize down with strong claws and pulls it apart with its beak, the loggerhead may hang prey on a sharp object so that it can perch next to it and rip off eatable chunks. Or the skewering behavior may be a food storage program. Sometimes bugs and small animals are found spiked but not dismembered. This leads to the suspicion that loggerhead shrikes may kill more than they can eat and then in lean times come back to their food cupboard. This theory is bolstered by the fact that loggerhead shrikes sometimes will press their dead prey snugly into the crotch of a tree rather than hanging it.

Maybe hanging meat in its territory is a male loggerhead's way of attracting female loggerheads, speculates the Utah Natural History Museum's Eric Rickart. "Everybody knows about this shrike behavior [spiking food on sharp objects] but I've never seen it. I'm not certain, but it may be male behavior that advertises the quality of its territory. Maybe

LOGGERHEAD SHRIKE

Status: Relatively common in Utah's west desert. Disappearing in northeastern states.

Tips for Viewing: They are slightly smaller than a robin; look for the black mask and heavy beak. The loggerhead shrike often perches on tree branches overlooking open fields.

males are making a statement to females, 'Look at *my* territory, there's plenty of food for a brood.'"

Certainly, when it comes to attracting mates, the loggerhead shrike shouldn't rely entirely on its song—if the human ear is any judge of romantic music. Though classified as songbirds, loggerhead vocalizations range from strangled gurgles and squeaky whistles to grating alarm shrieks. In fact, its name, shrike, is derived from the word shriek.

However unmelodic their tune, both males and females frequently break into song during spring courtship. They construct nests of twigs and grass in thorny shrubs like greasewood. Females lay and incubate a clutch of four to six eggs. The male feeds the female during incubation, bringing her bugs he's snagged. Eggs hatch after about two weeks, and then both mom and dad deliver food frantically to satisfy the fast-growing young birds. With a nest full of squawking beaks, loggerhead parents must deliver about 15 grasshoppers per hour, according to one study.

In two to three weeks, the young loggerheads are nearly as large as their parents are. They move to nearby branches during the day and gradually become self-sufficient. An adolescent loggerhead shrike's plumage is similar to an adult's except that its feathers are barred on the back of its neck and crown.

There are only two species of shrikes in the Western Hemisphere and during the winter you can see both in Utah. The loggerhead is a year-round Utah resident, while the northern shrike winters in northern Utah after breeding in the Arctic during the summer.

Once common all across North America, loggerhead shrikes have now vanished from the northeastern states and are declining in the Midwest. Two culprits are suspected: habitat loss and pesticides. Where loss of habitat pushes loggerheads to do their hunting on roadsides, they may collide with cars.

Where you can see loggerhead shrikes

★ Boise

★ Salt Lake City

★ Carson City

★ Phoenix

Loggerhead shrike.

© RICK A. FRIDELL

Electric fences are hazardous to perching loggerheads as well. California prison officials have executed 111 loggerhead shrikes—according to a *Deseret News* article—inadvertently electrocuting them on their brand-new, high-voltage penitentiary fences.

Luckily, loggerhead shrikes are still relatively common in Utah's arid, open spaces. And that's fitting. After all, here's a bird with its own food storage program that can probably eat more Mormon crickets than a seagull. It belongs here. 🌿

Bryce Canyon National Park.

PART II
What's Happening to Wild Places?

© DAN MILLER

© DAN MILLER

Sandhill crane.

CHAPTER SIX

Island syndrome extinctions

How small an area is too small for nature to carry on?

Islands cause extinctions, and Utah's wild places are rapidly becoming islands of natural landscape surrounded by a sea of human impact, say experts. Our national parks and other protected native landscapes were once shielded by buffer zones around them and by corridors of natural area between them. Now they are increasingly cut off and surrounded by human encroachments such as ranchettes, cabins, subdivisions, strip malls, over-grazed pastures, clear-cut forests, fenced farmlands, and highways.

Whether oceanic island or mainland island of wilderness, the smaller the size, the more extinctions, say ecologists. For example, Bryce Canyon National Park, which is only about five miles wide by twenty miles long, has lost 40 percent of its small mammal population since the park was created, including the spotted skunk, the red fox, and the white-tailed jackrabbit, notes David Quammen, who spent eight years studying island biogeography for his book *Song of the Dodo.* The larger Yellowstone-Teton national park system, on the other hand, lost one species, the gray wolf, in the same time period.

By making islands of wild places, we condemn many native species within them to extinction. It is a fact of biogeography that's true of islands on the ocean as well as islands of natural landscapes surrounded by a sea of human impacts. Island plant and animal populations are small and cut off, so they're vulnerable to extinction, Quammen remarks. "All populations fluctuate in size from year to year responding to good conditions—like gentle weather and abundant food—or bad conditions—like drought, harsh winters, and famine—that they encounter. Small populations are more likely to fluctuate to zero when conditions are bad because zero is never far away." A large, dispersed mainland population would survive the same population swing. Islands in the ocean are not completely isolated, Quammen notes; they have the traffic of seagoing birds. Similarly, artificial islands of wilderness in Utah are not absolutely cut off—what's an island to a chipmunk isn't one to an eagle—but the island paradigm holds true.

The rate of island syndrome extinctions can be predicted by the size of the park and the year it was established. The smaller the park and the longer it is isolated, the more species it loses, a recently updated study of western national parks found. "The premise behind establishing parks is that by protecting in perpetuity a patch of landscape, we can protect in perpetuity the ecological community within it," Quammen wrote for *The New York Times*. But most national parks are not large enough—as islands—to host their full complement of species over time. "Nature isn't convenient. Nature can't be compartmentalized. Nature is inherently big," he points out.

On the other hand, connections between protected natural areas and buffer zones of open land around them ensure the long-term health of the native landscapes that are designated as protected, says Eric Rickart, a local expert on island biogeography and curator of mammals for the Utah Museum of Natural History. "We need large areas protected; it's a law of biology. Large spaces support a large number of species. But they don't have to be huge untouchable areas. We need core wild areas, without roads or human disturbance, surrounded by areas of increasing human use."

Several groups of Utah animals are at high risk for extinction today: big predators like wolverines, lynx, and pine martin; amphibians, such as salamanders and frogs; and Bonneville and Colorado cutthroat trout. Also, Utah's share of plants awaiting listing as threatened or endangered, and its proportion of rare plants, is one of the highest in the United States, say local biologists.

Keeping open corridors of natural landscape, such as streams or drainages, to connect protected wild areas helps animals avoid island syndrome extinction, biologists note. However, different types of animals have different requirements. For example, grizzly bears are not known to travel within narrow corridors, while cougars will pad through a passageway as slim as an irrigation ditch. Native plants also rely on natural corridors. Often wild plants require shade or protection from drying winds in order to get started. If their seeds fall into a hayfield or a roadside, they may not germinate. But if blown or carried along a wild corridor, native plants will spread into other wild areas.

When protected natural areas become islands, the native plant and animal relationships within them begin to unravel, and the result is a cascading loss of species diversity. This makes a difference in our preservation priorities, Quammen observes. Wilderness supporters shouldn't define what's wild solely in terms of the human experience of solitude and natural beauty. We should protect landscapes that support the greatest richness of plants, animals, birds, amphibians, insects, and trees. We're overvaluing scenic landscapes and undervaluing biologically important ones, he said in an interview. "Our wilderness discussion has been confused by debates over what's 'natural,' what's 'pristine,' and what's 'wilderness' with a small 'w.' I don't believe we should debate definitions of wilderness. I think we should be concerned about preserving biological diversity. Biodiversity—the variety of life in a given area—is a form of richness, just like the Social Security Trust Fund or the books in our libraries," he says. "It belongs to future generations. You can't measure 'natural,' you can't measure 'pristine.' But you can measure and count biological diversity. Biological diversity is what's important in the long run, and what our standard should be in terms of protecting landscape." The Utah Wilderness Coalition wilderness proposals were not drawn up with preserving biodiversity as the primary objective, notes Dick Carter, longtime Utah wilderness advocate, but they do accomplish that. A large percentage of the acreage they recommend for wilderness designation adjoins or connects other already protected areas, such as national parks and monuments. Buffering and connecting these preserved tracts, as the wilderness proposals suggest, would help reduce the high risk of extinctions in protected natural areas.

In fact, Utah can become a trendsetter in applying biodiversity as a criterion for protecting native landscapes with wilderness designation, according to Quammen. He points to the landmark scientific paper by seven local scientists, including mammologist Rickart, "Selecting Wilderness Areas to Conserve Utah's Biological Diversity," published in the April 1996 *Great Basin Naturalist*. The paper outlines objective scientific standards for wilderness evaluation of Utah's Bureau of Land

Management land. "The use of biological and ecological criteria to designate Bureau of Land Management wilderness areas in Utah . . . would help to avoid future conflicts over resource management," these local scientists write.

Roadless natural areas are vital, the scientists argue, and it has nothing to do with backpackers. Cutting roads into native landscapes creates a pathway for the invasion of nonnative, or exotic, plant species. "The disturbance caused by road building gives aggressive and broadly adapted nonnative species [such as cheatgrass] a toehold. Later, wildfires allow exotic grasses to spread and crowd out native species. Nonnative grasses have greatly increased grassland wildfire frequency in Utah from former cycles of about 60–110 years to less than five-year cycles now," the paper's authors say. "Given the costliness of aggressive fire suppression and habitat restoration measures, the most economical strategy for preventing the spread of introduced [nonnative] grasses to areas that are still relatively pristine may be to maintain their roadless character," the paper said.

It just makes sense to use wilderness designation to protect native species, the local scientists argue. "Over the long term, it is both cheaper and easier to protect species . . . in their intact, functioning ecosystems than to conserve them individually in fragmented and decimated populations under the Endangered Species Act."

It's not only isolation on small islands of habitat that threatens native species with extinction, Quammen wrote in *Song of the Dodo*. Introducing exotic animal species into a native landscape causes a net loss of biodiversity as well, "With all exotics you can lose five or ten native species for every one exotic you introduce," he states. For example, in east Africa, the Nile perch was introduced to lakes because it's a larger fish and a better source of protein than native species. Trouble is, Nile perch outcompete and feed on the native fish, so nearly all of those natives are now extinct. The Nile perch itself may be doomed, having decimated its own food source.

In Utah, rainbow trout and mountain goats are two of many exotics introduced by the Division of Wildlife Resources for sport. But rainbow trout dominate native trout food sources and mate with native trout, endangering the gene pool of both the Bonneville and Colorado cutthroat. Aggressive feeders, rainbow trout may also threaten native Utah salamanders and frogs, critics say. Similarly, mountain goats overgraze their adopted home, damaging the plants that native elk and deer feed on.

But can't wildlife managers preserve habitat for popular game animals and at the same time help save other less charismatic species? "Yes," Quammen replies. "But that's not to say that everything good for deer is good for biodiversity. For example, encouraging a large population of elk and deer is not necessarily helpful, especially if you kill off their predators." Biologists point out that the destruction of willows and aspen seedlings on streambanks in Yellowstone is caused by the intensive grazing of its abnormally large elk herds; it's the elimination of predators in the past that allowed Yellowstone elk herds to grow huge. "Game animals have friends that endangered species would love to have. The white-tailed deer is never going to be an endangered species. It's got friends in high places," Quammen says. There are probably more deer in North America now than when Columbus landed. But nongame wildlife need advocates as well. And game managers can be voices of moderation to the hunting community, Quammen says.

Only 4 percent of the world is preserved in parks and protected areas, Quammen points out, and we can't give up on the other 96 percent. "We shouldn't separate ourselves from nature. We can't say, 'Nature will be in parks and preserves and we'll be everywhere else.' We can learn how to live and conduct our businesses in ways that encourage biodiversity. We should plant native species when landscaping our homes, stop using pesticides, and welcome back native birds and bugs. A lot of the landscape in the West is destroyed, not by mining and timber companies, but by liberal conservationists who want to have a cabin on twenty acres in the foothills. We all have friends and loved ones who are doing that and we need to speak up about it. People who want to live in the country and commute to town erode wild landscape. If you love the landscape, live in the city."

Quammen is encouraged by one political development in Utah: "Southern Utah's new Grand Staircase-Escalante National Monument—which reconnects two islands of natural landscape, Bryce Canyon National Park and Capitol Reef National Park—is the best news for biodiversity in the past ten years." ❦

Downy brohme.

Leafy spurge.

Purple loosestrife.

Yellow starthistle.

Spotted knapweed.

Pepperweed.

PHOTOS
© STEVE
DEWEY

CHAPTER SEVEN

Aliens have invaded!
Weeds take over habitat.

Wherever people live, work, or play, weeds follow like a dark shadow. When we visit natural areas to hike, bike, or take a Sunday drive, seeds of these alien travelers stowaway on us and invade our complex, yet balanced native ecosystems. These exotic hitchhikers root and spread quickly wherever humans have disturbed natural landscapes—places like roadsides, trail-heads, and cow-pounded pasture.

When this happens, a single variety of scrappy foreign plant will overrun many types of native plants—and the resulting weed field is either inedible or poisonous to wildlife. Consequently, weeds have become a major cause of habitat loss in the West. For example:

- A 1988 study in Glacier National Park found that invading weeds wiped out 6 of 21 of the park's native plant species in the rare category.
- Weeds have taken over important winter grazing areas in Montana and Wyoming, reducing elk and other wildlife populations, says Steve Burningham, a weed specialist with the Utah Agriculture Department.
- Whole ranches in Washington and North and South Dakota have been overrun by a weed called leafy spurge, forcing the owners to sell out, reports Larry O. Maxfield, Utah's Bureau of Land Management Weed Coordinator.

Ranchers, hunters, and conservationists all agree weeds must be con-trolled, yet the rate of infestation is snowballing. At least nine million acres of BLM land—that's the size of four Yellowstones—already have a serious

© ALAN HUESTIS / FAST FOCUS PRODUCTIONS

Weed-infested scenic area.

weed problem, and officials predicted the trouble would spread to a total of 19 million acres by 2000. On all Western public lands, weeds are spreading at a rate of seven square miles a day.

It's important to remember that the plants we call weeds are not pests in their native land, Maxfield points out. Where these robust plants evolved, natural predators, such as specialized bugs and diseases, keep them in check. For example, in China they spray insecticides on their native Asian tamarisk plants to kill the bugs that eat them. In Utah, where the nonnative Asian tamarisk has gotten loose, it encounters no such opposition as it overruns the state's riversides. We have to spray herbicides to kill Asian tamarisk because it has no native predators in Utah.

Without natural enemies, weeds quickly dominate natural areas, outcompeting the native plants for light and nutrients. They tolerate a broad range of climatic conditions and, once established, are tough to eliminate. Weeds reproduce abundantly; one yellowstar thistle plant, for example, produces

150,000 seeds. Wildlife can't eat weeds and some—like knapweed—are poisonous. In this way, weeds quickly turn a diverse, stable, native ecosystem into a near monoculture of exotic pests.

Utah's BLM office lists 17 weeds as noxious or dangerous. Of these, four are thistles and four are knapweeds. Some of them will fool you. "Lots of people see northern Utah hillsides covered with yellow flowers and think they're really pretty," says Maxfield. They don't know they're looking at an infestation of dyer's woad, a scrappy invader from Europe that takes over and won't go away.

Weeds arrive here from other continents, often brought intentionally as ornamental plants or accidentally along with livestock feed. Once here, they take us for a ride. Weed seeds stick to our shoes, clothes, tires, fenders, and domestic animals. They hitchhike on us, going where we go, sprouting wherever we seriously disturb the native vegetation.

Road building is a prime invasion pathway for weeds. A bulldozer's blade clears off native plant cover that would normally resist weedy intruders. The weeds are then free to sprout and spread on bare roadsides, and they quickly invade natural areas on either side. Humans build the roads, then disperse the weed seeds along them. It's an efficient system for the weeds. So effective that "introduced plants now form the dominant cover on many . . . landscapes in western North America and are widespread in Utah," according to local scientists in their paper "Selecting Wilderness Areas to Conserve Utah's Biological Diversity." These local scientists argue that it's cheap and effective land management to keep native ecosystems in one piece rather than allow them to be cut up with roads and then fight the resulting problems of weeds and loss of native plants.

Once weeds are established, there are several strategies to get rid of them; no one of them is completely satisfactory. Weeds on a one- or two-year life cycle, like thistle, can be yanked. These are annual or biannual plants, sprouting from seed. The hand-pulling technique worked well for Millard County, which held an annual Weed Day where hundreds of volunteers would pull scotch thistle out of wild areas. After a few years, Weed Day had to relocate for lack of weeds.

Perennial weeds such as knapweed and dyer's woad have a taproot that can drill a dozen feet into the ground. If you yank the top of one of these plants, it will just grow back from the root. In these cases, chemicals are the weapon of choice. "Herbicides are still the main tool" to control perennial weeds, says Burningham. "But biological control is our only hope in some places like wild and pristine areas, where you don't want to use chemicals."

Biological weapons, such as bugs that prey on weeds, are moving from the laboratory onto the range. Local land managers report they have introduced thistle head weevils into musk thistle infestations. This specialized insect bores into the thistle's seed head and destroys seeds.

But weed colonies have more lives than cats. With any weed-fighting strategy, people must go back to where the intruders are established and kill them year after year. For this reason, the most effective and highest priority technique of weed management is prevention, says the BLM. On 95 percent of BLM land, they point out, weeds are not yet a serious problem.

In the big picture, the most elegant strategy to keep natural landscapes weed free is to stop building new roads into them. But there are important ways hikers and mountain bikers can help the problem as well. Land managers ask recreationists to clean their boots, bikes, pets, and cars before heading into natural areas. For outfitters, it's the law that any feed for pack animals must be certified weed free. If you see thistle plants, yank them. If they're flowering or gone to seed, bag them and burn them at home. Report weed infestations you see in the backcountry to local land managers. These alien invaders are merciless—take no prisoners. 🌿

CHAPTER EIGHT

Western hydro-logic floods critical wildlife habitat.

RETHINKING LAKE POWELL

It took the soupy Colorado River 10 million years to sculpt Glen Canyon from a heart of radiant red and tan sandstone. It took federal Bureau of Reclamation engineers just 20 years to fill it to the rim with slackwater. A bureaucrat named the reservoir "Lake" Powell.

To John Wesley Powell, in 1869, Glen Canyon was an unexpected refuge from the roaring, whitewater chaos of Cataract Canyon and the wild upper Colorado River. His rapids-pounded wooden dories slowed to a crawl beneath towering walls with hanging gardens of fern and moss. Willows and cottonwoods fringed the riverbanks and deep alcoves echoed with birdsong and the trickle of chilly springs. For 150 miles, this unnamed canyon was a cool, serpentine oasis in the searing August slickrock. Powell found a "curious ensemble of wonderful features," in the canyon: "Carved walls, royal arches, alcove gulches." He chose the Scottish word glen, meaning a secluded, green valley, and named it Glen Canyon.

Fifty-five years later, Bureau of Reclamation surveyors saw it differently. Glen Canyon, they reported, was "of no particular value so far as is known." The Bureau of Reclamation had an attitude about the desert and its plumbing. Their "reclamation" mission was to irrigate naturally arid land for agricultural use. "The unregulated Colorado River is a son of a bitch," maintained Bureau Commissioner Floyd Dominy, ". . . either in flood or in trickle." Together with Western congressmen and lobbyists, the bureau proposed a

The reservoir named Lake Powell.

© DAN MILLER

"cash register dam" for Glen Canyon. Everyone will benefit, they argued. It will generate electricity to pay for irrigation projects, control both silt and floods, store water, and create a water sports haven for visitors.

They got their way. Then, even while the cement was still curing in Glen Canyon Dam in 1963, the Bureau of Reclamation turned its attention downstream to an even more ambitious scheme: they proposed building two dams in the Grand Canyon.

Today, Lake Powell's upstream end is rapidly filling with silt. The dam itself once caused a flood in the Escalante River's scenic Coyote Gulch, and its reservoir extends, despite Congress's intent, into Rainbow Bridge National Monument. It spouts clear, 46-degree water downstream, which has endangered native fish and scoured away Grand Canyon's beaches. The reservoir does store several years worth of water, but it's also a huge evaporation pond, losing more than a half-million acre feet of water a year and further mineralizing what's left. The dam generates electricity in a region of huge coalfields.

But they were right about visitors. Today, Lake Powell is more popular than either the Grand Canyon or Yellowstone National Park. About 3 million visitors come to Lake Powell each year—nearly the population of Los Angeles. Of course, that's become another problem.

Many visitors consider Lake Powell the Eighth Wonder of the World. Its beauty is surreal: an aquamarine sea lapping against bare domes of Navajo sandstone. That sandstone formation is unique in the world. For millions of years, rain, wind, and snow rapidly eroded the rock above the Colorado River, dissolving it at the geologically swift rate of a foot every two thousand years. Little soil was left for plants to take hold, and it became a vast petrified desert, known as slickrock.

Even conservationist David Brower predicted in 1963, "Lake Powell . . . will probably be the most beautiful reservoir in the world, though the best has gone under." Similarly, when writer Wallace Stegner was asked whether Lake Powell was a beautiful place, he said, "Yes. But it's like looking at a picture of Miss America with her legs covered."

What lies beneath Lake Powell's numbered navigational buoys? Few Americans alive today saw Glen Canyon as John Wesley Powell did. One of them is Ken Sleight, who guided river runners through the canyon from 1953 to 1963. Sleight is at a loss when asked to name his favorite place in pre-dam Glen Canyon. "There were so many beautiful places," he said. "Forbidding Canyon, Music Temple, Hidden Canyon. On each trip through Glen Canyon, I went to one place I hadn't been," he remembers. "I don't go to Lake Powell very often, it's too painful," he says. To the few that knew and appreciated Glen Canyon and its many side canyons, the buoys are as sobering as tombstones in a cemetery.

To the dam builders, cathedrals are built of granite and marble by the hand of man. But river runners found the canyon's dramatic wild places had spiritual qualities and named many of them after places of worship. Cathedral-in-the-Desert—now lying below Lake Powell's channel buoy number 68—was an immense vermilion alcove over 30 stories high, ribboned with silver-black desert varnish. High overhead, a small crack of sunlight streaked through narrow canyon walls, illuminating a jade pool fed by a slim crystal waterfall. Velvety moss blanketed the red sandstone. "It was the single most spectacular place I ever visited," writes Eliot Porter in *The Place No One Knew*.

Porter found another canyon named Cathedral a "journey reminiscent of Xanadu," referring to a mythical place of idyllic beauty. There he walked "through caverns measureless to man." Cathedral Canyon lies below Lake Powell's buoy number 45.5.

Pre-dam Glen Canyon was one of the most remote places in the United States. It was not until 1946 that a dirt road was completed across the area, linking Hanksville with Blanding. The road's ferry across the Colorado was a homemade contraption of planks hammered into a two-car size bridge and hauled by rusty overhead cables. It was the only crossing of Glen Canyon above Lee's Ferry, Arizona. Called Hite, or Dandy, Crossing, it now lies below buoy number 139.

But Glen Canyon was full of human history. The first visitors, small groups of stone-age nomads, hunted mammoth, sloth, and camel and gathered edible plants in the region about 9,000 years ago. Their few remains are flint chips, fireplace hearths, and grinding stones. Thousands of years later, Anasazi planted corn on the canyon bottom and wove baskets in the alcoves. Their adobe dwellings reveal that they favored Navajo Creek and Moqui, Forgotten, and Lake Canyons off the main stem of Glen Canyon. The first five miles of Lake Canyon, for example, had over three dozen stone and mortar dwellings. The massive rust and black-varnished cliff face of Wright Bar—now underwater across from Wahweap Marina—displayed a spectacular 50-foot panel of ancient drawings pecked into stone. Some petroglyphs dated from 100 B.C. Photos show that each of the hundreds of inscribed figures are unique, yet their combined effect suggests a prehistoric billboard or narrative. The Anasazi left Glen Canyon about A.D. 1300. Utes, Southern Paiutes, and later Navajos, ranged over parts of what's now Glen Canyon National Recreation Area but left few traces. Countless Native American artifacts lie beneath Lake Powell. The reservoir rose quickly and ended archeological survey in the canyon.

For most of the nineteenth century, southeastern Utah was a blank space on government maps. The Escalante River was undiscovered, and the nearby Henry Mountains were still unnamed. Powell, with four boats, 10 men, and a few brass scientific instruments, floated the Colorado River from Green River, Wyoming, into unknown territory. After weeks of tumultuous rapids, Powell washed into tranquil Glen Canyon. He wrote of leisurely passing by towering monuments, oak-set glens, fern-decked alcoves, and mural curves. They glided hour after hour stopping each time some new wonder arrested their attention.

Powell spotted a cleft in the canyon wall, almost hidden by cottonwoods, near the San Juan River's junction with the Colorado. Inside was a vast grotto over 200 feet high and 500 feet long. Deep inside, a clear pool mirrored columbines, ferns, and moss clinging to red walls. Powell's thermometer read 104 degrees on the river, but in the hollow it was cool and shady. A song in the alcove echoed to the river, a half mile away. It was "made for an academy of music" Powell said, and named it Music Temple. They stayed two refreshing days. His men carved their names in the alcove wall. Music Temple lies under the east side of Lake Powell near buoy number 55.

In the early part of the twentieth century, adventurous visitors came to float the river and see Glen Canyon. In 1940, Franklin D. Roosevelt's secretary of the interior, Harold Ickes, proposed a 4.5 million-acre national park, the heart of which was Glen Canyon. Called Escalante National Park, it was to include both sides of the Colorado River for 280 miles from Moab down to Lee's Ferry. It would cover the Green River from its confluence with the Colorado up to the town of Green River, and it would extend east, protecting 70 miles of the San Juan River. Lobbyists for mine owners and cattlemen, and the Utah congressional delegation, were incensed over the possibility that grazing permits and mining access would be restricted. They quickly mobilized and scuttled Ickes's plan.

After World War II, the Bureau of Reclamation proposed building dams in Dinosaur National Monument, Flaming Gorge, and Glen Canyon as part of the Colorado River Storage Project. While Midwestern and Eastern legislators complained that Western irrigation dams were government subsidies benefiting a few, Utah Senator Arthur Watkins denounced citizen dam opponents as "abominable nature lovers." No Western elected representative spoke in favor of preserving Glen Canyon.

To Sleight, it was senseless to drown 150 miles of canyon to generate electricity or store water while, just downstream, Lake Mead was full. He joined with river runners and other local outdoor activists to form a group called Friends of Glen Canyon. "We were too young back then," Sleight says of the group. "We didn't know how to protest or lobby to stop the dam. We were too timid. But some of us are not so timid now," he adds. Only five months after Glen Canyon Dam was authorized, the first bulldozers went to work. Back then, the law was not too concerned with environmental consequences. The Bureau of Reclamation wrote Glen Canyon's Environmental Impact Statement in 1995.

Dam in place, the reservoir's water rose quickly in the 1960s. A mile below Halls Crossing, in a side canyon named Lost Eden, a rookery hosting scores of great blue herons drowned. Up and down Glen Canyon that scene was repeated. Nesting grounds of egrets, pelicans, and other birds were inundated. Rising water submerged side canyons of willow and cottonwood, which had provided habitat for ringtail cats, deer, foxes, coyotes, bobcats, skunks, badgers, beavers, and cougars. Glen Canyon's seep-watered hanging gardens—so specialized they live in few places in the world—were the last to submit. The native squawfish, which grew to five feet long and one hundred pounds in Powell's time, all but disappeared. The bonytail chub, once the most common fish in the Colorado River, was also a victim of the dam's cold, clear water. Today, the reservoir's shoreline nurtures little vegetation or wildlife habitat because the water level fluctuates 20 to 25 feet a day.

Today's Lake Powell boaters get what was once a bird's-eye view of upper Glen Canyon. Waterskiers buzz around previously high and inaccessible cliffs, alcoves, and domes. But if you think about it, opponents say, "It's like flooding the Sistine Chapel so visitors can get a better view." Lake Powell has five marinas renting about six hundred boats. Figuring the lake has less than 300 square miles of surface area, the math seems scary at peak season density—even without counting private boats and jet-skis. Luckily, the reservoir has so many fingers that it can hide lots of watercraft. Both *Sea Kayaking* and *Backpacker* magazine publish articles about kayaking on Lake Powell, now that human-powered craft are a common sight. Boat launching, jet-skiing, swimming, fishing, and camping happen concurrently. Friction between rowdy watersports fans and visitors looking for solitude is continuous.

Still, there's only one town on Lake Powell—Page, Arizona—and it has fewer than 10,000 people. Glen Canyon's rims are bridged only at Hite on the north and at Glen Canyon Dam on the south. The reservoir itself is not natural, but the surrounding desert is remote and rewarding to the patient, attentive traveler. Also, the Colorado River never sleeps. As it flows into the still water of Lake Powell, it drops enough silt to bury more than fifty square miles of lake bottom a foot deep each year. Most of the sediment is upstream where the river first slows. "There is no question that at some point Hite Marina will silt in," the Park Service's John Rittenour notes. "But we have no immediate plans to move it." Eventually the Colorado will fill Lake Powell with sediment and make a waterfall of Glen Canyon dam.

There's a lesson in Lake Powell, Sleight contends. "Stop 'developing' wild places; you destroy what people come to see. It's happening over and over again in southern Utah." Sleight believes that the canyons now drowned by the reservoir would begin to regenerate if the Bureau of Reclamation reduced

Sandhill crane chick.

© MARK PARCHMAN

TreeUtah volunteers plant trees along the Jordan River.

© TREEUTAH

the water level. A group specifically organized for this purpose, Glen Canyon Institute, is lobbying to draw down the water level of the reservoir nicknamed "Lake Foul" and to restore the Colorado's natural riversides, which are critical habitat for many native plants and animals.

Of course, with its chalky bathtub ring of mineral deposits and 33 years of silt and man-made garbage, Glen Canyon will never be the same. But neither will the Bureau of Reclamation. In recent years, the bureau rethought its mission and announced that "Instead of constructing big water and power projects, we will concentrate on managing existing projects, conserving water and assuring good water quality and environmental protection."

JORDAN RIVERSIDES ARE BOTH BUFFER
AND BIRD BUFFET

Numbers tell this story: The 3 percent of Utah that is riverside supports three-quarters of the kinds of birds that visit or live in the state. Yellow warblers, northern orioles, willow flycatchers—there are more birds and more kinds of birds in the tangle of willows and cottonwoods bordering creeks and rivers than anywhere else in Utah. Many are songbirds who migrate here each year from South and Central America. Birds breed on Utah streamsides, like those along the Jordan River, because of the closeness of water, the cover, and the abundance of food.

Discouraging numbers: less than 5 percent of riverbanks in the American West remain in their natural condition. Nearly all of the West's streamsides—called riparian areas—have gone under the bulldozer's blade for such things as industrial parks, subdivisions, and golf courses or have been drowned for reservoirs. After 150 years of settlement, this is true of Salt Lake Valley as well; consequently, many songbirds are missing or have become a rare sight. "The Jordan River has the last riparian areas in the Salt Lake Valley," notes Vaughn Lovejoy, coordinator of TreeUtah, a local conservation organization. "All of the rest is developed." What natural riverside is left on the Jordan—hammered though it is—is especially precious now, so TreeUtah has taken on the task of restoring sections of it.

Soaring like a crow a few thousand feet above the Jordan River, you see that the riverside is a ribbon of green meandering alongside the waterway. Natural riverbanks are long, narrow woodlands that provide a corridor for plants and animals to go from one place to another. In the case of the Jordan, it's a passageway between Utah Lake and the Great Salt Lake. Also from high above, you can see that this border of vegetation along a river is a transitional zone from dry land to water. Natural riversides are both a link and buffer between land and water, and they're essential for a healthy river. The roots of the trees and shrubs that border the river form an underground mesh that stabilizes the river's banks and keeps topsoil from washing downstream. Plant roots also filter pollutants. Runoff water from surrounding areas percolates through streamside roots on the way to the river. A forested buffer to a river can filter 90 percent of the nitrogen in surface runoff from surrounding farmland, studies show.

Trees on the river's banks form a canopy that shades the river, reducing temperatures for cold-blooded creatures like fish and frogs and preventing a buildup of algae. When trees fall into the river, they provide nooks for fish to shelter, feed, and spawn. The leaves and needles decompose in the river and become food for bugs. Birds show up to chow on the bugs as well as the vegetation.

Left alone, it's an efficient system. But even as the pioneers were transporting granite blocks for the Salt Lake LDS Temple down the Jordan River to the city building site, they were also using the river as a sewer to carry waste to the Great Salt Lake. And because the Jordan floods occasionally, settlers dredged the river and straightened its winding path. This flood control work destroyed many of the Jordan's slow-moving eddies, pools, and side channels that are essential for juvenile fish.

In this century, when slaughterhouses, laundries, and mineral refineries moved nearby, they dumped their waste into the Jordan River. In particular, two industrial dumpsites—Sharon Steel and Midvale Slag—poisoned the Jordan with lead and arsenic. These toxins may have drifted as far north as Farmington Bay in the Great Salt Lake.

The natural river system took other hits as well. Nonnative weedy plants that thrive on bulldozed land and overgrazed pasture invaded the Jordan's streambanks. These aggressive, noxious plants crowd out native vegetation on the riverside and cause long-term problems. For example, specialized leaf-eating bugs that devour only one type of plant break down the leaves of native plants. When native trees are replaced by nonnative ones, the river is shortchanged of nutrients from the leaves that the bugs can't recycle. Of course, as the native bugs go out of business, the birds that migrate to the riverside buffet go away hungry. For this reason, critical remaining streamside areas—like the Jordan River in Salt Lake Valley—are not the places for golf courses and city-type parks. If landscaped with nonnative grass and ornamental shrubs, these human playgrounds won't support the rich variety of Utah's native birds and animals.

But here are some optimistic numbers: Thanks to the work of 800 TreeUtah volunteers and the U.S. Fish and Wildlife Service, 12,000 native trees and shrubs dot 20 acres of riverside along the Jordan. This partnership is restoring sections of the riverbanks by ripping out weedy intruders such as tamarisk and replanting with native vegetation like willows, chokecherries, and golden current. Recontouring sections of the riverbank for a more natural water flow is also on the to-do list. The future of Utah's remaining native species, like songbirds, depends on these numbers. 🎵

CHAPTER NINE

Can Utah's golf courses go green?

Chemical dependency is hard to kick. Take your local golf course's putting green. It's mowed down to a tenth of an inch tall. The stubble is seared by the sun, dried by wind, and stomped by humans in plaid pants. Underground, its unnaturally shallow roots are vulnerable to mold, fungus, and insects. Because a putting green is constantly on the ragged edge of survival, without regular fixes of fertilizer, fungicides, and insecticides, it's deader than Astro-Turf.

It's not just the greens either. In Utah, manicured tees and fairways planted with nonnative bluegrass require constant chemical maintenance as well. Without it, they won't have the intense green color and short, smooth turf golfers have come to expect from neighborhood courses.

Can local golfers change their expectations and accept a more natural setting that's less chemically dependent? "It's tough to change golfers attitudes when they see these nice green courses on television," says William Howard Neff, a golf course architect in Sandy, Utah. "Part of the cost of building a golf course is matching what local golfers see on TV." With emerald fairways and sapphire-blue ornamental ponds, classic golf courses like Georgia's Augusta National are Disneyesque caricatures of nature.

It wasn't always this way. Golf began as an unassuming, Scottish working-class game. Courses were pastures and open fields of unruly native grass. Hazards were sandy dunes and wild marshes. Even today, Scotland's natural golf courses, like St. Andrews, are less manicured and use fewer chemicals than courses in the U.S. Likewise, American golf course builders used to work with the shape and vegetation of the natural landscape. In the

1960s though, builders and architects began earthmoving to give their golf courses more dramatic layouts. As builders bulldozed hills and ponds, they had to use herbicides to control the weeds that thrive on disturbed landscape. They replanted with nonnative grass and ornamental vegetation that requires a regular fix of fertilizer, fungicides, and insecticides in order to thrive.

How bad did it get? Greenskeepers are more cautious today, but as recently as 1993 a course may have sprayed 21 different herbicides, 20 fungicides, and 8 insecticides. A typical course applied 18 pounds of pesticides per acre each year—seven times the amount used on farmland. Rain and sprinkling carry those chemicals into groundwater, wetlands, and rivers. A 1993 *Golf* magazine article cautioned players to "Clean your shoes immediately after your round and take a shower, especially if you've been wearing shorts . . . Clean golf balls with a towel, not your hands . . . Don't chew on tees."

Clearly, it was time for golf to check into its own chemical-dependency rehab program. "The trend in the game now is to take a minimal approach" toward altering the natural landscape, using nonnative grass, and applying chemical maintenance, reports Mark Passey, Southwest representative of the U.S. Golf Association. Environmental "awareness in the industry is growing," he said. "After all, most golfers are environmentalists too." Many environmentalists are golfers; one Sierra Club member in six is a golfer, a national poll revealed.

Golf course thirst for scarce, tax-subsidized Western water is another raw issue. A Southwestern golf course, like one in St. George, Las Vegas, or Phoenix, may use over 400 million gallons of water a year. But a new golf course design, called "links," reduces the total percentage of area of the course made up of tees, fairways, and greens. Those three features of a course are planted with nonnative grasses, like bluegrass, and so require intensive chemical maintenance and watering. A links-designed course may have up to three-quarters of its 150 to 200 acres in native grass and other local vegetation. Salt Lake's Wingpointe golf course, near the Salt Lake International Airport, is an example of a links course that's planted with mostly native grasses and so uses less water.

"The intensively maintained parts of a links course—the tees, fairways, and greens—require about two inches of water a week," course designer Neff points out. "The other parts, the roughs and far roughs with native

Utah golf course.

© DAN MILLER

grasses, may take a half inch of water—or will survive on what nature gives them." Neff says he is using salt grasses and alkali grasses in the roughs of a course in Syracuse, near the Great Salt Lake. He also points out that the recent 18-hole addition to Mountain Dell golf course, which is built in a watershed, was designed to drain into an artificial wetland for filtering.

Reducing water and chemical use by growing mostly native grasses and plants is a beginning step. But, as open green-space, golf courses also have the opportunity to provide habitat for the native bird and animal species displaced by humanity's relentless wildlife habitat destruction. Wildlinks, a program launched by the U.S. Golf Association in 1996, is the game's first methodical look at its relationship with wildlife and habitat. Wildlinks will inform golf course builders and owners of ways to preserve and protect habitat on golf courses. Meanwhile, the Audubon Society of New York established a set of criteria for Earth-friendly golf courses. The idea is popular.

About 15 percent of U.S. golf courses have applied for Audubon certification, among them are four Utah courses, including Homestead in Midway and Willow Creek in Sandy.

Some local golf courses, such as Wingpointe, were built to rehabilitate already-damaged landscape. Wingpointe sits over the old Salt Lake City landfill and brings a former eyesore back into productive use. For plants and animals, better a golf course than a shopping mall. But the best habitat for native plants and animals is one left in its natural state. Golf course pesticides eliminate bugs that native birds and animals feed on; they are also passed up the food chain to predators—and to humans. Some golf course greenskeepers are experimenting with an integrated pest management program. It employs various holistic techniques, such as using bugs to eat other bugs and using diluted bleach to reduce fungi, rather than applying full-strength chemicals. Today, club owners may tell golfers to spray themselves with insect repellent in the clubhouse so greenskeepers don't have to spray the entire golf course with pesticide as frequently. In addition, courses can apply organic fertilizer, such as composted turkey manure, for a slower-greening, but biodegradable, grass food.

It remains to be seen whether local golfers are willing to adjust to brown grass during certain times of year. Also, longer, rougher native grasses may cost strokes or lost golf balls, and those bird-friendly buffers of thick vegetation around water hazards will eliminate dramatic, edge-of-water shots. But if local golfers can learn to play on courses that reduce the spread of chemicals in drinking water and encourage native birds and animals to visit, it's a small price to pay. Nobody said rehab was easy. 🦋

CHAPTER TEN

Transforming the Wasatch Mountains into an amusement park.

DOWNHILL DEMOGRAPHICS

Go figure. The number of skiers in the U.S. is falling as the Baby Boom generation ages, so why do Utah ski resorts expand facilities each year and crowd further into what was once wildlife habitat?

It's a fact: as skiers age, they ski less. Boomers are now 35 to 55 years old, and the U.S. skier market has gradually shrunk by about 15 percent in the 1990s. It's 18 to 24 year olds who ski more than anyone—about one in ten ski. But there aren't enough Gen Xers to make a statistical dent in general skier declines because Boomers make up fully one-third of the population. Yet all local ski areas, except Alta, are busy replacing double and triple chairlifts with expensive four- and six-person lifts. They're cutting new runs, widening established ones, and installing artificial snowmaking.

And they're not cutting prices. Lift tickets are becoming even more expensive as many Utah resorts turn themselves into sprawling complexes of fancy restaurants, 100-room lodges, luxury spas, multilevel parking lots, towering condominiums, and even gated communities of million dollar, single-family homes.

What happened? Skiing used to be a simple sport focused on the thrill of sliding down a mountain on boards. Has it become merely a front for Robin Leach-style mountain home developments and Disneyland-esque family entertainment?

From a commercial point of view, alpine skiing is a scary business. It's capital intensive and weather dependent and has high liability costs. Now its core market is shriveling. Historically, ski resort profits skyrocketed in the 1970s when Boomers were young adults. At that time, short skis and plastic boots had drastically reduced the skill level needed to ski. In the 1980s the ski industry advertised heavily in southern states like Texas and Georgia, attracting a new market of skiers. Then, in the '90s the number of "skier visits" in the United States—roughly equivalent to lift tickets sold—flattened, hovering at about 53 million. Snowboarders now buy 15 percent of ski passes, but shredders are not an additional market because they are already counted in the number of "skier" visits.

Ski resorts can no longer depend on what used to be their core market—the 18 to 24-year-old age group of skiers—to fill their chairlifts; the demographics have changed. The industry has learned that it must continue to cater to aging Boomer skiers and their growing families.

The implications are significant. Older skiers have more money and want more comforts than younger skiers. They also take the skiing experience slower. Younger skiers will scarf down a hot dog for lunch, then rush off to squeeze in the maximum number of ski runs. Older skiers want a sit-down restaurant, high-quality food, premium beer, and espresso. Sophisticated ski service consumers, Boomers expect to be whisked quickly to the mountaintop, without waiting in lift lines. Killington, in Vermont, built a high-speed, eight-person chairlift with heaters on each chair. Park City recently installed Utah's first six-passenger, high-speed lift; named Silverlode, the lift moves skiers up 1,300 vertical feet in five minutes.

As the skier market flattens and the percentage of older skiers increases, industry investors have discovered that more skiers go to the larger, destination ski resorts. Disney World has become the business model for these destination ski resorts, writes Randall Lane in *Forbes* magazine. Boomers bring their whole families to high-end ski resorts and pay Dumbo prices. They expect tennis courts, luxury accommodations, shopping, and game rooms. "Like Disney, ski resorts have learned that one new ride each year is enough to bring customers back, so major resorts strive to offer a new feature every year—another 'super' lift, another new bowl opened. Though these expansions are concentrated at larger resorts, competitive pressures will force the smaller ones to upgrade."

Marketing correctly also means indulging Boomers' desire to live in mountain communities, says Leisure Trend's Joy Spring, whose marketing research company completed an extensive skier survey on the subject during the 1997 season. The Park City area destination resorts are spending tens of millions of dollars in a major expansion of homes, hotels, and lifts on surrounding private and public land. Park City ski resort is building an eight-story hotel, 600 condos, parking for 3,000 cars, as well as new lifts and runs. Deer Crest, by Deer Valley, is building a 100-suite hotel and spa, 255 multi-family homes, and a gated, private community of million-dollar single family homes. And that's just for starters. North America's largest ski resort owner, American Ski Company, has plans to extend their resort, The Canyons, from Bear Hollow to Park City. A resort that size will be the second largest in the U.S., after Vail in Colorado.

Older skiers' rising expectations are digging deeply into resort owners' pockets. Smaller ski resorts already have less ability to weather poor market conditions and easily suffer big declines in profitability, according to the National Ski Areas Association survey. Economies of scale favor large resorts and play an important role in their long-term financial health. With new ski lifts costing over $2 million each, rising expenses in a stagnant skier market may spell trouble for debt-laden smaller local resorts.

In contrast to its neighbors, Little Cottonwood's Alta ski resort has "no plans for expansion of lifts or buildings," Otto Wierenga, general manager, reports. "Looking down the road five years, we'll have the same number of lifts, though some may be upgraded, and same number of buildings, though some may be replaced. People tell us all the time, 'Don't mess up a good thing.' We're happy the size we are and we're careful not to change that."

Alta caters to local skiers, but the Wasatch resorts that market to out-of-staters are steering a different route. Apart from Alta, each of the other Salt Lake and Summit County ski areas is expanding in size—adding new ski lifts, new ski runs, luxury lodges, or restaurants.

For example, Alta's neighbor, Snowbird, just can't let neighboring turf sit. It's erecting two new ski lifts into Mineral Basin, high in Utah County's American Fork Canyon, which is on the other side of the mountain ridge from Snowbird's base. Lift towers, a warming hut, and a road are going into a steep, 9,500-foot bowl that has no permanent structures now. Utah County planners allowed this although they classify this alpine area as a critical environmental zone. Snowbird's using 100 acres of U.S. Forest Service land besides 400 private acres it bought.

Snowbird claims the expansion into Mineral Basin is necessary to keep up with resorts in Colorado and Park City, which are constantly adding new lifts. They have a point. A few years ago, for example, the U.S. Forest Service, landlord for many Western ski resorts, approved Telluride's ski resort's proposal to nearly double its size on public land and allowed Steamboat a similar increase. Both resorts are in Colorado. Utah's Park City-area ski resort expansion is on private land and doesn't need U.S. Forest Service approval.

Snowbird's high-rise base facilities are shoehorned into Little Cottonwood Canyon, one of two canyons that provide Salt Lake with most of its drinking water. A narrow, two-lane blacktop road connects Snowbird with Salt Lake Valley. The highway, which cannot be widened without substantial damage to the watershed, was already over capacity in 1989 when Salt Lake County's canyon master plan was written.

Snowbird operates mostly on U.S. Forest Service land and has several other expansion plans in the hopper. They're planning to build a three-story restaurant with a conical roof on Little Cottonwood's ridgeline and to add a day lodge, and they want to install a ski lift and runs in neighboring White Pine Canyon. Snowbird has already enlarged its Mid-Gad restaurant, and built Baby Thunder lift, clear-cutting slopes for nine more ski runs. They also rigged the Gad 1 lift to carry twice as many skiers.

Ski lifts in Mineral Basin will cost at least $2 million apiece. Snowbird's current financial condition is known only to the U.S. Forest Service and to Snowbird insiders, but in the past, Snowbird has been burdened with crushing debt. Texan Rick Bass, the feisty entrepreneur who built Snowbird, has publicly joked about how much money Snowbird loses. And Snowbird's not alone. One-third to one-half of U.S. ski resorts fail to make a profit each year, according to 1996 congressional testimony by ski industry experts. A 1995 National Ski Area Association's economic analysis of its Rocky Mountain members showed resort expenses are rising faster than revenues.

"Judging by the number of condos going in and ski slope acres the resorts are grooming, you'd think the number of skiers is exploding," said Tom Berggren of Salt Lake City's Committee to Save Our Canyons. "But the market is not growing. Each resort is cannibalizing the same group of rich Americans who can afford to decide whether to go to Aspen or Snowbird."

Are local Forest Service officials concerned about the consequences of allowing ski resorts to expand while the number of skiers shrinks? "Yes," says Dick Kline, Forest Service public affairs officer for the Wasatch-Cache National Forest, "we do weigh that. But you can also argue that we have encouraged private enterprise to fill the niche of skiing as a legitimate use of the land and we must be conscious of making it financially viable." The Forest Service does not consider whether a ski resort's proposed project is a good investment, only whether the party is financially capable of completing it.

But past market cycles put ski areas out of business without leaving the Forest Service funds to reclaim the mountainsides, recalls John Hoagland, now the Forest Service's director of planning for the 2002 Olympics. In the '60s and '70s, mom-and-pop day ski areas went out of business when larger ski resorts lured customers away. Blue Mountain ski area in Utah's Manti-LaSal National Forest went out of business, and "because it was operated by an association that dissolved," the Forest Service could hold no one responsible for restoring the land, Hoagland says. Hidden Valley, Pike's Peak, and Geneva Basin, all in Colorado, went out of business during that time as well.

Those unprofitable day-ski areas were often just a towrope and a gravel parking lot. But a resort like Snowbird is a village with high-rise buildings, sewer lines, and dozens of clear-cut ski runs. Will Utahns be saddled with reclamation expenses from a round of ski area bankruptcies if the market demographics change five years from now? "The risk of bankruptcy is high, as in any business, but the likelihood of a ski resort owner just walking away is low," concludes John Carpoff, professor of finance at the University of Washington. "However, if they did, reclamation cost would be high."

Save Our Canyons' Berggren believes that far more likely than abandoning a resort like Snowbird because it can't make money on lift tickets and hotel rooms, new owners in a bankruptcy would look for ways to develop land adjacent to the resort. If new owners believe they can make money on private real estate development, money-losing resorts will always find a willing buyer, he said.

Hoagland agrees: "You can't build a ski resort any more without private real estate development at the base. Resorts just can't make money without it. The Forest Service will only let ski area permittees build public facilities—no condos or private dwellings. That's why resorts push to get title to Forest Service land with land exchanges."

"The way the system works now, it forces commercial real estate development at the ski resort's base. That's why the precedent set by Snowbasin [outside Ogden, Utah] is so disturbing," Berggren adds. Snowbasin ski resort, owned by oil company millionaire Earl Holding, said it needed title to 1,300 acres of Forest Service land at its base to build facilities for the 2002 Winter Olympics. In 1996, Congress approved the trade. Only after approval did Snowbasin reveal plans to build 1,500 private condos, town-houses, and homes on the land.

For investors, maybe the chairlifts are half full rather than half empty. Natalie Gochnour, director of demographic and economic analysis for Utah's Office of Planning and Budget, doesn't believe demographics are an accurate indicator of Utah's skiing future. "We used to track the Baby Boom numbers very closely," she says. "It looked like a flat market and we were not very optimistic. But we find that the Baby Boom phenomenon is not so significant to Utah's experience." Gochnour points out that Utah's number of resident skiers—a market younger than the national market—is growing more slowly than the number of destination skiers coming to Utah. "Utah's out-of-state skier numbers are increasing while the number of resident skiers—which has all the demographics going for it—hasn't been growing as fast," she says.

While expanding ski resort capacity in a shrinking skier market may seem counter-intuitive to some, it appears inevitable that Utah ski resorts will continue to grow at the expense of mountain habitat.

WHAT HARM CAN A SKI RUN DO?

As local ski resorts grow, a lot of trees are chainsawed. "When you cut a ski run into a stand of conifers, you lose bird nesting habitat," explains Larry Dalton of the Utah Division of Wildlife Resources. "People think that the displaced bird can just move next door. That's not true. The nesting area next door is already taken by a bird that's defending its territory. The displaced bird must move to a less secure nesting site that's more apt to be exposed to weather or predators. And it's unlikely that the bird will successfully reproduce." As humans reduce wildlife habitat, the displaced animals die without reproducing and rearing young. Dalton notes that the Wasatch's elk were eliminated by this kind of habitat destruction. The steady creep of new subdivisions built up the foothills destroyed the elk's critical winter range in the foothills.

Another problem with ski runs is that "the grassy opening changes the mosaic of the natural alpine community by favoring different small animals—with unpredictable consequences," Dalton says. A ski run can create habitat inviting to nonnative animals like house mice or roof rats that don't belong there, points out local zoologist George Oliver. Weeds are another problem.

Construction that churns up alpine turf, such as slope grading or road building, creates a path along which aggressive nonnative plants, a.k.a. weeds, invade the mountainsides. These aggressive and broadly adapted plants that follow human disturbance eventually crowd out native vegetation.

Cutting up the mountains with runs and roads can cause local extinctions, say experts. An alpine biological community needs to be contiguous to function over time. For example, some native rodents won't cross a road. If a small population of them is trapped on one side of a road, it can easily die out. Of course, if the rodents in an area die out, the owls, hawks, and coyotes that feed on them disappear as well. Oliver points out that pika populations, on mountainside scree slopes, are widely separated and isolated. Further isolation through habitat destruction makes the many pika subspecies vulnerable to extinction during naturally harsh climate cycles. Another example is the Wasatch's black rosy-finch, which lives at high elevations and nests in crevices on talus slopes. This finch is not a wide-ranging bird, so it is especially vulnerable to habitat loss as well, he notes.

Ironically, Park City, Solitude, and Snowbird are building extensive artificial snowmaking facilities, though Mother Nature's own snowmaking system dumps hundreds of inches on them most years. "Utah resorts are investing heavily in artificial snowmaking equipment as much for marketing [to out-of-state-skiers] as for operational reasons," says Mark Menlove, former president of the Utah Ski Association. Advertising artificial snowmaking capability assures out-of-staters—who must make their ski vacation reservations months in advance—of skiable snow when they arrive. Installing snowmaking equipment requires digging trenches up mountainsides and burying pipes. Charlie Lansche, spokesperson for Park City ski resort, says they try to run the pipes along existing ski runs to avoid cutting down more trees.

The Wasatch Mountains are a watershed, providing 60 percent of the drinking water for Salt Lake City and County. In an effective watershed, rain and snow are slowed up and filtered through the natural community of scrub, trees, tundra, and soil. Each new construction project or ski run incrementally reduces the ability of the mountainside to filter drinking water—and to act as habitat for native mountain wildlife. 🌿

Sonoran Desert.

PART III
What Does the Future Hold?

© MARK HENGESBAUGH

Black bear.

© UTAH DIVISION OF WILDLIFE RESOURCE

CHAPTER ELEVEN

The legacy of predator control

STATE-RUN ANIMAL FARM

Some animals are less equal than others. It's government policy.

Take predators. Until as recently as the 1960s, Utah's predators were officially considered vermin. Grizzly bears, wolves, and wolverines have been wiped out. Most of Utah's surviving four-legged carnivores—such as cougar, black bear, and fox—are still trapped and hunted both for sport and to keep their populations low. The coyote is officially considered a pest and is actively exterminated still.

On the other hand, Utah's wildlife managers have encouraged the growth of prey herds, such as elk and mule deer, for the enjoyment of human hunters. Game officials have imported exotic prey species, like pheasant and mountain goats, and have decimated native predator populations to ensure that hunters' targets will flourish.

But are pheasants more important than fox? Are mule deer more important than cougar? Government officials decide every day. Wildlife managers promote or suppress various populations on the premise that wild animals are crops to be "harvested" from the state's animal farm. Hunters pay the animal farm's bills. All but $4 million of the Division of Wildlife Resource's budget of $28 to $32 million comes from the sale of hunting and fishing licenses.

But further reduction of Utah's remaining predator populations may be devastating to the balance of natural landscapes, scientists say. If predator populations are not maintained to keep deer and elk numbers in check, we risk transforming entire biological communities in Utah.

How many of Utah's native predators remain? It's an official guess. To estimate fox populations, for example, the state's Division of Wildlife Resources counts the number of fox pelts taken by trappers each year. DWR also monitors fox sightings, the animal's prey base, and reported encounters with livestock growers. No estimate of total population is made, but a "harvest" is recorded. Boyde Blackwell, DWR mammal project coordinator says 500 kit foxes and 1,000 gray foxes are taken each year on a 10-year annual average. Red fox populations, which thrive in agricultural settings, are growing. Blackwell says increasing red fox numbers are inferred from the fewer number of days it takes to trap more red foxes each year. In 1982, 564 red foxes were caught. The number has steadily increased to 4,000 in 1996.

"We don't hear much about fox in Utah because not much is known about them," observes Dick Carter of the High Uintas Preservation Council. "The premise of the few studies done is, 'Do we have too many fox?'" When you begin from that perspective, he notes, you don't get the data you need to know if the population is viable over time. A Utah State University (USU) study proposed to exterminate every fox and ground-based predator in 16-square-mile zones to study the decline of Utah's pheasant populations. They intended to compare later the number of pheasants in those predator-free zones with other study zones that have the usual complement of predators. "This 'study' is not science," Carter, a USU graduate, wrote to the school. It amounts to simply killing predators to see what happens. The research is funded by upland game—that's bird—hunting licenses and is mandated by the Utah legislature. Pheasant and other game birds are the third highest money generator for DWR after mule deer and elk.

The way we view predators is as important as the habitat that we leave for them, Carter says. For example, USU also has a cougar study going on, paid for by DWR and the state legislature. "The question they're asking is, 'Are there too many cougar?' We should be asking, 'Is the cougar's genetic base dangerously reduced?' Rather than, 'Are cougars causing problems with deer and elk?' which make money for the state government through the sale of hunting licenses."

Local extinctions of predators from specific areas can happen more easily now because Utah's wild areas are fragmented and small groups of predators are cut off from each other. Though to a layperson one cougar looks like another, cougar populations in one location have slightly different genes than groups in other places. That genetic variation in the larger population

Kit fox.

© RICK A. FRIDELL

is essential to avoid inbreeding and to avoid a catastrophe such as a single virus wiping out an entire population that's genetically similar.

Blackwell reports that research shows 20 percent of a cougar population is about the maximum you can kill over time and keep a viable population. However, if prey is low, human contact is high, and reports of cougar eating livestock are frequent, that 20 percent can be raised for a time, then reassessed. The DWR believes Utah has 2,000 to 3,000 cougars, Blackwell says. In 1995–96, DWR issued 872 cougar hunting permits and hunters killed 452 cougars. Total known mortality, including poached, killed by government animal control, and road kill, was 510 that season.

Cougar killing has steadily increased this decade. The 1995–96 number of 510 cougars killed is double the number of each year's take from 1990 through 1992. It's also grown from the annual number killed from 1993 to 1995. In one season, an entire cougar population in a given area can be killed off through overhunting, Craig Axford of the Utah Cougar Coalition suggests. "In the Henry Mountains, we think the DWR has allocated more cougar hunting permits than there are cougar. They've allocated 10, and so far have only taken one cougar. Between 1989 and present, a total of only 10 cougar have been taken in the Henry Mountains area." A recent cougar hunting regulation change allows unlimited access to 13 of 39 hunting areas. The goal is to hunt cougar in those areas until 250 are killed.

Carter claims "it's irresponsible to guess" how many cougar are left in Utah. "DWR is just guessing. The data that exists doesn't suggest—doesn't come close to suggesting—1,500 or 2,000 Utah cougars. But total population size is irrelevant anyway. What's relevant is how many cougars there are in particular, distinct populations. What's important is the number of cougars within those groups that are of reproductive age. Evidence shows the ratio is not good. Some populations are mostly females of breeding age; others, mostly male."

Ditto, Carter says for Utah's black bear. But with black bears, it's even trickier. "I know of no one who believes black bear populations are healthy in all of their individual locations in Utah. Hunters are finding only very young bears to shoot now. They're taking very few old bears," Carter notes. "Black bears don't reproduce until they're four to seven years old, then they have only one or two cubs. Scientists and wildlife managers can cruise along for years watching what seems to be a stable population of bears. Then, boom: almost no females in the Book Cliffs area, and almost no males in the Abajos."

Coyotes, at least, are doing very well in Utah. Ironically, coyote populations have grown in size and spread in territory because of the elimination of another canine predator—the wolf—from most of the West. Some studies show humans would have to kill 75 percent of the coyote population over five years—without a let up of even one year—to permanently reduce the population. The number of coyotes killed in Utah has been steady, DRW's Blackwell observes. Each year Federal Animal Damage Control hunters and trappers kill about 4,500 coyotes and others take about 4,500. "The Utah coyote population is steady," says Carter, because the more coyotes you kill, the faster they reproduce. Carter said a Mt. Naomi, Utah, study showed coyote females as young as six months old were producing pups. In Yellowstone, where coyotes are not trapped and hunted, the average female coyote produces her first pups at two years old.

In Yellowstone, coyotes are no longer top dog. Since the reintroduction of the gray wolf into Yellowstone National Park, the park's coyote population is plummeting, Carter said. The wolves kill and disperse bands of coyotes. Utah may see this phenomenon as well. Utah wildlife officials announced that migration patterns suggest the gray wolf and the grizzly bear might return to Utah's Uinta Mountains from the Yellowstone area within the next several years.

In many ways, Utah's predator policies mirror citizens' concerns: Will predators eat the profit out of livestock growing? Will they leave enough deer, elk, and game birds for human hunters? Will a cougar or black bear "harvest" a picnicker or hiker?

If a predator kills a human, it's news precisely because it is so rare. Biologist Paul Beier studied every cougar attack on a human in the past 100 years in western North America. Beier found 53 attacks, 9 of which were fatal. By contrast, each year deer kill about 130 humans (mostly in car wrecks), bees kill about 45 humans, and dogs kill about 15 humans. Even rattlesnakes, spiders, and lightening are greater threats to human safety than predators. And game managers shouldn't hold out hope that hunting cougars will reduce the risk of attacks on humans. Beier's study showed that most cougar attacks were in British Columbia, where cougars are intensively hunted.

But Utah's predators do kill many sheep and cattle each year. Livestock grower groups complain they lose millions of dollars to predators. The U.S. Department of Agriculture Animal Damage Control's draft 1996 annual report shows that 12,398 cattle and sheep were lost in Utah to cougars, black bears, foxes, and coyotes. "I don't know any livestock growers who advocate extinction of predators," says Tom Bingham of the Utah Farm Bureau Federation. "But we need balance. We realize that even under the best circumstances, some losses will occur. However, losses to predators are right up there with the top two or three problems, like market prices and weather, that livestock growers face."

Utahns raising sheep and cattle point out that they tap a renewable resource providing both food and clothing for the rest of us. Perhaps more important, they maintain vital open spaces. If a rancher or farmer is driven out of business by predator losses and other contributing factors, their land is usually subdivided and sold. Each year America loses over a million acres of farmland to suburban creep. That's a bad deal for all wild animals.

It's often said that predators help maintain healthy herds of wild prey by killing the weak and the sick in them, but even that is controversial. Don Peay, of Utah Sportsmen for Fish and Wildlife, claims predators routinely take healthy prey as well as the sick and weak. "Predators are opportunistic," Peay says. He notes a study of a 300-member herd of bighorn sheep found 100 of them were killed by cougars. "That's more than the sick and young," Peay says.

But Cougar Coalition's Axford says that predators' year-round culling of deer and elk herds keeps them moving, which prevents overgrazing. Predators eat sick prey, which limits the spread of disease within a herd, he argues. Cougars do compete with human hunters for mule deer. Axford reports that a male cougar will take one deer every two weeks, while a female cougar with cubs will kill a deer every seven to ten days. If there are 2,000 cougars in Utah, then they kill and eat about 80,000 mule deer each year.

Some Utah hunters blame an increase in cougars for the recent drop in mule deer populations. In the past though, DWR officials have said cougar populations fluctuate with the deer population, but that it takes a couple of years for the populations to level out. Axford claims fewer deer should be killed to allow the herd to grow, rather than killing more cougars. But fewer deer licenses sold means less revenue for DWR.

Whatever else one says about Utah hunters, they have shown a willingness to tax themselves to improve their chances in the field. Peay points out that his group spearheaded the effort to require hunters and fishers to buy a $5 habitat authorization fee with their licenses. The $2.5 million revenue raised is spent on improving habitat for wildlife. Peay says that by protecting mule deer habitat you preserve cougars too.

With such sharply conflicting opinions, you may think that DWR would increase its reliance on science to make wildlife policy. No such luck. There are many allegations that within Utah's DWR, science must follow politics. In an anonymous letter to *Outdoor Life* magazine, a group of employees of DWR wrote that Governor Mike Leavitt and his appointees "have destroyed a professional wildlife-management agency and its dedicated personnel . . . Morale has never been lower or prospects for scientific management bleaker." According to Hartt Wixom, a longtime Utah wildlife writer, biology is not allowed to conflict with politics in the DWR now. For example, all DWR personnel who investigated trout whirling disease, which spread from the Leavitt family's trout hatcheries, were terminated or hounded out of their jobs. DWR professionals were cautioned not to speak out against a scientifically risky livestock industry attempt to legalize elk farms. Wixom's remarks were printed in a *Salt Lake Tribune* op-ed piece.

With Utah's increasingly urban population, nonconsumptive wildlife activities, such as birdwatching and wildlife photography, are becoming more popular. But state wildlife officials are still conditioned to respond to consumptive users—hunters and livestock growers. And even as the controversy over the health of Utah's cougar population raged, the Utah legislature reduced the penalty for poaching cougar from a felony to a misdemeanor. Legislators offered no scientific basis for the change.

TOUGH TIMES FOR ADOLESCENT PREDATORS

"Look it straight in the eye," is the advice of wildlife experts if confronted by which one of the following predators?

- A. Grizzly Bear
- B. Cougar
- C. Coyote
- D. Jackalope

Think about it. As Utahns move into native predators' shrinking habitat, encounters with them are more likely. That's true for at least one generation of predators in an invaded area. Then, the loss of habitat will usually keep the animal from successfully reproducing and rearing offspring. Soon after, they'll disappear from the area.

Ironically, intensive hunting may make human-predator encounters more likely as well. Biologist Paul Beier's study of cougar attacks on humans in western North America showed many attacks came from juvenile cougars. Most of the cougar attacks were in British Columbia, where the relentless cougar hunting often prematurely orphans juveniles. Beier theorized the juveniles were probably not fully trained by their mothers.

At best, a male predator's young life is not easy. "Betas—young male bears and cougars—are chased out of the territory in which they were born as soon as they reach the age they can reproduce. This is because, evolutionarily, they shouldn't mate with their sisters, who stay in their home areas," notes Dick Carter of the High Uintas Preservation Council. "Looking for a territory of their own, these roving male juveniles are treated by other members of their species in the same way you or I would treat a burglar in our homes. If they kill a prey in another bear or cougar's territory, they're treated as if they stole something from that predator to whom the territory belongs. "Predators are space dependent in this way," Carter says, not dependent on the amount of prey in the area.

Craig Axford, of the Utah Cougar Coalition, points out that "juvenile cougars may have to travel 300 to 600 miles to find a territory that's not occupied by other cougars. For juvenile cougars, hunting in those circumstances is

© MARK PARCHMAN

Cougar, also known as mountain lion.

difficult because they can't cache a kill for a second meal, so they kill more prey when transient." When humans build homes or cabins on the finger ridges of mountains, they cut off critical traveling corridors for these juvenile cougars.

Once, huge areas of backcountry gave predators security. Not anymore. Technology has reduced the effectiveness of predators' habitat as protection. "Cougar hunters are not chasing their dogs in the backcountry on snowshoes. They're driving snowmobiles. This renders ineffective what little habitat cougars have left. Habitat is not only lost directly by such things as building subdivisions in winter range. Habitat is also rendered ineffective by the intrusion of snowmachines and dogs," Carter comments.

Likewise, black bears are hunted in Utah by dog teams wearing radio collars. Lack of effective habitat may be the reason that there aren't as many cougar and black bear in the Uintas and Wasatch as experts say there should be, Carter argues.

Occasional attacks notwithstanding, humans aren't cougar prey. "Cougars evolved to hunt ungulates with long necks," Axford notes. "Human necks are short."

Coyotes, on the other hand, will mug your cocker spaniel, but they won't hurt you. Government predator control programs, though, might foster adolescent coyote attacks on domestic animals, Conger Beasley, Jr., wrote for *Buzzworm*. "Stable, undisturbed populations of coyotes tend to live in packs and forage cooperatively . . . When extensive culling throws their social equilibrium out of whack, younger, restless leaders emerge who do not know how to forage efficiently, and are much more likely to go after livestock." Beasley said some biologists think that predator-control projects were responsible for the creation of "a 'supercoyote': stronger, smarter, tougher, more apt to succeed in bringing down domestic livestock when it suits its purposes to do so."

"Coyotes are the most researched animal in the U.S. on how to kill them," says Carter. Still, studies show that killing coyotes in one area prompts immigration into the area by other coyotes and promotes the fertility of female coyotes at a younger age.

The answer to the quiz at the beginning is B. Experts say that if you find a cougar is watching you or stalking you, talk loud, and stay upright, above the lion. Don't even consider running, as cougar prey would do. Even Olympic sprinter Marion Jones can't outrun a cougar. ❦

© MITCH MASCARO / HERALD JOURNAL

Hunter in the field.

CHAPTER TWELVE

Decline of hunting leaves habitat hurting

Utah hunters are becoming an increasingly rare breed. And that's not necessarily good for the state's wildlife.

Yes, you read that right. Here's why: During each recent fall season, fewer than 80,000 Utahns line up their rifle sights for a deer hunt that, in the past, drew 200,000 residents. What wild animals will be missing is not the crack of hunters' gunfire, of course, but the money those absent hunters have been contributing to preserving habitat and wildlife for 60 years. A national "guns and ammo tax"—an assessment on the manufacture of firearms and ammunition since 1937—together with the sale of hunting licenses, has allowed Utah's Division of Wildlife Resources to spend millions each year on habitat preservation and wildlife. The large majority of Utahns who are not hunters think that somewhere, some state agency is spending significant amounts of money on nongame animals. It's not so. As the sport of hunting's popularity continues to decline, so does money for wildlife management.

The words "wildlife" and "management" don't sit together easily. Wildlife management is an oxymoron. After all, are these animals wild or are they managed? The stewardship DWR has embraced for generations is full of contradictions as well. For example, DWR has killed off predators, such as cougar, to increase mule deer herds, and they have introduced exotic game animals, such as pheasants, at the expense of native birds and animals. DWR admits that its wildlife management has favored hunters' targets and has not been holistic. But hunters have been paying DWR's bills, and hunters have been calling the shots. Regardless, DWR's management of game animals and habitat has had a residual effect that's beneficial for Utah's nongame wildlife. For example, increasing big game winter range also preserves habitat for migrating songbirds. And lately, DWR has been working to save nongame wildlife threatened by extinction.

As funding sources go, the DWR is all Utah's wild animals have got. No other state agency is spending money, in any significant amount, on wildlife and habitat. Who will make up the missing bucks to pay for wildlife habitat management as hunting continues to decline in popularity along with its associated habitat revenue?

The decline of participation in hunting is a nationwide phenomenon and promises to be long-term. National polls show that only half as many 18- to 24-year-old Americans hunt today as hunted a decade ago. The percentage of the Utah population that hunts has been decreasing for the last fifteen years. The decline has been so steep that the total number of Utahns who hunt was fewer in 1996 than in 1960—even though Utah's population doubled in that time. In 1960, Utah had 184,000 hunters, about one in five of the state's population. In 1996, Utah had 167,000 hunters, one in twelve. "Utah is no different from other states" in the decline of participation in hunting, remarks Steve Phillips, DWR information specialist, though in Utah, some unique factors have exaggerated the dropout rate, he notes. "Hunting is a tradition that's not handed down as it was," Phillips says. Utahns who grew up on ranches and farms or in small towns learned to hunt at an early age and continued hunting throughout their lifetimes, even if they later moved to the city. Often though, while the first generation of rural people who move to the city still hunt, the second and third generations do not take it up. City dwellers hunt less often than their rural counterparts, and Utah has become one of America's most urbanized states.

The decline in the number of Utahns who hunt deer affects other kinds of hunting. The rifle deer hunt was the traditional way Utahns entered the sport of hunting. It was Utah's most popular event as well. In 1980, for example, when Utah had 250,000 hunters, 200,000 of them headed into the backcountry to hunt mule deer with rifles. By 1993, however, a series of severe winters decimated the deer herds and Utah's swelling human population transformed much of mule deer winter range into subdivisions and strip malls. The DWR was forced to limit deer hunting permits. That year alone, 30,000 fewer hunters bought licenses. The rifle deer hunt has not recovered. In 1996, DWR sold only 77,596 permits to Utahns, and the decline may continue each season.

Utah's DWR is relying on national surveys to find out why fewer people are taking up the sport, but often the complaints are too little game and loss of habitat at favorite hunting spots. This destruction of wildlife habitat will get worse. Utah grew from one million people in 1965 to two million in 1995. The third million Utahns will appear in half the time—only fifteen years. The quality of the hunting experience has degenerated with the habitat loss. Hunters using four-wheel, off-road vehicles reduce the effectiveness of the wildlife habitat that's left. A mechanized hunter covers many more miles than a walking hunter does, so fewer hunters disturb a larger area. Some hunters—in order to experience the adventure, challenge, and solitude that the sport can offer—are switching to hunting with bow-and-arrow or muzzle-loading guns. Both methods have their own seasons, and nationally, these are the fastest growing segments of the sport.

The DWR is offering programs to make it easier for Utahns to take up hunting, and they're recruiting from nontraditional sections of the population. The DWR operates a nationally funded "outdoorswomen" program that targets female, single heads of households. They also offer a Spanish-speaking hunter education class for Utah's fast-growing Hispanic population. Also, the Utah legislature lowered the legal hunting age from 16 to 14 years old—over the objections of many experienced hunters.

But no one predicts the number of Utah hunters will increase significantly. Even if it does, wildlife biologists say that Utah's range no longer has the carrying capacity to allow, for example, 100,000 rifle deer hunters. The habitat is gone. Along the Wasatch Front, as in countless places around Utah, mule deer winter range has been turned to suburbs and mountain cabins.

The decline hits DWR in the purse. Eighty-five percent of DWR's budget comes from the sale of hunting and fishing licenses or from the federal government, which allocates money to Utah based on the number of hunters and anglers the state has. Nearly one-quarter of DWR's budget, about $5.8 million, comes from two federal programs. The Pittman-Robertson Act is a surcharge on gun and ammunition manufacturers; money it raises goes to the states for their hunting programs and to manage game species. A similar program for fishing, the Dingell-Johnson Act, has been in effect since 1954.

No one argues whether DWR's wildlife management efforts have been skewed toward game animals. "No state with big game and fishing programs will ever spend the same amount on nongame as game," says Bob Williams of the U.S. Department of Fish and Wildlife's regional office. "Part of the reason is that the money that comes back to the states, like the Pittman-Robertson money, must, by law, be spent on the game programs. It's not that Utah's DWR doesn't care about nongame species," he insists. "Lately, DWR has provided money to species listed as sensitive, like the spotted frog, the Bonneville cutthroat trout, and the Colorado cutthroat trout. DWR's strategy is to invest money before a species is listed as endangered, because once that happens, DWR has less flexibility under federal law."

Utah's DWR is also feeling the heat of changing public opinion about wildlife. "We have about six hundred vertebrate species in Utah," DWR's Phillips observes. "Fewer than fifty are hunted or fished. So, it's true that nongame wildlife haven't been given the attention they deserve. We're trying to manage wildlife and habitat more holistically now, not only because it's good science, but because the public attitude is requiring it." For the more than 550 nongame vertebrate species in Utah, DWR has only one person whose time is dedicated solely to monitoring and managing them.

Williams of the U.S. Fish and Wildlife Service believes that it's time to tax citizens to the degree to which they are responsible for damage to wildlife and habitat. A habitat impact fee on Utah homebuyers, developers, and industry is a logical, but politically incorrect, alternative to charging outdoorspeople. "The Utah legislature debated a bill that would have taxed water users for their effect on sensitive species," Williams says. "It didn't pass, but around St. George especially, the increased human population and development are having a huge impact on wildlife."

Outdoor recreationists such as hikers, campers, and bird watchers are also negatively affecting wildlife, he notes. "The term 'nonconsumptive' just means a person doesn't take wildlife home and eat it," says Williams. "It doesn't mean they have no impact." On the contrary, "nonconsumptive users are having a huge impact on wildlife."

The shift of outdoorspeople from hunting to nonconsumptive sports puts new burdens on wildlife managers and animal habitat. The large number of people involved magnifies the wear and tear on natural areas. It's not just public access, such as trails and wildlife viewing areas, that's needed. What's needed is an inventory of nongame wildlife—measuring existing biodiversity—and creation of habitat management plans to save what open space is left for them. Outdoorspeople expect this, but there is no funding for it.

The DWR dusted off an old program—the Wildlife Heritage Certificate, which costs $20 and gets the buyer DWR magazines and newsletters, a Watchable Wildlife Guide, and free admission to seminars on such subjects as backyard birdfeeding and landscaping for wildlife. It's also free admission to DWR-guided field trips to see such critters as burrowing owls and ospreys. Most important, Wildlife Heritage Certificate buyers must first pay a $5.25 habitat authorization fee. The fee is a tax put on hunters and anglers in 1996. DWR says the money will be used to preserve and enhance wildlife habitat and to provide public access to it.

But will a birdwatcher's $5.25 tax go toward improving mule deer habitat for hunters? Theoretically, Phillips says, the money goes to nongame programs if it comes from the certificate program. If it comes from hunters, it goes to preserving game habitat. If it comes from anglers, it goes toward water projects. "However, it's a gray area," Phillips continues. "If we protect streamsides for anglers, it saves game and nongame bird habitat as well. Let's look at the common ground: We're nowhere without habitat," he emphasizes.

There are solutions. The rise in the number of wildlife watchers and the decline in the number of hunters point to one. A national coalition of hunters and conservationists called Teaming With Wildlife (TWW) proposes we copy the tried-and-true "guns and ammo" tax to raise funds for nongame wildlife. TWW's initiative calls for legislation that would put a national 3- to 5-percent tax on the production of outdoor recreational equipment, such as binoculars, hiking boots, and backpacks. The money would be returned to the states in a formula weighted by population and land area. Utah's general fund would have to match the incoming money at a ratio of $1 state to $3 federal. TWW figures it would mean about $4 million annually to Utah's Division of Wildlife Resources and Department of Parks and Recreation—all for nongame wildlife and habitat. "The initiative itself has been building support and has 3,000 businesses and organizations supporting it," reports Terry Messmer, who represents TWW in Utah. Audubon, Ducks Unlimited, the National Wildlife Federation, the Nature Conservancy, and the Wilderness Society all are supporters.

Studies show that overcrowded and poorly maintained outdoor facilities along with lack of access to wild places chill a child's interest in outdoor sports. Outdoor manufacturers need to know that and support the proposed tax to assure their future sales, TWW said. Of course, outdoor equipment manufacturers will pass the increased expense along to buyers. But nonconsumers of Utah wildlife will discover what hunters have known for years: If you want wildlife and habitat, you have to pay to manage and preserve it. 🌿

© DAN MILLER

The Nature Conservancy of Utah's Layton Wetlands Preserve.

CHAPTER THIRTEEN

The Nature Conservancy of Utah
Wheeling and dealing in race with extinction.

Unless you're a bug or a biologist, this swamp is not pretty. But the Nature Conservancy of Utah's Layton Wetlands Preserve—a sweep of mudflats, pickleweed, and brine flies that smells of rot—is paradise to birds; they come here to rest and nest by the millions. The preserve, six miles along the Great Salt Lake's eastern shore, hosts some of the largest concentrations of wildlife ever counted on a lake that's teeming with birds: for example, a million northern pintail ducks, a half-million sandpipers, a quarter-million American avocets. Utah's wetlands are comparable to rainforests in the number and variety of species they support, so the Conservancy's Salt Lake office snatches them up whenever they're for sale.

The Nature Conservancy isn't in the business of buying pretty scenery. Organized forty years ago around what was then a little-known branch of earth science called ecology, its mission is to preserve native plant and animal species and the natural communities that support them. Headquartered in Washington, D.C., the Conservancy has protected over nine million acres of ecologically important land—that's larger than Connecticut, New Jersey, and Delaware combined.

Because property rights rule, the Conservancy buys private land to protect nature. They offer the carrot of hard cash, not a stick, only buying from willing sellers. The Conservancy's low-key negotiators—such as Salt Lake field office's Chris Montague—frequently spend years building up trust with owners and neighbors and write contracts that satisfy the concerns of each party.

The Conservancy has toiled quietly in Utah for 16 years. Despite achievements, they're not exactly headline news. For example, the Conservancy expanded the Bear River Migratory Bird Refuge, owned by the U.S. Fish and Wildlife Service, by 10 percent with one transaction. Few Utahns heard about it. Long before that purchase, Montague called on the private owners of nine square miles of wetlands next to the refuge. Then, for seven years, Montague kept in touch with them and developed a rapport. The Conservancy finally bought the marsh in 1992. They resold it within days—as agreed—to the Bear River refuge. "The Nature Conservancy is very professional and skilled at what they do," says Al Trout, manager of the Bear River refuge. "That adjacent land purchase was very complicated. But because they're a private organization, they bring a perspective and leverage that we in government don't have."

The Nature Conservancy's scientists set land protection priorities. Then its field offices find the best ways to preserve targeted areas. Later, Conservancy land managers tend purchased landscapes and experiment with ways humans can live and work there without harming native plants and animals. In the West, that means they work to make ranching an Earth-friendly enterprise.

While rhetoric and confrontation fuel the political debate over wilderness on Utah's public land, the Conservancy finds ways to work and play well with others in preserving natural areas. "Wilderness is not our issue," explains Libby Ellis, the Salt Lake field office's director of development. "We don't need the legislature to do our job." The Conservancy's stand—that nothing should go extinct—is spurred by knowledge that at least three plant or animal species disappear each day. That pace is 1,000 times faster than the background rate shown in Earth's fossil record. "We are in a race with extinction. We couldn't possibly buy all the land that needs protection—and most of it is not for sale anyway. So we know we have to cooperate and form partnerships," Ellis says.

On Utah's Book Cliffs, for example—a forested plateau-and-gulch landscape with few humans but plenty of black bear, elk, and cougar—four ranches control all grazing rights. In 1990, the Conservancy brought together the Rocky Mountain Elk Foundation, ranch owners, the federal Bureau of Land Management, and the Utah Department of Wildlife Resources to create a conservation plan. The Conservancy bought one ranch along with its water rights and grazing permits; the Rocky Mountain

Elk Foundation bought another. Both intend to maintain them as working ranches but to repair damaged streamsides and allow more forage for wildlife. The remote Book Cliffs is home to a dozen rare and endangered plants and animals.

But why is the Nature Conservancy trying to save every kind of bug or rare herb? "The Earth is a machine like an airplane," Ellis comments. "You can pop out a few rivets from the airplane's hull, but eventually removing one more rivet will bring the airplane crashing down. It's the same way with species on Earth. We don't know which species lost may finally bring down the whole system." When one species goes extinct, biologists say, others that depended on it also die out. Ecosystems become unstable as they lose species and subspecies: one type of parasite or virus may wipe out an entire race. A wide range of plant and animal species in an environment—biodiversity—brings self-regulation to a biological system.

Whether or not it is morally wrong to cause a species to go extinct, "each species holds a wealth of information to scientists," Ellis points out. For humankind, allowing unknown plants to go extinct is like throwing out nature's medicine cabinet. About 25 percent of our pharmaceuticals come directly from plants, and many more from studying plant chemistry. Even so, relatively few known plants have been studied for beneficial drugs, and many more plants are thought to be unknown than are known to science. Viruses and bacteria, which prey on humans, evolve at a much faster rate than the human immune system. As a rare plant goes extinct, we may be losing a medicinal compound that cures an evolving disease. Also, wild plant foods, such as native species of corn, contain traits that modern farmers eventually need. Two decades ago, scientists had to mix strains of wild corn with field corn because 20 percent of American farmers' crops withered from a disease to which cultivated corn had no resistance—but its wild cousin did.

Saving Earth's biodiversity, as a goal, grew over time for the Conservancy. Before 1975, the Conservancy bought or collected through donation small patches of land with no particular ecological significance or economic value. Often these parcels were undisturbed because they were too steep to farm or too wet to subdivide. A Conservancy scientist, Bob Jenkins, convinced other members that they should be preserving the gene pools of species, subspecies, and unique biological communities that are disappearing because of human activity. The Conservancy soon found that the idea of buying a small parcel of land—like a spring with an endangered flower or a pasture with a rare kind of prairie dog—was flawed. Small, isolated populations of plants and animals suffer high rates of extinction, and they are easily overrun by aggressive, nonnative species. The Conservancy began to look for complete biological systems that were large enough to host their full complement of species over time.

In Utah, preserving a complete biological system "was one of the things that attracted us to Dugout Ranch," said Montague. The Conservancy purchased this ranch adjacent to Canyonlands National Park several years ago. The property includes 42 miles of cottonwood and willow riverside and the water rights to keep a steady streamflow from the nearby Abajo Mountains. This kind of intact streamside habitat is rare in southeastern Utah. The ranch and its quarter million associated acres shelter at least four globally rare wildflowers. Ellis says, "We try to protect species before they're put on the endangered list." It's costly for the U.S. Fish and Wildlife Service to do their job of preserving plants or animals under the Endangered Species Act after populations are decimated and their habitat is biologically unraveled.

Nature Conservancy biologists survey and identify rare plants, animals, and biological systems; then they decide which ones are in danger of disappearing first. To help states keep track, the Conservancy developed the State Natural Heritage Inventory Program. It's a computer catalog that allows you to type in real estate survey coordinates and get back a list of rare plants and animals in the area. The government has taken over the system in most states, including Utah.

Once Conservancy scientists target critical areas, field offices find the best ways to preserve them. Because so much land needs protection and because funds are limited, the Conservancy is always looking for ways to leverage its efforts. Field office personnel policy was finding "people who like to get a good deal," according to Pat Noonan, an early director. Conservancy field officers don't have to know an oriole from an Oreo, but they quickly become experts on real estate law, gift tax incentives, and public land management. Frequently the Salt Lake office will do all the legwork on a property—find a seller, survey, appraise, and title search—so another buyer can preserve it.

The Salt Lake field office has been especially clever in preserving wetlands using the Central Utah Project's (CUP) money. As part of Congress' reauthorization of CUP four years ago, it required states to replace in other areas—to mitigate—wetlands habitat destroyed by dams. The Conservancy's Salt Lake field office draws up protection proposals for Great Salt Lake wetlands, primarily in Davis County, and the CUP Mitigation Commission purchases them. "This CUP mitigation money is especially helpful now," said Montague. "The population of Davis County is expanding rapidly, subdivisions are creeping closer to the lake, and land prices are skyrocketing. Ten years from now, most of this land would be gone."

Each Conservancy field office is responsible for raising all the money for projects in its state. The national organization does have a fund of over $150 million from which Utah can borrow for a quick purchase if necessary. But the loan must be paid back with interest.

After a field office has found donors to purchase land, the Conservancy's stewardship branch takes over. "However, the Conservancy itself only manages property if it makes sense for us to do so," notes Ellis. For example, in February of 1996, the Conservancy bought a 700-acre parcel in the Snake Creek drainage at the top of Big Cottonwood Canyon that was threatened by Brighton ski resort's expansion. The Conservancy immediately turned around and sold the mountainside to the Utah Department of Parks and Recreation, which manages Wasatch State Park next door. This way they avoided duplicating land management efforts. Whenever the Conservancy resells land, the contract includes a conservation easement that permanently protects the land. In the Snake Creek purchase, the easement protects the acreage in perpetuity for watershed and wildlife habitat.

Increasingly the Conservancy buys conservation easements to ranches and farms. The Conservancy pays the rancher or farmer an agreed-upon price. In return, the rancher or farmer will continue to graze or farm their land but cannot sell it to be subdivided. It's either cows or condos in the new West, according to Dave Livermore, the Conservancy's Utah State director. "We can't afford to buy all the land that needs protection—and strip malls, subdivisions, and ranchettes will replace ranches" unless we work with the best rural stewards of the land.

Next door, Colorado loses 90,000 rural acres each year—over 140 square miles—to suburb creep. "Rural communities in Utah are under tremendous pressure from the forces of development," Ellis says. Expanding suburbs can cause property taxes to rise for rural residents and force them to sell to real estate agents and construction companies. "We want to work with rural property owners," she says. On the Conservancy's Book Cliffs ranch and in the Dugout Ranch deal, the Conservancy will continue to work the properties as ranches. This makes the Conservancy a good neighbor in two ways: local businesses get money from ranching purchases, and the property stays on the county tax rolls, continuing to pay property tax. Successful examples of sustainable ranching "that make money but also take care of the land and can teach others to do the same" would be real leverage in these purchases, Livermore observes.

Dugout Ranch has had a reputation of excellent land stewardship, notes Montague. Heidi Redd, Dugout's long-time owner, found ways to keep her quarter-million acre allotment of grazing land in good condition, even during drought years. "Heidi moved her cows frequently, and covered lots of ground so no one area was hit too hard. She has always been open to new ideas, was interested in native grasses, and never tried to eliminate predators, such as cougar and coyotes. She figured that some livestock losses are part of the deal," Montague says. The Redds sold the ranch to the Conservancy at a substantial discount from its appraised value of $6.3 million.

Even when protecting entire biological systems, the Conservancy has to worry about long-term global changes affecting large preserves. For example, acid rain may kill all the fish in a preserved lake; a temperature increase from the greenhouse effect may kill plant species blocked from spreading north; or the reduction of Earth's ozone layer may kill off all the frogs in an area. And ultimately the interests of nature and humans are the same. "Everything plants and animals depend on, such as clean air and water, humans depend on too. We're part of the food chain," Ellis emphasizes.

With vast natural landscapes to protect and climbing real estate prices, the Nature Conservancy of Utah is raising its profile to bring in more donors. Contributors get results for their money—the Conservancy is known for action, not talk. "To a donor, the way the Nature Conservancy works makes a lot of economic sense," says Scott Lee, professor of finance at Texas A&M University and long-time Utah conservationist. "Instead of paying legislative lobbyists each year, the Conservancy buys property rights to critical natural areas. When you buy land to protect it like they do, it's like money in the bank." 🌿

CHAPTER FOURTEEN

Birdwatching in the Beehive State
Its popularity soars.

URBAN PEOPLE CONNECTING WITH NATURE

According to the latest count, the state of Utah has two bird watchers in the bush for every hunter out there. Over a quarter of a million people watch birds in the Beehive State as an outdoor activity each year, according to U.S. Fish and Wildlife Service estimates. It's Utah's fastest growing outdoor sport.

Birdwatching has a new constituency too. "When I was in school, they called me 'birdman'—and bird watchers had the image of little old ladies in tennis shoes," recalls Sugar House ornithologist Mark Stackhouse, whose ebony beard and full head of hair betray no signs of gray—even at his temples near the gold loop in one ear. And Stackhouse's business—a tour company that guides birders to Utah's Bohemian waxwings and bald eagles—is soaring on a rising thermal of interest in the sport. It helps that Utah hosts a rich variety of birds and has a world-famous shorebird refuge. But the growing popularity of birdwatching reflects a national demographic trend too: a population that's increasingly urban shuns the rural tradition of hunting but still wants to connect with nature.

Birders watch their quarry in backyards as well as in the backcountry. In fact, it may appear that there are two species of bird watcher. One type puts out feed near a window and watches birds come to them. Another kind troops out into the backcountry, binoculars in hand, for an avian treasure hunt. However, the domestic bird-feeder type often evolves into the second, more mobile variety, and there's plenty of crossover. In Utah, you'll find birders who will jet to Bali for a rare glimpse of the white-feathered, blue-eyed Rothschild starling—and feed the song sparrows in their own backyard as well.

Owen Hogle caters to both species of birder and attests to their increasing numbers. "After gardening, backyard birdwatching is the second highest home hobby expenditure now," he says. On weekends, Salt Lakers flock to his Wild Bird Center in Holladay to pick up feed, binoculars, bird books, and advice. "My demographic studies show that the valley can support eight more bird stores like mine." Birdwatching in Utah is an easy sell, he explains. "There are 900 bird species in North America, and in Utah we have the opportunity to see over 400 of them." Birders from other states covet birds that Utahns take for granted. "I get phone calls all the time from birders passing through Salt Lake International. They say, 'I'm out at the airport and have a three-hour layover; where can I see a black-billed magpie?' chuckles Hogle. "I tell them to walk a few hundred yards from the terminal and they'll see one."

Entry costs to the hobby are low. All you need to get started are a pair of binoculars and a decent bird book (see "Choosing a Field Guide to Birds" at end of this chapter). Usually people begin birdwatching by noticing neighborhood birds. Patty Johnson, now tagged "The Bird Woman of Holladay" by her friends, got started this way. She has five bird feeders in her yard and sometimes can see two dozen quail milling outside her door. It's peaceful and therapeutic to watch birds, Johnson comments. "It's magical to look closely at them and notice all the details. I love the close contact with nature."

It's easy to make a backyard bird-friendly. To attract the widest variety of birds possible, experts suggest that you add shelter and water along with feed. By adding different heights of vegetation, you'll draw different types of birds. For example, birds such as sparrows and doves prefer low-growing cover, while robins perch in the highest trees. Chickadees and wrens nest in vegetation of medium height. If you add standing water to your yard—or let a hose trickle over rocks—many birds will arrive just for a bath and a belt. If you do enough, your backyard can be certified by the National Wildlife Federation as a bird and animal sanctuary, notes Lorie Millward, a naturalist with the Utah Museum of Natural History. Her one-third acre lot in Riverton is a year-round haven to hummingbirds and other hardy species.

Bird watching in Utah.

© JOHN WILKIN / HERALD JOURNAL

When backyard birders study their neighborhood birds, the big talents of these small creatures often surprise them. For example, that jewel-like hummingbird buzzing a Salt Lake feeder is a member of a species that can fly backwards at 40 miles per hour, cruise (forward) nonstop for 500 miles, fly to South America, and maintain a heart rate of 600 beats a minute. And while the free room and board a person doles out to their feathered neighbors may appear to have a big impact on the birds, "the biggest effect of a backyard bird feeder is on the human who fills it up with seed," observes Stackhouse, who regularly finds that backyard bird watchers develop into full-fledged, list-keeping birders.

Commonly, those who begin by watching birds in their backyard soon find themselves in the backcountry, out to observe as many other kinds of birds as possible. And because birds migrate seasonally, birders want to be at particular places during certain times. Spring and early summer are spectacular seasons to birdwatch in Utah. During this time, birds are pumped with hormones and out in the open singing and defending territory and displaying their most colorful plumage. It is the height of the breeding season. On every Utah birder's spring visiting list is the world-renowned Bear River Migratory Bird Refuge, just west of Brigham City. Here you can drive out into the Great Salt Lake's freshwater marshes on top of miles of man-made dikes. From a car, you'll see tens of thousands of birds and scores of species. The east shore of the Great Salt Lake is internationally recognized as essential habitat for a notable portion of the world's birds.

There's more to birding Utah than the Great Salt Lake, however. The state is on the itinerary of another type of migrating bird. In the spring and fall, Utah's mountains are corridors for migrating raptors—birds of prey. To save energy, these large-bodied meat eaters ride the updrafts created by ridges. On a mountaintop in spring you can watch—at eye level—golden eagles and red-tailed hawks glide in the breeze or see a falcon hover, then tuck wings and dive like an F-16. An hour before sunset, migrating raptors find a place to spend the night. "One of the most memorable sights I've seen," recalls Salt Laker Laurel Casjens, whose birdwatching has taken her around the world, "is watching hundreds of bald eagles roost in a canyon just north of Ogden."

During the migration, you may see a dozen raptors soar past each hour. Along the Wasatch Front, Squaw Peak road in Provo Canyon is a premier raptor observation site. Further north, Farmington Canyon will lead you to lookout places on Francis Peak and Bountiful Peak.

To see songbirds and perching birds, go to Heber Valley and walk the banks of the Provo River. Farther south, "Utah's canyon country is less bird-ed than other parts of the state," Stackhouse says, so there are great places yet to be discovered.

One southern Utah area that's legendary among Utah birders is the Lytle Ranch Preserve, southwest of St. George. The ranch preserves a piece of the Mojave Desert that spills up into Utah's borders. Among the Joshua trees, mesquite, and creosote bushes, you'll spot birds that are seldom seen else-where in Utah, such as the gray flycatcher.

Any place with unusual birds will draw seasoned birders like sunflower seeds attract chickadees. Casjens and husband Carlton DeTar flew to a small national park in the northwest corner of Bali, Indonesia, for a chance to see a Rothschild starling. "There are only 25 Rothschild starlings in the wild," Casjens explains. "And we saw two of them." Dedicated bird watchers are also known for writing inventories of the species they've seen and identified. These are lists of what they've watched in the backyard, in the state, during their lives, or on their best day watching. "Bird watchers who keep lists are sometimes called 'bird golfers' by those who don't—because they keep score," jokes Stackhouse, whose own best-day-in-Utah list is more than 180 species long.

Identifying 180 bird species in one twenty-four-hour period is quite a feat, but in the future it may not be possible to match in Utah. Ironically, the increase in birdwatching's popularity is happening at a time when wildlife habitat is disappearing at an unprecedented rate because of an expanding human population. Loss of habitat is a death sentence for individual birds because "basically, all suitable habitat is already filled with birds," explains Stackhouse. Adjacent areas are already saturated with other birds who defend their territories. The displaced birds can no longer make a living for them-selves or successfully reproduce. Take away enough natural area—or com-promise critical habitat like the east shore of the Great Salt Lake—and you wind up with endangered bird species or extinct ones.

"Just in the five years I've been birdwatching, I've already noticed a loss in bird habitat," says Larene Wyss, who belongs to Salt Lake Birders and is helping to organize a statewide birdwatching organization, partly for the lobbying power it would provide. "Now I know how important wetlands are and that if you take them away, you never get them back," she says. "Before I started birdwatching, I'd have been sitting on the fence about the Legacy Highway." The west Davis County stretch of the proposed Legacy Highway, to which she refers, would pave over 150 acres of east shore Great Salt Lake wetlands and isolate thousands more from the natural water flow.

If bird lovers don't figure out how to protect Utah's wildlife habitat, bird watching's popularity may shrink the way the number of hunters has. It was habitat loss, not just a loss of rural traditions, that was responsible for a crash in the number of those hunting in Utah. But Wyss has hope: "The more people know about birds, the more aware of nature they become and the more they want to protect the environment."

CHOOSING A FIELD GUIDE TO BIRDS

A field guide to birds is a compact book used for identifying wild species. Each picture in it is accompanied by notes pointing out significant differences identifying a bird as one species rather than another. "There are only two field guides to consider for beginners," according to ornithologist Mark Stackhouse: *Peterson's Field Guide to Western Birds* and the more advanced *National Geographic Society Field Guide to the Birds of North America.* "And be sure to read the front part of the field guide," Stackhouse advises. "It tells you how to use the book; don't just look at the pretty pictures." Field guides that use photos as references for identifying birds are not as good as those that use artists' illustrations, Stackhouse says. Avian plumage varies seasonally and differs among individual birds of the same species, so a photograph can't show enough examples. On the other hand, an artist's illustration is a more generalized impression of the species.

Amateurs make the mistake of trying to identify birds by noting their color and size, Stackhouse observes, but both are deceptive. Plumage varies with individuals, and the bird you want to identify is seldom near a reliable size reference. "It's much more accurate to go by profile of the bird and by its behavior, such as its flight pattern."

Most bird watchers end up with more than one field guide. Golden's *A Guide to Field Identification, Birds of North America; The Audubon Society Field Guide to North American Birds;* and *Watchable Birds of the Rocky Mountains,* by Mary Taylor Gray are other available field guides.

OTHER RESOURCES FOR BIRDERS
Utah Birdline: (801) 538-4730

Videos
Audubon Society's Video Guide to the Birds of North America. The Backyard Birdwatcher, with George H. Harrison. *John James Audubon: The Birds of America.*

Stores
Wild Bird Center: 4898 Highland Drive, Salt Lake City, UT, (801) 277-4544. Rocky Mountain Wild Bird Station: 875 Iron Horse Dr., Park City, UT, (435) 647-5990.

Organizations
Salt Lake Birders: Larene Wyss, Membership Chair (801) 278-8758. Great Salt Lake Audubon Chapter: 4726 Wallace Lane, Salt Lake City, UT. Utah Museum of Natural History: (801) 581-6927. Utah Division of Wildlife Resources and the Watchable Wildlife program: (801) 538-4700, <www.nr.state.ut.us/dwr>. Tracy Aviary: (801) 466-0920. U.S. Fish and Wildlife Service: (801) 831-5353, <www.fws.gov>. Utah Society for Environmental Education: <usee@sisna.com>. HawkWatch International: (800) 726-4295 or (801) 524-8511, <www.info-xpress.com/hawkwatch/>. Nature Conservancy of Utah: (801) 531-0999. North American Bluebird Society: (435) 649-6982. Audubon Society: (303) 499-0219, <www.audubon.org>. Utah Wildlife Federation: (800) 477-5560 or (202) 797-6800, <www.nwf.org>

Wetlands Organizations
Friends of Great Salt Lake: (801) 582-1496, <www. xmission.com/~fogsl>. Utah Wetlands Foundation: (801) 364-2045. Wetlands Information Hotline: (800) 832-7828, <www.epa.gov/OGWDW/wetline>. Wetlands Workshop: (801) 538-4864, <www.nr.state.ut.us/dwr>. Ducks Unlimited: (801) 364-9672.

Where To Go
Great Basin. Bear River Migratory Bird Refuge: Fresh water marsh fringing the Great Salt Lake, with 12 miles of roads, over 200 species of birds. Take I-15 north to Brigham City, go west 15 miles.

Ogden Bay Waterfowl Management Area: On the Great Salt Lake. Migrating ducks in September, hiking trail, and automobile loop.

Farmington Bay Waterfowl Management Area: On the Great Salt Lake. Wetlands, sweeping views, many species of shore, wading, and migratory birds.

Stockton and Vernon, Utah: Wintering bald eagles which feed on the blacktail jackrabbit population; rough-legged hawks and prairie falcons also in winter.

Antelope Island: A wildlife sanctuary on the Great Salt Lake, with hiking trails. More rare birds are reported from the Antelope Island causeway than from any other single spot in Utah; also sanderlings, sandpipers, plovers, and eared grebes in great numbers. In winter look for unusual ducks. On the island: loggerhead shrikes, sage thrashers, and chukars.

Rocky Mountains. Red Butte Gardens: On the Wasatch foothills east of Salt Lake City, (801) 581-5322.

Midway Fish Hatchery: In Heber Valley, Utah, northeast of Deer Creek Reservoir. Osprey in spring, black-crowned night herons, great blue herons, and sandhill cranes.

Deer Creek Reservoir: East of Provo, Utah. Common loons and terns in the spring; in nearby fields are white-face ibis.

Cutler Marsh: West of Logan, Utah, on the Little Bear River off Highway 30. American bitterns, marsh wrens, yellow-headed and red-winged blackbirds, pied-billed and western grebes, and warblers.

Bear Lake National Wildlife Refuge: North end of Bear Lake in Idaho.

Wellsville Wilderness: On the southwest side of Cache Valley, Utah. Annual raptor migration, including northern harriers, kestrels, goshawks, red-tailed hawks, and golden eagles.

Pineview Reservoir: East of Ogden, Utah, the North Arm viewing site has a nature trail. Songbirds such as the yellow warbler, lazuli bunting, white-crowned sparrow, and northern oriole; also shorebirds, swimming birds.

Cascade Springs: East of Provo, Utah. Trails built over mountain springs, songbirds each spring.

Ouray National Wildlife Refuge/Pariette Wetlands: In Colorado. Waterfowl, shorebirds, wading birds spring through fall.

Huntington Canyon: Streamside zones, many songbirds in the turnouts.

Canyon Country. Lytle Ranch Preserve and Beaver Wash: Southwest of St. George, Utah.

Scott M. Matheson Wetlands Preserve: 850 acres along the Colorado River near Moab, Utah, (801) 259-4629, <www.netoasis.com/moab/matheson>.

CHAPTER FIFTEEN

Watching wildlife in wild places

MOJAVE DESERT SPRINGTIME: A FESTIVAL OF LIFE

Most of the year, southwestern Utah's Mojave Desert is an intimidating stretch of stone, sand, and silence. It's hotter and drier than the Great Basin desert on its north, so outside of St. George, cedar and sage hillsides give way to a rocky landscape bristling with yucca, Joshua trees, and spine-tangled cacti. In summer, the three-digit Mojave heat is stunning. In winter, the desert lies freeze-dried, awaiting a meager few inches of annual rain.

But spring is different. This time of year, bouquets of delicate wildflowers erupt in rock washes and even the stubborn cacti bloom. Songbirds and butterflies scout the crystal air. Desert tortoises, like rocks that have sprouted legs, emerge from burrows and plod off on urgent turtle business with solemn yellow eyes.

Visiting hours for the Mojave begin in May. When the temperature moderates, the spare landscape reveals a web of weird and wonderful life; for example, it's the only place in Utah you'll find Gila monsters, roadrunners, and sidewinders. But even at the peak of its spring vitality, a trip to the Mojave Desert is not about an overwhelming abundance of life. It's still a rock garden—more stones than living things.

Because desert life is secretive, subtle, or just rare, it's worthwhile to tag along with desert experts who know where to find it. St. George's Desert Wildlife Festival, held each year in May, is a locally organized program of field trips and classes designed to teach people about the hardy plants and animals that make this place home. For two days, the area's experienced desert ramblers lead hikers to the Mojave's hidden corners and, there and in classrooms, teach participants desert lore, from medicinal plants to venomous reptiles.

© MARK HENGESBAUGH

Mojave Desert.

The festival has a devoted following. "Some Utah families get together each year for the deer hunt. Our family gets together for the Desert Wildlife Festival," says Marshall Topham, father of six and principal of St. George's Pine View High School. "Even my two kids in college try to come back for it. On a festival hike last year we saw desert tortoise hatchlings, Gila monster tracks, and a sidewinder."

Wild desert life is out there, if you know where to find it. "When I take people out into the desert, they're always amazed at the variety and amount of life we find," notes wildlife biologist Ann McLuckie, who's with the Utah Division of Wildlife Resources, one of the festival sponsors. But it's a tough place for life to take hold, so plants and animals are more dispersed in the Mojave. This part of Utah gets only 6.7 inches of rain a year, McLuckie points out, less than half of Salt Lake City's total, and most of that falls between December and February.

Mojave plants employ strange and elegant ways to cope. Cacti grow shallow roots to suck up the slightest rain quickly and store it in expandable trunks. Barrel cacti have accordion-like pleats that swell, then shrink as they use up water reserves. Other plants, like mesquite, drill deep roots and tap into underground water. A mesquite tree's muscular root can grow to 80 feet and may be thicker than its trunk.

In a climate that is either scorching or freezing most of the time, desert annual flowers sprint through their life cycle in spring. They send up stalks in days and then bloom quickly, taking advantage of tolerable temperatures to deposit seeds for future generations. These tough kernels may lie in the dirt for years before conditions are again right to sprout. Desert soil is a seed bank with dozens of seeds in each scoopful. But on this vast, convoluted landscape, knowing exactly when a type of wildflower should be blooming—then finding it—is tricky. For this reason, the festival's guided wildflower walks are popular. Desert blossoms are not only short lived, but "they are often tiny and delicate as well. You need to get out on foot to see and appreciate them," says McLuckie.

"Our goal is to acquaint people with the desert," notes Marilyn Davis, St. George native and a public contact representative for the Bureau of Land Management, another sponsor of the festival. "A little education goes a long way, then most people can get out and discover more for themselves, which is fun." Organizers enjoy the festival as much as the participants do. "We set up birdwatching blinds on the Virgin River during the festival so that people can get a close look at the egrets, avocets, and other birds that migrate here in spring," says Davis, a birdwatcher. One memorable morning "we were walking down to a blind when four mule deer popped up and splashed out across the water." People learn that the "Virgin and Santa Clara Rivers are a lifeline for the birds and animals here."

Water—how desert creatures find, conserve, recycle, and even manufacture it—is key to their survival. Kangaroo mice, for example, never drink standing water; they produce all the water they need by eating dry seeds. Desert tortoises recycle the moisture in their bladders when needed.

Such resourcefulness rules the Mojave. Clever prehistoric humans used a much wider variety of desert life for food and medicine than modern humans do and not all this folklore is forgotten. The festival holds a popular class on edible and medicinal desert plants, although most participants lead urban or suburban lives and will never need to tuck into a plate of prickly pear fruit.

But city dwellers or not, a growing number of Utahns of all ages show a desire to connect with the natural world. "As a high school principal, I see many of our students attend the Desert Wildlife Festival," notes Topham, who's also on the festival board. "One of our students is skilled at identifying birds, so he's a presenter at the festival. Another one of our students went on a festival night hike to see bats. That trip inspired her to do a science project on bat houses. It placed so high in the regional science fair competition that she was invited to show her project at the International Science and Engineering Fair," Topham reports with pride.

As the public learns more about desert life, Topham hopes they'll take it for granted less often. There was a time when the general public thought of desert as wasteland, as in "You can't really hurt it—it's only desert." The sprawling human population in Washington County, which doubled between 1980 and 1990, reflected this attitude, causing serious wildlife declines. For example, local officials recently had to commit to a habitat conservation plan to protect the area's endangered desert tortoise—Utah's only native turtle species.

Topham comments, "I think we've realized that we have a very unique environment here and we have a responsibility to make others more aware of the sensitive species in it. We have a responsibility to educate people about this special place."

DESERT NATIONAL WILDLIFE RANGE: 99.9 PERCENT PURE MOJAVE

Tired of tame parks with entrance fees and souvenir shops? Looking for raw wilderness without hiking trails or interpretive nature centers?

Have I got a refuge for you. Southern Nevada's Desert National Wildlife Range is 2,200 square miles—half the size of Connecticut—preserved as habitat for desert bighorn sheep. It's the largest wildlife refuge in the lower 48 states. And, other than a couple of really rough roads and a few picnic tables, it makes no accommodation for human visitors. It's wild country preserved for native wildlife. You gotta love that.

The eastern half of the Desert National Wildlife Range is open to hiking, backpacking, and car camping. Here lies a thousand square miles of silent Mojave Desert with two major mountain ranges made from rippling, twisted layers of brilliant sedimentary rock.

The western one-thousand square miles of the Desert National Wildlife Range is part of the Nellis Air Force Bombing Range. I asked Marti Collins, refuge manager, if the pneumatic screech of jets and aerial bombardment

Desert National Wildlife Range in Nevada.

© MARK HENGESBAUGH

made the bighorn sheep on the military side of her refuge skittish. Collins says the Air Force tested bighorns for stress by connecting them to remote control heart sensors. Researchers watched for heart-rate increases during bombing nearby, and they detected no rise. One question, Collins says, is whether the bighorn sheep were already adapted to the commotion before the test.

Maybe they're deaf by now. Anyhow, don't go into the bombing range. The tourable part of the preserve is about 20 miles wide and 50 miles long. It sits deep in southern Nevada where the state's shape is squeezed to a point from California on the west and Arizona on the east. The range has no hiking trails; the few walking visitors wander up its remote washes. If you stay overnight, you must camp out of sight of, and a quarter of a mile away from, the springs or you'll scare away the wild customers.

The Sheep Mountains, rising to nearly 10,000 feet, run the full length of the public side of the wildlife range. The Las Vegas Mountains run parallel to the Sheep mountains, then they merge. Climate in the wildlife range depends on elevation. The valley floors, at 2,500 feet, get four inches of rain each year. These popcorn-dry lowlands are paved with sandblasted gravel and are sparsely covered with creosote bush and white bursage. Climbing a few thousand feet, spear-pointed yucca and Mickey Mouse-eared cactus poke up. At 6,000 feet, pretzel-like Joshua trees—actually a gigantic member of the lily family—and furry-spined cholla take over.

Above 6,000 feet, the desert shrubs give way to woodlands of juniper and sagebrush. Bighorn sheep and mule deer live near the springs here. Pinyon jay and broad-tailed hummingbirds are common as well. The 7,000 to 9,000 foot elevations may catch 15 inches of rain and snow annually. Green pockets of ponderosa pine and white fir thrive. Fewer mule deer or bighorn hang here, but there are some cougars. Plenty of sagebrush lizards, Clark's nutcrackers, and canyon wrens dart through. Approaching 10,000 feet, you'll find the wizards of the tree world—bristlecone pines.

The wildlife range is Mojave Desert preserved for bighorn sheep habitat, but in saving this island of natural landscape from human renovation, it also protects all the usual suspects: badgers, bobcats, foxes, coyotes, mountain lions, and over 260 species of birds, including roadrunners and golden eagles.

Most visitors enter the range through its Corn Creek Field Station, 23 miles northwest of Las Vegas on U.S. Highway 95. Corn Creek is a marshy spring-fed oasis that was once a stagecoach stop on the route from Salt Lake City to Los Angeles. Now it provides R and R for hundreds of birds species during their spring and fall migrations. The flint chips scattered around Corn Creek show it was a campground for Southern Paiutes. Later it was a freight wagon stop; it still has a blacksmith shop and a storehouse built of railroad ties from that era. The range is home to another stagecoach stop, called Mormon Well, at a 6,000-foot pass between the Sheep and Las Vegas Mountains. In a clearing of cedars, the stage stop's original corral—an enclosure of skinny, charcoal-black sticks rammed into the ground—stands next to a forgotten wagon track.

The range has two through roads. The Mormon Well Road runs northeast from the Corn Creek Field Station to Highway 93. The Alamo Road runs north from Corn Creek to Highway 93 at Pahranagat National Wildlife Refuge. Both roads are rutted and have long sections of loose rock. A high-clearance vehicle is essential; four-wheel drive is recommended.

You should reserve a whole day, even for just a drive-through. But definitely get out and walk some. Just a short stroll from your car, the range's vast spaces and interplanetary quiet conspire to lower your blood pressure. The crystal air telescopes scenery, bringing grand sweeps of tan desert floor and magenta mountain walls up close. A short walk off the Mormon Well Road are two prehistoric crock pots. Like traditional Hawaiians, Southern Paiutes and Virgin Branch Anasazi roasted meat and vegetables underground in pits lined with limestone cobbles and covered with earth. Succeeding generations left piles of white rocks in coffee-table size mounds, called agave roasting pits. You can still see chunks of charcoal among the stones.

When I was there, we took a brief hike away from the Alamo Road to an old Indian cave. It's a low den in lava rock with a sandy midden, or ancient trash heap, out front. Someone had been digging into the midden carelessly. Gray potsherds, flint chips, and bird-size bones lay all mixed up worse than Fido's breakfast. Looking out from the cave, the Mojave was a spiky sea of glowing Joshua trees and swordlike yucca in the low afternoon sun. A spray of mountain bluebirds shot by with two needle-beaked flickers in hot pursuit.

The range's 850 desert bighorn sheep are more difficult to spot. Their numbers are down, range manager Collins says. Biologists believe it may be drought, disease, or predation by mountain lions that's causing the decline, which is serious because scattered bands of 50 or fewer desert bighorns rarely last 50 years. Compared to mountain bighorn sheep, desert bighorns are smaller and lighter colored and have a wider flare in their horn curls. Genetically, though, the mountain and desert bighorn are closely related. Desert bighorn travel only about a mile or two on an average day and live their entire lives within a 10 to 20 mile area. They have preferred travel paths to water and feed and to cliffs; ewes pass this knowledge on to succeeding generations. Rams and ewes roam separately, each with a group leader, who also acts as the sentinel. Standing watch, the leader signals danger with a snort. When breeding time approaches, the groups join and rams sort out leadership. Most duels are one-butt skirmishes, but occasionally they can last 24 hours. Bighorns stay lean on their diet of grass and desert shrubs; they also scour the desert for cactus fruits, jojoba nuts, and the fruiting heads of brittlebush.

Desert bighorn are tough to see in the wild. You'll be wishing they wore fluorescent orange vests, like deer hunters. The color of a bighorn's coat— drab brownish-gray that fades into a small white rump patch—blends perfectly with desert mountainsides. The sheep are wary, and just after hunting season—when we were there—they make themselves scarce. A ranger at Lake Mead comments, "I took a class to learn how to spot bighorn sheep in the wild, and still I have a hard time seeing them." Collins recommends that if you just want to see desert bighorn sheep, go to Boulder City's Hemenway Valley Park, near Lake Mead National Recreation Area. A herd of bighorn is often seen nearby. To see bighorn sheep on the Desert National Wildlife Range, it's best to drive the Gass Peak Road in August.

If you're lucky enough to see a bighorn sheep in Desert National Wildlife Range, that's wonderful. But just to walk in this Mojave wilderness is magnificent.

If You Go

Entry: There are three entries to the public side of the refuge, one of them is unsigned. The southern entry is the Corn Creek Field Station, which is 23 miles northwest of Las Vegas off Highway 95. The northern entry is at Pahranagat National Wildlife Refuge, which is about 60 miles directly north of Highway 93's junction with I-15. An unsigned entry is at Elbow Canyon, two miles south of state road 168's junction with Highway 93. Look for the intersection of the east-west and north-south power lines and for a small substation. The entry is the rough gravel road on the west side of Highway 93.

Getting Around: The public side of the range has two through roads. Both are rough; a high clearance vehicle with four-wheel drive is recommended.

Hiking: The entire east half of the refuge is open to hiking. There are no designated hiking trails. The most popular canyon hikes are Hidden Forest and Cow Camp Spring off the Alamo Road, and Sawmill Wash and Pine Nut Road, both off the Mormon Well Road.

Camping: Roadside camping is allowed along routes signed as open to vehicles. Camps must be at least **one-quarter** mile from, and out of sight of, water sources.

Backpacking: Hidden Forest Canyon and Sawmill Canyon are five-mile hikes that go to springs amid conifer trees. Again, camp one-quarter mile away and out of sight of water sources.

Map: U.S.G.S 30 x 60 "Indian Springs."

Hotels: Hotel rooms are relatively expensive and occasionally booked up in nearby Las Vegas. However, in Mesquite, 80 miles northeast of Las Vegas, rooms are cheap and plentiful. Call ahead and ask for specials in effect when you're visiting.

Weather: Winter weather is mild. Temperatures range from freezing at night to 75 degrees during the day. In the summer, daytime highs usually exceed 100 degrees.

More Information: Martha K. Collins, refuge manager, Desert National Wildlife Range Complex, 1500 North Decatur Boulevard, Las Vegas, Nevada 89108-1289; (702) 646-3401. Ask for a free map and brochure. The Corn Creek headquarters area is open every day from sunrise to sunset.

CABEZA PRIETA: A SONORAN SAFARI

It was a smuggler's nightmare. At the shoulder of a rocky ridge, we heard the hollow thump-thump of an approaching U.S. Border Patrol helicopter long before we could see it. Only a few dozen feet off the ground, it came straight to us, like a giant dragonfly tracking lunch. The whirlybird's bronze-tinted bubble windshield reflected the ragged Agua Dulce Mountains as it turned and landed. We were amazed. In a sea of rock and cactus about the size of Delaware, a lone Border Patrol crew located us two walkers as easily as if we'd phoned in G.P.S. coordinates.

I was glad our paperwork was in order.

"The Border Patrol has a tough, no-win job out here," Virgial Harper, Cabeza Prieta National Wildlife Refuge's recreation planner, told me earlier that morning as I applied for an entry permit. The Border Patrol tracks the footprints of illegal immigrants through the refuge, which shares 56 miles of border with Mexico. Too often where the tracks stop, ill-shod campesinos are found exhausted or dead from thirst and exposure.

The Cabeza Prieta refuge is more than three-quarters of a million acres of protected Sonoran desert that spills into southern Arizona from Mexico. It is the third largest wildlife refuge in the continental U.S. "It's a complicated wildlife refuge to operate," Harper said. Coordination of federal agencies is tricky. Not only is Cabeza Prieta patrolled for smuggling and illegal immigration, but the U.S. Air Force uses it to practice bombing runs.

Cabeza Prieta is not for everyone. Visitors must apply for a permit from the U.S. Fish and Wildlife Service and sign a hold-harmless agreement for the Air Force. A four-wheel drive vehicle is required to handle its solitary two-rut road, which becomes impassable after a spit of rain. And yes, Cabeza Prieta does have rattlesnakes—six species of them. Easy to see why the refuge is a chunk of nearly unspoiled Sonoran real estate still. The summer heat is extreme. Ground temperatures can hit 175 degrees. The refuge wrote just over 1,500 visitor entry permits last year, reports Don Tiller, refuge manager. Only one of them during July.

161

But the Sonora gets furious thunderstorms in the summer and soaking rains in the winter, which allow it to support a vast array of plants and over 40 species of mammals, from the endangered Sonoran pronghorn to pocket mice. Year-round moisture—though it amounts to only a few inches—keeps the Sonoran desert more biologically diverse than the Great Basin and Mojave deserts to the north or the Chihuahua desert to the east.

We crossed the remote northwestern corner of Organ Pipe Cactus National Monument to enter Cabeza Prieta on a winter afternoon. The road is a knotted, twisting groove in the desert floor, sliced by silty runoff channels. It took two-and-a-half hours to penetrate twenty miles into the refuge from Ajo, Arizona.

Twelve mountain ranges, not much higher than 3,000 feet but extremely rugged, corrugate the desert floor. The landscape is dominated by telephone pole-sized saguaro cacti, their upcurved branches frozen in a stiff "Howdy." Many of these giants are over one hundred years old. A hawk with a toast-colored head and creamy breast perched on a lofty saguaro and examined us curiously as we bounced past.

The refuge is a cactus cornucopia. Every turn offers new varieties: Mickey Mouse-eared prickly pear cactus, fishhook cactus, pencil cactus, as well as several species of cholla with spines so fine and dense they appear to be blond fur. Whiplike ocotillo, olive creosote, and ironwood scrub—along with cacti—create a sparse forest with a wind-blasted, gravel floor. The mountains are steep heaps of bowling ball-sized rocks dotted with thorny brush and cactus.

We camped in a low pass and lit out on a walk. It was then the Border Patrol's flying welcome wagon landed—not to check our entry permit—but to kindly inform us that the road ahead was flooded. The refuge has only one east-west avenue for visitors. A section of it, nicknamed El Camino del Diablo, or "Devil's Highway," dates back to 1540 as a risky shortcut for travelers from Mexico to California. At one time, human graves lined the road like milestones; 65 tombs were dug near Tinajas Altas (High Tanks) alone. In 1855, U.S. Army Lieutenant N. Michler wrote, "Death has strewn a continuous line of bleached bones and withered carcasses . . . to mark the way" along the Devil's Highway. For Cabeza Prieta travelers today, one road forks from the Devil's Highway. It heads north, passing a pale granite peak with a black volcanic layer on top, Cabeza Prieta, or "Dark Head." That road eventually meets up with Interstate 8 after it leaves the refuge. Refuge rules allow vehicles to park within 50 feet of its two roads for camping. This corridor is the only place vehicles are permitted. The refuge has no maintained hiking trails. The result is an enormous, untrammeled wilderness, perfect for animal watching.

At camp in the morning, we watched a pair of racoon-masked cactus wrens perch on the grill of our truck and knock flattened bugs off the radiator. Then they dropped to the ground to savor the dehydrated treats. In the afternoon, a clack of rocks tipped me off that a large creature was near. I turned to see the ghostly pale butt of a desert bighorn sheep warily traversing the ridge just 50 yards away. The color of its coat blended so well with the surrounding rock, all I could see at first were two white hind legs. Looking carefully, I could make out a white dot of fur at its nose and two spiked nubbins on its head. It was more than twice as large as a domestic sheep. When the ewe caught our scent, she bounded straight up the steepest part of the facing ridge. Cabeza Prieta is home to approximately 400 of these desert bighorn sheep.

That evening, the Sonoran sky turned peach as the sun dropped behind interlocked purple and gray mountain ranges. When the night went crystal black, a lone coyote whined into the eternity of stars. All night long, owls hooted.

A morning walk flushed three sturdy mule deer out of a nearby wash. One had an enormous Bullwinkle-size rack. The dry washes in the Sonoran desert create a microclimate that support much of its wildlife. Like coral reefs in the ocean, Sonoran washes provide food, shelter, and denning sites for animal life. Between mountain ranges, Cabeza Prieta is a web of washes. Walking near one overgrown ravine, a palo verde bush rustled, and out stalked a javelina, or peccary, a stocky, piglike animal with tusks and long charcoal-black fur. Awakened early from siesta, the peccary turned to confront me, planting stumpy forepaws in the turf like an NFL lineman.

My U-turn deflected that challenge. Soon after, a creosote bush erupted in front of me as I flushed a gang of Gambel's quail. Clucking like chickens chased by a cat, the plump birds rushed crazily back and forth, each with a plumed topknot jiggling before its two beady eyes. In a few minutes, my heart stopped hammering.

Cabeza Prieta Wildlife Refuge will surprise you. Some days, you'll encounter sternum-rattling ker-BLOOMS as low-flying warplanes scream by. The Air Force uses electronic targets these days, so the only explosions you'll encounter will be flushed birds or beasts. Although it takes planning to get the necessary entry permit, Cabeza Prieta is as untamed and exciting as any natural landscape left on Earth.

Thoreau nailed it about places like Cabeza Prieta: "It is a world more wonderful than convenient, more beautiful than it is useful; it is more to be admired and enjoyed than used."

If You Go

Permits: An entry permit from the refuge headquarters in Ajo, Arizona, is required. You must also sign a military hold-harmless agreement. Necessary paperwork can be done in advance by fax and mail; refuge headquarters is not open on weekends or holidays.

Entry: From Ajo via Bates Well Road; from Tacna, exit 42, off Interstate 8; from Wellton, exit 30, off Interstate 8. The Charlie Bell Trail goes a short distance into the refuge; take Rasmussen Road out of Ajo. Get permits before entering the refuge.

Getting Around: A four-wheel-drive vehicle is required. Traveling in parties of at least two vehicles is safest. The refuge requests that "to protect historic trails, and for your protection, avoid using the roads during wet conditions and especially at times when rutting or potential for erosion is high." There are no regular patrols for the assistance of visitors; if you break down at certain times of year, such as summer, it may be a month before someone finds you. Bring plenty of gas, water, a hat, and sun protection. Mountain bikes are permitted on designated four-wheel-drive roads only. Allow at least two days to drive the 124-mile Camino Del Diablo from Wellton to Ajo.

Camping: Car camping is permitted within 50 feet of the road. The refuge requests that you camp at already-impacted areas. No camping within a quarter mile of waterholes. No wood fires.

Hiking: No trails, but you can hike washes and ridges.

Map: Available in downtown Ajo at a store named "Si Como No."

Hotels: There are at least two in Ajo, Arizona.

Weather: October to April the days are sunny in the 60s and 70s with occasional light rains. May through September the temperatures often exceed 105 with brief violent thunderstorms. Nights are cooler than days year-round.

Warnings: Don't collect cultural artifacts or military hardware or fall into mine shafts. Carry one gallon of drinking water per person per day plus a reserve.

For More Info: Cabeza Prieta National Wildlife Refuge Headquarters, 1611 North Second, Ajo, AZ 85321; (520) 387-6483, fax (520) 387-5359. Headquarters are in north Ajo on the west side of Highway 85. 🌵

CHAPTER SIXTEEN

The Blame Game
Whose responsibility is habitat loss?

In the mid-1800s, American philosopher Henry David Thoreau noted that his experience in the New England forest—because it was lacking so many native plants and animals—was like hearing a symphony performed with most of the instruments missing. Even in Thoreau's time, only 200 years after the first pilgrims arrived on the east coast of North America, a drastic simplification and dismantling of the natural landscape of New England had already occurred.

In the Intermountain West we are luckier than residents of many other locations, but we do listen to a similarly impoverished orchestra today. Native plants and animals are only expressions of natural landscapes; as these places disappear so do the creatures that inhabit them. The destruction didn't begin yesterday and it won't end tomorrow. We can be certain it won't end tomorrow because our civic debate—a long-running cat fight in the media spotlight—focuses on a power struggle between special interest groups rather than on individual responsibility for the problem of preserving habitat.

Blaming others allows individuals to shrug off personal responsibility and continue on a comfortable course. A suburbanite may throw up his hands and blame local ranchers and farmers for blocking the reintroduction of wolves into the Intermountain West. The same suburbanite, however, could replant his subdivision property with native plants and, if he stops using pesticides, could welcome back the native bugs and birds his own landscaping kills off and drives away. The tendency of urban and suburban non-hunters to demonize individuals who hunt is another example. An ethical elk hunter may kill one animal a year, but the foothill subdivisions and golf courses built by urban and suburban people eliminate whole herds of elk permanently by destroying their winter range. Of course, sympathy with the plight of an individual animal is not a character defect; honest hunters feel it too. But ethical hunters limit their kill and know they must preserve elk's winter and summer range, however inconvenient, in order to keep these animals around.

At the same time, many wildlife policies promoted by special interest groups in the name of hunters, ranchers, and farmers *should* cause alarm. Definitely, our present habitat conservation problems are intensified when, through cultural inertia, we follow wildlife policies of the past. Until the middle of the twentieth century, while the Intermountain West was powered by an agricultural economy, wildlife management centered on the goals of a rural population. Ranchers and farmers didn't want predators, such as wolves, bears, and cougars, around to prey on their domestic animals, so native predators were treated as vermin and exterminated. This is still happening to some extent today. Also, when Utah's population was primarily rural, hunting and fishing were the most popular outdoor sports. Catering to sportsmen, wildlife managers introduced exotic species, such as pheasant and rainbow trout, to the detriment of native animals.

Persecuting native predators and using wildlife management to promote a cash crop of game species seems strange—even offensive—to today's primarily urban and suburban population. Interest in hunting has declined dramatically, and today's Intermountain West residents are likely to spend their time outdoors mountain biking, picnicking, or wildlife watching. Wildlife managers are turning to more holistic ways of dealing with wildlife and habitat.

The crash in the popularity of hunting has another, less beneficial, consequence. In the past, wildlife managers funded habitat management and preservation with the taxes and licenses paid by people who hunt and fish. With the decline in hunting, money for protecting habitat—game or nongame—is scarce. Most urban and suburban people think that somewhere, some state agency is spending significant amounts of money on nongame animal habitat. But that's not happening.

Worse, those most often responsible for wildlife habitat loss today are urban and suburban people who pay no direct remedial costs for it. Often city-dwellers believe they're part of the solution to environmental problems simply because they're not overgrazing public land with livestock or not hunting mule deer. But urban and suburban growth is fueling the new dams, highways, subdivisions, strip malls, golf courses, and ski runs that collectively are having a colossal negative impact on native wildlife habitat today.

Undoubtedly, water projects are most devastating to native wildlife. Dammed rivers drown riparian habitat underneath reservoirs. These riversides are critical habitat for native wildlife. For example, streamsides support three-quarters of the kinds of birds that visit Utah. The water level of man-made reservoirs rises and falls on a daily cycle—sometimes by twenty feet—as it fills and empties according to needs of dam operators. Evolution hasn't prepared native species to live on this type of constantly fluctuating shoreline, so reservoirs support very few native species. Drowning the critical habitat of riversides for water projects is recklessly wasteful when you consider that half of the water is used to keep ornamental lawns green in urban and suburban areas.

Turning native landscapes into outdoor playgrounds, such as golf courses and ski resorts, is another example. These modified environments support many fewer native species and encourage nonnative species to invade. Of course, the problem isn't a few ski runs or a few holes of golf. It's the relentless nibbling to death of native landscapes by a growing urban population that's divorced from natural processes. We value what we know and we no longer know what's wild.

In fact, we no longer require wildness from our wilderness areas. Because so few natural landscapes survive, the ones that remain—national and state parks and wildlife refuges—are becoming islands of natural habitat in a sea of land transformed for human use. But preserving pockets of native landscapes surrounded by areas of severe human impact doesn't work over meaningful periods of time. Nature's not just a place, it's a process; and natural processes are often big and inconvenient. Native landscapes need buffer zones and connections with each other or the woven fabric of plant and animal interactions begins to unravel. But we treat these parks as playgrounds—big outdoor adventure parks—complete with paved roads, a surrounding fence, and ticket booths and souvenir shops at the entrance, and nature won't stay behind the gate—remember *Jurassic Park?* More to the point, fences won't keep weeds and feral animals from invading these remaining natural areas and taming them over time.

NATURE'S BOUNDARIES ARE FEATURES such as watersheds, but humans divide land into private and public ownership. There is as much critical wildlife habitat on private land as there is on public land, but nearly all attention in the conservation debate is focused on how much public land—Bureau of Land Management and U.S. Forest Service land—to preserve in formal wilderness areas.

The 1964 Wilderness Act set up the National Wilderness Preservation System, which was intended to ensure that some public landscapes could be preserved in a natural condition for the benefit and enjoyment of current and future generations of Americans. The Wilderness Act shouldn't be confused with the 1973 Endangered Species Act, which the U.S. Congress passed to preserve native plants and animals identified as threatened by extinction.

When it comes to preserving Utah's remaining federally owned natural areas by means of the Wilderness Act, interest groups on one side of the debate say the cost in lost economic opportunities is too high; they point out that mining and timber harvest are banned within designated wilderness areas (though grazing domestic animals is allowed). Also, opponents say that wilderness designation puts economic limitations on surrounding communities and limits land management and motorized recreation options within these areas.

Those in favor of formally designating many millions of acres of Utah public land as wilderness point out that while extractive industries, like mining and timber, were an important part of the state's economy in the past, that's no longer true today. Wilderness supporters say preserving these remaining natural landscapes will draw tourists and recreational visitors, thereby benefitting the businesses in the surrounding communities who cater to them.

The argument that protecting large natural areas with wilderness designation will create magnets for tourists makes an economic point. On the other hand, it emphasizes the preservation of aesthetically pleasing mountains and canyons as outdoor playgrounds, rather than the protection of the less charming places, such as wetlands and creek drainages that, while not dramatic, are much more important to native wildlife. In the current public land debate, protecting habitat takes a back seat to tourism and outdoor recreation.

Still, it is true that many of the remaining native plants and animals in our region can be protected by official wilderness designation of public land. The scientific overview is already done. As pointed out in earlier chapters, seven scientists from Brigham Young University and the University of Utah assessed the potential of designating wilderness areas in Utah specifically to conserve native ecosystems. The result was a paper entitled "Selecting Wilderness Areas to Conserve Utah's Biological Diversity," published in the April 1996 *Great Basin Naturalist.* "Among the significant ecological functions of wilderness areas is their role in conserving biological diversity," these local scientists write. And, as opposed to scenic values and outdoor recreation, the local scientists suggest these criteria for designating wilderness areas:

> (1) ensure the long-term population viability of native animal and plant species, (2) maintain the critical ecological and evolutionary processes upon which these species depend, and (3) preserve the full range of communities, successional states, and environmental gradients . . . to protect large, contiguous areas, and to buffer wilderness areas with multiple-use public lands . . . conserve entire watersheds . . . and protect native communities from invasions of exotic species.

The logic is tough to dispute. The Endangered Species Act commits Americans to preventing extinction of native wildlife, so it makes sense to protect their functioning habitat while it's still in one piece.

Using scientific criteria for determining wilderness designation, as these local scientists propose, can bring diverse groups, such as hunters, wildlife watchers, and conservationists into the same camp. Scientific criteria is not like aesthetic criteria; it's objective. Biodiversity can be measured and counted.

A wild place without wildlife is just pretty scenery, and that's not sufficient for those who know and value wildness. Fortunately, wildlife watching is quietly becoming one of the most popular outdoor activities with the Intermountain West's urban and suburban population. In fact, bird watching is the fastest growing outdoor sport in Utah. This will increase the public's biological literacy and may change the wilderness debate. Wildlife watching is a path that begins with appreciating species, then leads to valuing the biological diversity of the native landscapes they depend upon. After all, birdwatchers soon learn that creatures like native bugs, which few people prize in themselves, play a critical role in attracting birds and preserving the natural system in which everything else they value can thrive. Wildlife watching is recreation but it's also an education.

The growing popularity of wildlife watching is no secret to state and federal wildlife managers; they are beginning to manage natural areas so the public can watch nongame animals. Across the country, wildlife managers have collaborated with conservation organizations in a program named Watchable Wildlife. The first phase of Watchable Wildlife's program, state-by-state publication of wildlife viewing locations, is completed (see Appendix C). In the future, wildlife managers will be adding viewing blinds, platforms, parking, and restrooms at wildlife watching locations.

While the noisy civic debate is over conservation of public land, many nonprofit organizations are quietly working to set aside private land as open space and habitat. These groups range from the Nature Conservancy, which buys land operating on the principle that nothing should go extinct, to Ducks Unlimited, which protects and restores wetlands. With these goals, they don't have to worry whether habitat will get support from a majority of the public because it's not pretty scenery.

The natural landscapes of the Intermountain West are still reeling from many of yesterday's wildlife management practices. At the same time, we increasingly pave over what's left to accommodate today's intense human population growth. That means many native plants, animals, and habitats are in a race with extinction. Hunters, ranchers, farmers, and city-dwelling conservationists can, as individuals, each help protect remaining open space and reclaim some of what is lost. It takes a commitment to understand, to acknowledge, and then to reduce individual contributions to the problem of habitat destruction.

It's not too late. We in the Intermountain West are privileged to still have wild places in which we can see, for example, a dusty bighorn ewe and lamb crossing an impossibly narrow canyon ledge, or places where we can spend a mountain morning watching a chubby pika fussily arranging its tiny haystack of dried grass. So, don't wait to get out there to see them. Do it now. 🌿

Appendix A
Utah Sensitive Species List

This list is courtesy of the Utah Division of Wildlife Resources and is current as of February 1998. Please see <www.state.ut.us/dwr/> for complete text and references.

DEFINITIONS

For the purposes of this list, wildlife includes all vertebrate animals; crustaceans, including brine shrimp and crayfish; and mollusks in Utah that are living in nature, except feral animals.

Extinct Species: any wildlife species that has disappeared in the world.

Extirpated Species: any wildlife species that has disappeared from Utah since 1800.

State Endangered Species: any wildlife species or subspecies which is threatened with extirpation from Utah or extinction resulting from very low or declining numbers, alteration and/or reduction of habitat, detrimental environmental changes, or any combination of the above. Continued long-term survival is unlikely without implementation of special measures. A management program is needed for these species if a Recovery Plan has not been developed.

State Threatened Species: any wildlife species or subspecies which is likely to become an endangered species within the foreseeable future throughout all or a significant part of its range in Utah or the world. A management program is needed for these species if a Recovery Plan has not been developed.

Species of Special Concern: any wildlife species or subspecies that: has experienced a substantial decrease in population, distribution and/or habitat availability, or occurs in limited areas and/or numbers due to a restricted or specialized habitat, or has both a declining population and a limited range. A

management program, including protection or enhancement, is needed for these species.

Conservation Species: any wildlife species or subspecies, except those species currently listed under the Endangered Species Act (ESA) as threatened or endangered, that meets the state criteria of Endangered, Threatened, or of Special Concern, but is currently receiving sufficient special management under a Conservation Agreement developed and/or implemented by the state to preclude its listing above. In the event that the conservation agreement is not implemented, the species will be elevated to the appropriate category.

BIRDS
Extinct Species

Passenger Pigeon (*Ectopistes migratorius*): The Passenger Pigeon has been extinct since 1914. Both overhunting and habitat loss have been cited as reasons for the species' demise. There is archaeological evidence from a prehistoric site that Passenger Pigeons may have occurred in Utah; however, the species was probably never an important part of the state's avifauna.

State Endangered Species

Bald Eagle (*Haliaeetus leucocephalus*): The Bald Eagle is a federally listed threatened species. There are only four known bald eagle nest sites in the state, they are located in riparian habitat along the Colorado and Jordan Rivers and in a shelterbelt near the town of Castle Dale. Migratory eagles winter throughout the state in riparian, low elevation forest, and desert habitats. The bald eagle is threatened by loss of habitat and environmental contaminants. The species is recovering across its range;

however, the number nesting in Utah remains extremely low.

American Peregrine Falcon (*Falco peregrinus anatum*): The American Peregrine Falcon is a federally listed endangered species. Peregrines nest on cliffs in association with riparian wetland habitats statewide, except in the western basin and range. The species is threatened by environmental contaminants and loss of habitat. While the Colorado Plateau portion of the falcons' population is currently recovering, the northern Wasatch portion has not reestablished a self-sustaining breeding population.

Southwestern Willow Flycatcher (*Empidonax traillii extimus*): This neotropical migrant ranges and nests primarily in mid to low elevation (less than 2,600 meters [8,500 feet]) willow habitats. The southwest subspecies occurs in southern and southeastern Utah and is difficult to separate from the northern subspecies. The southwestern willow flycatcher is adversely affected by loss of habitat from agricultural and grazing practices, water development, and replacement of native riparian habitats by nonnative plant species. Additional information is needed to more accurately determine the degree of population declines of this species in Utah.

State Threatened Species

Ferruginous Hawk (*Buteo regalis*): This raptor nests at the edge of juniper habitats and open, desert and grassland habitats in western, northeastern, and southeastern Utah. The species is highly sensitive to human disturbance and is also threatened by habitat loss from oil and gas development, agricultural practices, and urban encroachment. The ferruginous hawk, a neotropical migrant, has declined across much of its range and has been extirpated from some of its former breeding grounds in Utah.

Yellow-billed Cuckoo (*Coccyzus americanus occidentalis*): This neotropical migrant species nests in localized riparian valleys statewide. The species is threatened by loss of habitat from agricultural, water, road, and urban development. The species has declined significantly across its range.

Mexican Spotted Owl (*Strix occidentalis lucida*): The Mexican spotted owl, the only subspecies of spotted owl that occurs in the state, is federally listed as threatened. It is a permanent resident that nests in canyon land habitats of southern Utah. The owls exist in small isolated subpopulations; it is potentially threatened by habitat loss and disturbance from recreation, overgrazing, road development, catastrophic fire, timber harvest, and mineral development. There are currently approximately 90 known spotted owl sites in Utah.

Species of Special Concern (Declining Populations)

Northern Goshawk (*Accipiter gentilis*): This neotropical migrant raptor occurs statewide in scattered populations primarily in mature mountain forest and valley cottonwood habitats. The species is adversely affected by loss of habitat from timber harvest and development in riparian areas. Because goshawks occur in low density populations, they are particularly susceptible to population loss. The goshawk's population appears to have declined across the range and particularly in the Colorado Plateau ecoregion.

Swainson's Hawk (*Buteo swainsoni*): This neotropical migratory raptor nests in trees near open desert grasslands, shrub-steppes, and agricultural fields primarily, but not exclusively, in the northern valleys and West Desert of Utah. While Swainson's hawk populations in Utah have declined from historical levels, the species had exhibited a population increase in Utah and across its range from 1966 to 1994. However, pesticide poisonings of tens of thousands of Swainson's Hawks have occurred since 1994 in Argentina, where at least a portion of Utah's population winters. The species should be closely monitored on its nesting grounds to determine if winter mortalities are threatening the Utah breeding population.

Caspian Tern (*Sterna caspia*): This species nests colonially on Great Salt Lake wetlands, islands, and dikes and occasionally on similar habitat in Utah Lake. The species is sensitive to human disturbance and predation by California Gulls. Colonies are also adversely impacted by water level fluctuations.

Black Tern (*Chlidonias niger*): This species nests colonially in wetlands associated with northern Utah lakes, such as Utah, Pelican, and Great Salt Lake, and the Green and Bear rivers. Much of the insectivorous tern's habitat has been lost to agricultural and commercial development. Populations appear to be declining and information is needed to accurately determine the degree of decline which has occurred.

Burrowing Owl (*Athene cunicularia*): The burrowing owl is adversely impacted by agricultural and residential development though it may be able to adapt to minor disturbances. The owl, a neotropical migrant, nests in desert valleys and grasslands and is often found in association with prairie dog colonies. The owl's population appears to have declined across its range; its distribution has been localized in many areas of Utah.

Common Yellowthroat (*Geothlypis trichas*): The yellowthroat population has declined significantly in Utah. This neotropical migrant nests in riparian and wetland habitats statewide and is negatively impacted by loss of habitat from a variety of development activities.

Short-eared Owl (*Asio flammeus*): This raptor is a permanent resident of central and northern Utah wetlands and deserts. The species appears to be declining. It is adversely impacted by loss of habitat to agriculture and urban development.

Species of Special Concern (Limited Distribution)

American White Pelican (*Pelecanus erythrorhynchos*): This species nests in a large colony on Gunnison Island in the Great Salt Lake (and formerly on Utah Lake) but forages in freshwater wetlands and lakes. The species is extremely sensitive to human disturbance on its nesting grounds and is adversely impacted by loss of foraging (wetland) habitat, environmental contaminants, and water level fluctuations. The nesting colonies in Utah are among the largest in North America and account for a significant proportion of the North American population.

California Condor (*Gymnogyps californianus*): There is limited evidence that the California Condor occurred in Utah historically. The entire wild population was taken into captivity in the late 1980s and has been successfully bred. Condor were reintroduced into the wild in northern Arizona, 20 miles from Utah, in 1996. The range of this reintroduced population is expected to include southern Utah. These birds are classified as an experimental/nonessential population by the U.S. Fish and Wildlife Service.

Osprey (*Pandion haliaetus*): This piscivorous raptor is sparsely distributed around mountain lakes and on the Green River. Its historical range has been substantially reduced in the state and nearly all known nesting occurs at Flaming Gorge Reservoir. Osprey are adversely affected by habitat loss and are susceptible to environmental contamination.

Sharp-tailed Grouse (*Tympanuchus phasianellus columbianus*): Distribution of the Columbia sharp-tailed grouse has been reduced to a remnant of its former range. In Utah, the subspecies is now limited to a few scattered, mostly isolated populations in the northern counties; historically its range covered almost half of the state. The subspecies is threatened by continued loss of habitat from agricultural and urban encroachment. The bird nests in dry grasslands and relies on a variety of grasses and forbs for cover and food; cultivated crops and scattered shrubs and trees are also used as forage.

Williamson's Sapsucker (*Sphyrapicus thyroideus*): This woodpecker nests in high elevation (2,400 meters [8,000 feet] to timberline) mountain forests (primarily Ponderosa, Conifer-Aspen) habitats statewide. The species is negatively impacted by habitat loss from timber harvest practices. Additional information is needed to more accurately determine the extent of population reductions for this neotropical migrant.

Three-toed Woodpecker (*Picoides tridactylus*): This species nests and winters in mountain forest conifers, usually above 2,400 meters (8,000 feet) elevation in the Wasatch, Uinta, and southern Utah ranges. The population densities of three-toed woodpeckers are low across Utah. The species is negatively affected by forest management practices such as clearcutting and fire suppression.

Species of Special Concern (Declining Populations and Limited Distribution)

Sage Grouse (*Centrocerus urophasianus*): Sage grouse populations have declined across the range of the species, including Utah. Since 1967 in Utah, the abundance of male grouse attending breeding grounds has declined by approximately 50 percent in Utah. Brood counts and harvest data show a similar downward trend. Historically, the range of sage grouse in Utah was nearly continuous, including portions of all 29 counties; currently sage grouse exist in scattered populations in only 19 counties. Habitat loss and fragmentation from agricultural encroachment, urbanization, and overgrazing are the primary threats to the sage grouse.

Mountain Plover (*Charadrius montanus*): This neotropical migrant species nests in upland grass and shrub habitats and is frequently associated with prairie dog colonies; the total plover population is from 4,000 to 5,000 birds and is declining significantly across its range. A small population of plovers is known to

nest in the Uinta Basin. Additional information is needed to more accurately determine the status of this species in Utah; however, it is negatively impacted by loss of habitat from agricultural encroachment and may be affected by mineral development activities.

Long-billed Curlew (*Numenius americanus*): This neotropical migrant shorebird nests in the upland meadows and rangelands of northern and central Utah valleys. It forages in moist meadow wetlands and upland habitats. The curlew is adversely affected by human disturbance and habitat loss from agricultural practices. The species' range has been substantially reduced and current information indicates that the population is declining regionally.

Black Swift (*Cypseloides niger*): In Utah, black swifts nest in small colonies near or behind waterfalls. They forage for aerial insects up to several thousand feet above the ground and may forage great distances from their nests. Pairs typically lay only one egg per year and incubation (approximately 30 days) and fledging (approximately 45 days) are both prolonged in this neotropical migratory species. Nesting has only been documented at a few sites in Utah in the Cascade and Timpanogos ranges. While the Utah population's status is uncertain, the species is declining significantly rangewide.

Lewis' Woodpecker (*Melanerpes lewis*): This woodpecker is a scattered permanent resident found primarily in the riparian habitats of the Uinta Basin and along the Green River. Some portions of the Utah population may migrate to the neotropics. Formerly common in several areas of the state, the species distribution is currently reduced and the species is experiencing a rangewide decline. This woodpecker usually feeds on flying insects in the spring and summer and thus forages in open areas interspersed with trees. It feeds on mast in the fall and winter. It is adversely affected by loss of habitat from water development and agricultural practices. It is also increasingly affected by competition for nest cavities from non-native bird species.

Crissal Thrasher (*Toxostoma crissale*): This species is a permanent resident in southwestern Utah. It nests in dense mesquite and streamside shrubs in the Virgin River and its tributaries. The thrasher is adversely affected by riparian habitat loss from agricultural practices, and water, road, and urban development. Information indicates the species is declining in Utah.

Bell's Vireo (*Vireo bellii*): This neotropical migrant nests in streamside willows of the Virgin River and Beaver Dam Wash in southwestern Utah. The species is very limited in its distribution in Utah and is declining across its range. It is negatively impacted by riparian habitat loss from agricultural, water, road, and urban development.

Blue Grosbeak (*Guiraca caerulea*): This neotropical migrant nests in thickets of lowland riparian habitat primarily in the Colorado River drainage; scattered populations are also known from southwestern and central Utah. The species has experienced significant declines over the past five years in Utah. It is negatively impacted by riparian habitat loss from agricultural, water, road, and urban development.

Grasshopper Sparrow (*Ammodramus savannarum*): This neotropical migratory species was considered to be historically abundant in the state. Currently only a few grasshopper breeding sites are known from northern Utah grasslands. Much of this species's former habitat has been lost to overgrazing and agricultural and urban encroachment. The species has declined significantly across its range. These birds nest in semi-colonial groups in dry grasslands characterized by short to mid-height clumps of grass with few to no shrubs.

Bobolink (*Dolichonyx oryzivorus*): This neotropical migrant was historically common but is now a rare nester in flooded grasslands and wet meadows of northern Utah. The range of the bobolink has decreased in Utah because of habitat loss; the species has exhibited a significant long-term population decline across its range in North America. Local populations are threatened by habitat loss from drought and agricultural practices such as early season hay cutting, grassland conversion, and overgrazing.

MAMMALS
Extirpated Species

Grizzly Bear (*Ursus arctos*): Once occurring throughout Utah except the western desert areas, it is commonly believed the last grizzly was killed in Utah in 1923 in Logan Canyon, Cache County. The closest population to Utah is in the Yellowstone ecosystem with an occasional report in New Mexico and Colorado.

Fisher (*Martes pennanti*): Fishers are large members of the weasel family thought to have once occurred in Utah in the Uinta Mountains and possibly the northern Wasatch Mountains. However, Utah is at the southern fringe of their range, and whether there ever existed a stable population within the state is unknown. The only known proof of them inhabiting Utah are tracks that were observed in 1938 in the Trial Lake area of the Uinta Mountains. In Utah, fisher would most likely be found in dense lowland forests containing spruce-fir and spruce-aspen stands and an extensive overhead canopy. They avoid open spaces with no overhead cover. Fishers are opportunistic feeders that feed predominantly upon snowshoe hares, porcupines, rodents, and carrion. Availability of prey species is thought to dictate fisher habitat use and preference. Fishers are thought to be extirpated from Utah, and no populations are known to occur within the state.

Gray Wolf (*Canis lupus*): Formerly found throughout Utah and most of the United States, several small populations are now located in the extreme northern United States. The last wolf reported and confirmed was from San Juan County in Harts Draw on February 11, 1937. No other confirmed records have occurred since then.

State Endangered Species

Black-footed Ferret (*Mustela nigripes*): The black-footed ferret is considered the rarest mammal in North America. It was once common throughout the Great Plains (Canada to Texas), Montana, Wyoming, Colorado, and Utah. Ninety percent of their diet is prairie dogs. The decrease in prairie dog populations as a result of habitat alteration and poisoning has led to the probable extirpation of this species in the wild. Efforts by many agencies have established a successful captive breeding program, and ferrets are now being reintroduced into historical habitat. Efforts are underway in Utah to bring this species back to historical ranges if suitable conditions are present.

State Threatened Species

Utah Prairie Dog (*Cynomys parvidens*): The Utah prairie dog population once numbered approximately 95,000 individuals. It is found only in southwestern Utah. By 1976 its numbers had declined to about 2,000, and it was listed as an endangered species. In 1984 it was reclassified as threatened. Efforts to establish four self-sustaining populations on federal lands have been in progress since the 1970s.

Wolverine (*Gulo gulo*): Utah is the southernmost range extension for this species. The last confirmed sighting was in 1924 near Brighton, Salt Lake County. Several unconfirmed sightings have been reported in recent years near Mt. Timpanogos.

Species of Special Concern (Declining Populations)

Spotted Bat (*Euderma maculatum*): This bat is distributed throughout the West. Very little specific life history information is available on this species. It is found in very small numbers throughout its range and in association with other bat species. Indications are that its numbers have declined in historical trapping locations.

Species of Special Concern (Limited Distribution)

Fringed Myotis (*Myotis thysanodes*): The distribution of this bat is listed as statewide, however, voucher specimens have been collected only in the southern and east central portions of Utah. The fringed bat inhabits caves, mines, rock crevices, and buildings at relatively higher elevations (1,217 to 2,438 meters [4,000 to 8,000 feet]).

Allen's Big-eared Bat (*Idionycteris phyllotis*): The distribution of the big-eared bat, according to Durrant (1952) in *Mammals of Utah*, appears to be wide through the lower two-thirds of the state. This may have changed in the past 50 years. There may have been changes in their numbers and habitat. Work needs to be done to determine current distribution.

Dwarf Shrew (*Sorex nanus*): Found only in southeastern Utah. It is extremely rare but can occur in high densities locally.

Desert Shrew (*Notiosorex crawfordi*): This species occurs only in the southern portions of Kane and San Juan Counties. They inhabit a variety of many different habitats within their range.

Chisel-toothed Kangaroo Rat (*Dipodomys microps celsus*): This subspecies of kangaroo rat is found in an isolated population only in Washington County. It is classified as sensitive in distribution because of its isolated location in Utah. Pritchet, in 4,895 trap nights, only collected one specimen in 1993.

Abert Squirrel (*Sciurus aberti navajo*): This subspecies of Abert squirrel is found only in San Juan County on the Abajo Mountains and Elk Ridge and on the LaSal Mountain range in the Manti-LaSal National Forest. Although limited in distribution in Utah, its status is currently considered to be stable. It is totally dependent on the ponderosa pine for most aspects of its life cycle (food, nest material, space, and escape cover).

Belding Ground Squirrel (*Spermophilus beldingi*): Distribution of this species is restricted to extreme northeastern Utah in the Raft River Mountains.

Thirteen-lined Ground Squirrel (*Spermophilus tridecemlineatus*): Distribution restricted to the Uinta Basin in Utah. Habitat includes grasslands with well-drained soils, disturbed areas, and semi-desert shrub lands.

Spotted Ground Squirrel (*Spermophilus spilosoma*): Distribution restricted to the southeastern portion of Utah in San Juan County. Occurs in high desert areas with dry, sandy soils and sparse, shrubby vegetation.

Wyoming Ground Squirrel (*Spermophilus elegans*): Listed in Durrant (1947) as a species that may occur in Utah but a record is lacking. May be present in northwestern Box Elder County and northeastern Daggett County.

Yellow Pine Chipmunk (*Tamias amoenus*): This species occurs only in the Raft River Mountains in the northwest corner of Utah. It has a wide distribution in the northwestern United States. Habitat includes young immature conifer forests. Tend to frequent shrubs, slash piles, and stumps.

Rock Pocket Mouse (*Chaetodipus intermedius*): This species is restricted in Utah to the Rainbow Bridge-Navajo Mountain area of San Juan County. Their distribution is restricted to lava flows in sparsely vegetated desert habitats.

Olive-backed Pocket Mouse (*Perognathus fasciatus*): Their range in Utah is confined to the extreme northeast corner of Daggett County. It occurs in open areas with sparse vegetation and sandy soils.

Merriam's Kangaroo Rat (*Dipodomys merriami*): Has an extensive range in other southwestern states but is restricted to Washington County in Utah. Habitat includes sagebrush, shadscale, creosote brush, and other desert shrub communities.

Cactus Mouse (*Peromyscus eremicus*): Utah is the northernmost extension of their range. Habitat includes riparian zones. Found in lower population densities than most mouse species. Inhabits areas where lower habitat productivity is evident. It's low tolerance for each other makes low population numbers.

Southern Grasshopper Mouse (*Onychomys torridus*): Southern grasshopper mice are found only in Washington County. They are found in the hot, dry, low-lying desert habitat. They are insectivorous, feeding on scorpions, grasshoppers, spiders, and insect cocoons.

Marten (*Martes americana*): Their distribution is restricted to dense conifer stands of fir, spruce, and lodgepole. Sensitive to habitat alteration, the dead, downed, and woody debris found in old undisturbed forests is a critical component of marten habitat.

Pika (*Ochotona princeps*): Durrant (1952) describes five subspecies of pika. More may be present in Utah mountains. Work is needed to determine the amount of genetic isolation present in these isolated populations.

Ringtail (*Bassariscus astutus*): Most often found in rocky, boulder-strewn riparian areas, most often within a quarter mile of a water source. Dense cover is preferred, providing them with seclusion and prey availability.

Northern Flying Squirrel (*Glaucomys sabrinus*): The northern flying squirrel is well distributed through the major mountain ranges of central and eastern Utah. It is primarily found in the riparian zones of this area. Loss of riparian habitat adversely impacts northern flying squirrel populations.

Species of Special Concern (Declining Populations and Limited Distribution)

Western Red Bat (*Lasiurus blossevillii*): This bat could potentially occur in most counties in Utah; however, it has been confirmed in only Washington and Carbon Counties. Several state mammalologists have recommended this species be looked at to determine status.

Big Free-tailed Bat (*Nyctinomops macrotis*): The northern range of the big free-tailed bat extends to the southern two-thirds of Utah. Their presence within this range is very rare. Use of caves and mines for maternal colonies makes them very vulnerable to human disturbance.

Brazilian Free-tailed Bat (*Tadarida brasiliensis mexicana*): This species is migratory and forms large maternity colonies in caves and mines in southern Utah. These large congregations are subject to disturbance and indiscriminate killing by humans.

Townsend's Big-eared Bat (*Plecotus townsendii*): Although statewide in its distribution, the communal roosting habits of this species make it sensitive to the closure of caves and mines.

Desert Kangaroo Rat (*Dipodomys deserti*): Has an extensive range in other southwestern states but is restricted to Washington County in Utah.

Northern Rock Mouse (*Peromyscus nasutus*): Found in Colorado, New Mexico, and central Mexico, but restricted in Utah to southwestern San Juan County in the vicinity of Navajo Mountain.

Stephen's Woodrat (*Neotoma stephensi*): Distribution of this species is limited to Navajo Mountain in San Juan County.

Virgin River Montane Vole (*Microtus montanus rivularis*): Restricted in distribution to the Virgin River drainage and environs (Durrant 1952). Very restricted distribution to riparian habitat adjacent to the Virgin River in Washington County. Recent changes in land use patterns and resulting loss of riparian habitat have impacted this small rodent.

Mexican Vole (*Microtus mexicanus*): Only southwestern vole in Utah. Habitat includes yellow pine forests and dry sparsely vegetated grasslands. Also use typical mountain meadows and wet areas.

Northern River Otter (*Lutra canadensis*): Northern river otter have been extremely rare in Utah for the past 100 years. River otter have been documented in the Raft, Weber, Provo, Bear, Colorado, and Green River drainages. Their present range and abundance in Utah has been reduced. River otter are known to occur in the Green River, Colorado River, and Raft River drainages. A few sightings have been reported in the Weber and Provo River drainages in recent years.

North American Lynx (*Felis lynx canadensis*): This species inhabits the higher elevations of Utah. These areas include the slopes of the Uinta Mountains, south to the Fish Lake National Forest. Their present distribution is limited to the southern slopes of the high Uintas. Lynx use a variety of forest types but generally inhabit those habitats with snowshoe hare populations. Due to the remoteness of their habitat and nocturnal nature, very few sightings have been reported and fewer have been verified over the past ten years.

AMPHIBIANS
Extinct Species

Relict Frog (*Rana onca*): This species once occurred around streamsides and several springs along the Virgin River in Washington County. No individuals were observed in recent surveys (Jennings et al. 1995) of amphibians in the Virgin River Basin. Habitat loss and degradation are thought to be the cause of the extirpation of this species in Utah.

Species of Special Concern (Declining Populations)

Arizona Toad (*Bufo microscaphus*): This species inhabits loose gravelly areas of streams and arroyos in drier portions of its range and along sandy banks of quiet water in other areas. The range of this species is highly fragmented. Its distribution in Utah is limited to the southwest corner of the state, which is its northernmost range extension. Noticeable declines have been observed in this species; however, the reasons remain unclear.

Boreal Toad (*Bufo boreas boreas*): This species inhabits areas near springs, streams, meadows, or woodlands at higher elevations. Beaver ponds with abundant riparian vegetation appear to be its preferred habitat. Recently, this species has experienced declines in many areas of the Rocky Mountain region. These declines may be related to one or a combination of factors. These include habitat loss and degradation, environmental contaminants, disease, and ozone layer depletion. In Utah, this species has been noticeably absent or greatly reduced in numbers in previously occupied areas. Additional surveys are warranted to better document distribution of this species in Utah. This species is currently listed as a candidate species for listing under the ESA in Colorado, New Mexico, and Wyoming.

Lowland Leopard Frog (*Rana yavapaiensis*): Inhabiting areas close to springs and pools along rivers in deserts, grasslands, and oak and oak-pine woodlands, it is only known in Utah from an area near St. George. It is thought that reproductive mechanisms have isolated this species from other ranids within its range. It is not know if any viable populations of this species still exist in Utah or in adjacent states.

Species of Special Concern (Limited Distribution)

Pacific Chorus Frog (*Pseudacris regilla*): Pacific chorus is chiefly a ground dweller, found among low plant growth near water in a variety of habitats. These include grassland, chaparral, woodland, forest, desert oases and ditches, reservoirs, and slow streams. A few specimens exist from southeastern Washington County and unverified records have been reported from extreme northwestern Utah. The current status and distribution of this species remains unclear.

Conservation Species

Spotted Frog (*Rana pretiosa*): This species inhabits shallow, spring- or creek-fed marshes, seeps, and springs along the Wasatch Front and in the West Desert. Further genetic analysis may indicate that some populations of spotted frog in Utah may become classified as a separate subspecies, *Rana pretiosa luteiventris*. Recent surveys and monitoring indicate that the Wasatch Front populations are declining, fragmented, and of limited size. Habitat loss due to human growth and water development is the major threat to the Wasatch Front populations. Currently, West Desert populations appear to be somewhat stable. Several populations of this species, however, are currently candidates for listing under the ESA, including the Wasatch Front populations in Utah. As part of recovery efforts, several agencies are working cooperatively under a conservation agreement to eliminate or significantly reduce the threats facing this species.

REPTILES
State Endangered Species

Banded Gila Monster (*Heloderma suspectus cinctum*): This species occurs in arid and semi-arid areas of gravelly and sandy soils, especially areas with shrub and some moisture. In Utah its distribution is limited to the extreme southwest corner of the state, primarily in the Mojave desert ecosystem of Washington County. It is currently threatened with extirpation due to limited numbers, overcollection, and habitat loss.

Desert Tortoise (*Gopherus agassizii*): The desert tortoise is the only native turtle to Utah. It occupies desert habitats with washes, dunes, and rocky slopes that consist of creosote bush and Joshua trees. Like the Gila monster, the distribution of this species in Utah is limited to the Mojave desert ecosystem in extreme southwest Utah, including the Beaver Dam Slope and other areas near St.

George. This species is in danger of extirpation due to habitat alteration and loss, impacts of cattle grazing, and introduction of disease. Populations are thought to have declined by as much as 75 percent in Utah. Currently, recovery efforts are being directed by the Desert Tortoise Recovery Plan and the Washington County Habitat Conservation Plan.

Species of Special Concern (Declining Populations)

Utah Mountain Kingsnake (*Lampropeltis pyromelana infralabialis*): This colorful tri-colored snake occurs in disjunct, localized populations in many of the central Utah mountain ranges. Its habitat includes chaparral woodland and pine forests in mountainous regions, bushy rocky canyons, and talus slopes and near streams and springs above 850 meters (2,800 feet). Population declines, although difficult to detect in this secretive species, are thought to be due to habitat impacts and over collection.

Utah Milk Snake (*Lampropeltis triangulum taylori*): Often nocturnal, this species inhabits semi-arid regions, pine forests, deciduous woodlands, and suburban areas. It is spottily distributed in the mountain regions of eastern and central Utah. Attractive to snake fanciers, overcollection as well as habitat impacts may be factors in its apparent decline.

Species of Special Concern (Limited Distribution)

Desert Iguana (*Dipsosaurus dorsalis*): This species occurs in sandy and rocky arid and semiarid areas where creosote bushes are abundant A fairly common species in the southern part of its range, its distribution is limited to the extreme southwest corner of Washington County in Utah.

Utah Banded Gecko (*Coleonyx variegatus utahensis*): This species occurs in very dry habitats with rocky tracts, canyon walls, and sand dunes. Its distribution in Utah is limited to the extreme southwest corner of the state.

Utah Night Lizard (*Xantusia vigilis utahensis*): This Utah endemic subspecies is limited to one area in the southeast corner of the state. Typical habitat includes arid and semiarid granite outcroppings and rocky areas. Population densities of this subspecies are unknown within its limited distribution.

Desert Night Lizard (*Xantusia vigilis vigilis*): The desert (common) night lizard is fairly common throughout its range; however, in Utah, the distribution is limited to the southwest corner of the state in Washington County. Its typical habitat includes arid and semiarid rock outcroppings and rocky areas among fallen leaves and trunks of yuccas, agaves, and Joshua trees.

Mojave Zebra-tailed Lizard (*Callisaurus draconoides rhodostictus*): This species is typically found in areas with hard-packed soils and sparse vegetation associated with sandy washes. Occasionally it can be found among small rocks. Its distribution in Utah is limited to the extreme southwest corner of the state in the Mojave desert.

California Kingsnake (*Lampropeltis getula californiae*): This species occurs in diverse habitats, including dry, rocky wooded hillsides, river wetlands, desert, and chaparral. Its range in Utah is limited to the southwest part of the state, particularly in Washington County. Only the black and white-banded color morph occurs in Utah and is prohibited from collection.

Southwestern Black-headed Snake (*Tantilla hobartsmithi*): This species occurs in open areas of the southwest, particularly in areas with canyons and arroyos ascending into open forests, as well as along river corridors. Because it is an extremely secretive, ground-dwelling snake, its status remains unclear. Its distribution in Utah is limited to areas along the Colorado River Valley.

Desert Glossy Snake (*Arizona elegans eburnata*): Habitats include dry, open sandy or loamy areas; creosote-mesquite desert; and sagebrush flats. Its distribution in Utah is limited to the southwest portion of Washington County.

Painted Desert Glossy Snake (*Arizona elegans philipi*): Habitats include dry, open sandy areas; creosote-mesquite desert; sagebrush flats; and oak-hickory woodlands. Its distribution in Utah is limited to the southern portions of Kane and San Juan Counties.

Sonora Lyre Snake (*Trimorphodon biscutatus lambda*): Chiefly a rock-dwelling species of lowlands, mesas, and lower mountain slopes, it can be found in desert grassland, creosote-bush, desert scrub, and chaparral up to evergreen forests. The range of this species is limited to the lower portions of Washington and Kane Counties in the southwest corner of the state.

Utah Blind Snake (*Leptotyphlops humilis utahensis*): The habitat of this snake includes deserts, grassland, scrub, canyons, and brush-covered mountain slopes with moist sandy or gravelly soil suitable for burrowing. The range of this species is limited to the southwest corner of Washington County.

Mojave Patch-nosed Snake (*Salvadora hexalepis mojavensis*): This species occurs throughout the Mojave desert in areas of barren creosote bush, desert flats, sagebrush, semidesert, and chaparral. In Utah, it only occurs in most of Washington County and the western part of Kane County.

Southwestern Speckled Rattlesnake (*Crotalus mitchellii pyrrhus*): A rock-dweller, this species inhabits rocky terrain, rock outcrops, deep canyons, talus slopes, and chaparral amid rock piles and boulders. It may also be found occasionally on loose soil or in sandy areas. This species only occurs in Utah in the extreme southwest part of Washington County.

Mojave Rattlesnake (*Crotalus scutulatus scutulatus*): Chiefly inhabits upland desert and lower mountain slopes in habitats ranging from barren desert, grassland, and scrubland to open juniper woodlands. This species only occurs in Utah in the extreme southwest part of Washington County.

Mojave Desert Sidewinder (*Crotalus cerastes cerastes*): The sidewinder inhabits arid desert flatlands with sandy washes or mesquite-crowned sand hammocks and occasionally rocky areas. In Utah, this species only occurs in Washington County where the Mojave Desert extends.

Species of Special Concern (Declining Populations and Limited Distribution)

Glen Canyon Chuckwalla (*Sauromalus obesus multiforaminatus*): This species is a rock dweller which occurs in arid and semiarid areas with open flats and rocky areas with large boulders. Its distribution extends from the Colorado River at the Glen Canyon Dam at Page, Arizona, to near Hite and the Henry Mountains in Utah. This subspecies is threatened due to habitat loss and over-collection.

Western Chuckwalla (*Sauromalus obesus obesus*): This species is a rock dweller which occurs in arid and semi-arid areas with open flats and rocky areas with large boulders. Its distribution in Utah is limited to the extreme southwest corner of the state and in some areas in south central Kane County. This subspecies is also threatened due to habitat loss and overcollection.

Many-lined Skink (*Eumeces multivirgatus gaigeae*): This species is only known to occur in the lower southeastern part of the state in San Juan County. Since few locations have been documented, it is unclear what its actual distribution in Utah is. Declines in these areas have been observed. Typical habitat of this species includes areas of rocks and small brush in open grassy plains, sandy hills, and desert. It has also been observed in mountainous wooded areas.

Plateau Striped Whiptail (*Cnemidopherus velox*): Typical habitat of this species includes pinon-juniper woodlands and ponderosa pine forests at elevations between 1,700 and 1,800 meters (5,500 and 6,000 feet). Few locations are known in Utah. The known distribution is limited to the lower southwest part of the state.

Great Plains Rat Snake (*Elaphe guttata emoryi*): This species is common throughout its range; however, the populations in Utah consist of a unique color morph, making it a target for overcollection. Very few individuals of this race have been documented in Utah. Its distribution appears to be limited to areas in eastern Utah in San Juan, Grand, and Uintah Counties. Its habitat includes woody groves, rocky hillsides, and meadowlands along water courses and springs.

Smooth Green Snake (*Opheodrys vernalis*): The smooth green snake typically inhabits meadows, grassy marshes, and moist grassy fields along forest edges. Its distribution is somewhat unclear. This snake occurs in the upper northeast part of the state in the Uinta Mountain region.

FISHES
Extinct Species

Utah Lake Sculpin (*Cottus echinatus*): This species once occurred only in Utah Lake. It was probably extinct by the 1950s.

State Endangered Species

Bonytail (*Gila elegans*): Bonytail are endangered under the ESA and are endemic to the Colorado River Basin. Bonytail have been severely reduced in numbers with no wild bonytail being captured for several years. Flow regulation, habitat loss/alteration, and introduction of nonnative fish have been identified as causes for decline. The only significant numbers of these fish known to exist are held in culture facilities. Reintroduction efforts have begun to reestablish this species

Colorado Squawfish (*Ptychocheilus lucius*): Colorado squawfish are endangered under the ESA and are endemic to the Colorado River Basin. Presently, Colorado squawfish are only found in the upper Colorado River Basin, upstream of Glen Canyon Dam. Reproduction is known to occur in a few locations in the Green River, and the Ouray reach has been identified as an important nursery habitat area. Flow regulation, migration barriers, habitat loss/alteration, and introduction of nonnative fish have been identified as causes for decline.

Humpback Chub (*Gila cypha*): Humpback chub are endangered under the ESA and are endemic to the Colorado River Basin. Humpback chub have been severely reduced in numbers. Canyon areas with deep, swift water and rocky substrates on the Green and Colorado rivers have been identified as important habitat for this species. Flow alteration has been identified as a significant cause of decline.

Razorback Sucker (*Xyrauchen texanus*): Razorback sucker are endangered under the ESA and are endemic to the Colorado River Basin. Adult razorback sucker prefer slow runs, pools, and eddies. The Green River has the only known spawning areas; however, only extremely limited recruitment of this species has been documented in the last 30 years. Young razorback sucker likely require backwaters and flooded bottomlands. Flow regulation, habitat loss/alteration, and introduction of nonnative fish have been identified as causes for decline.

Woundfin (*Plagopterus argentissumus*): Woundfin are endangered under the ESA and are endemic to the Colorado River Basin. Woundfin have been severely reduced in numbers and distribution; they are now restricted to the Virgin River Basin. Flow regulation and introduction of nonnative fish have been identified as causes for decline. Runs and riffles close to channel banks have been identified as important habitat for the woundfin.

Virgin River Chub (*Gila seminuda*): Virgin River chub are endangered under the ESA and are endemic to the Virgin River. This species has been severely reduced in numbers and distribution. Deep runs and pools with adequate cover have been identified as important habitat for the Virgin River chub. Flow regulation and introduction of nonnative fish have been identified as causes for decline.

June Sucker (*Chasmistes liorus*): June Sucker are endangered under the ESA and are endemic to Utah Lake. Only extremely limited recruitment of this species has been documented in the last 30 years. Flow alteration and introduction of nonnative fish have been identified as causes for decline.

State Threatened Species

Lahontan Cutthroat Trout (*Oncorhynchus clarki henshawi*): Lahontan cutthroat trout are not native to Utah. The species was introduced and has persisted in a few streams in western Utah. It is listed as state threatened because it is federally listed as threatened under the ESA.

Roundtail Chub (*Gila robusta*): Roundtail chub are endemic to the Colorado River Basin. Runs and pools of streams and rivers have been identified as important habitat for roundtail chub. Roundtail chub have been reduced in numbers and distribution. Flow alteration and the introduction of nonnative fish have been identified as significant causes of decline.

Species of Special Concern (Declining Populations)

Leatherside Chub (*Gila copei*): Leatherside chub have been extirpated from much of their historical range. Pools and riffles in cool to cold streams and rivers have been identified as important habitat for leatherside chub. Introduction of nonnative fish and habitat alteration have been identified as the primary causes for decline.

Flannelmouth Sucker (*Catostomus latipinnis*): Flannelmouth sucker are endemic to the Colorado River Basin. Rocky pools and slow-flowing, lower gradient reaches in larger rivers have been identified as important habitat for flannelmouth sucker. Flannelmouth sucker have been reduced in numbers and distribution. Flow alteration, habitat loss/alteration, and the introduction of nonnative fish have been identified as significant causes of decline.

Bluehead Sucker (*Catostomus discobolus*): Bluehead sucker have been reduced in numbers and distribution. Fast-flowing rocky riffles in higher gradient reaches of small to large rivers have been identified as important habitat for bluehead sucker. Flow alteration, habitat loss/alteration, and the introduction of nonnative fish have been identified as significant causes of decline.

Species of Special Concern (Limited Distribution)

Bonneville Cisco (*Prosopium gemmiferum*): Bonneville cisco are endemic to Bear Lake. Bonneville cisco are sought as a sport fish. They are managed under an intensive fishery program at Bear Lake.

Bonneville Whitefish (*Prosopium spilonotus*): Bonneville whitefish are endemic to Bear Lake. Bonneville whitefish are sought as a sport fish. They are managed under an intensive fishery program at Bear Lake.

Bear Lake Whitefish (*Prosopium abyssicola*): Bear Lake whitefish are endemic to Bear Lake. Bear Lake whitefish are sought as a sport fish. They are managed under an intensive fishery program at Bear Lake.

Bear Lake Sculpin (*Cottus extensus*): Bear Lake sculpin are endemic to Bear Lake.

Desert Sucker (*Catostomus clarki*): Desert sucker are restricted to the Virgin River Basin. Flow regulation and introduction of nonnative fish have adversely affected this species's populations.

Conservation Species

Colorado River Cutthroat Trout (*Oncorhynchus clarki pleuriticus*): Colorado

River cutthroat trout are one of two native subspecies of cutthroat trout inhabiting Utah waters. Special emphasis, including the development of a conservation strategy and agreement, has been given to this species for several years. Habitat alteration and introduction of nonnative fish have contributed to their decline.

Bonneville Cutthroat Trout (*Oncorhynchus clarki utah*): Bonneville cutthroat trout are one of two native subspecies of cutthroat trout inhabiting Utah waters. Special emphasis, including the development of a conservation strategy and agreement, has been given to this species for several years. Habitat alteration and introduction of nonnative fish have contributed to their decline.

Virgin Spinedace (*Lepidomeda mollispinis mollispinis*): Virgin spinedace are endemic to the Colorado River Basin and are now restricted to the Virgin River Basin. The species is severely reduced in numbers and distribution. Special emphasis, including the development of a conservation strategy and agreement, has been given to this species for several years. Flow regulation and introduction of nonnative fish have been identified as causes for decline.

Least Chub (*Iotichthys phlegethontis*): Least chub are proposed to be listed as endangered under the ESA because they have been extirpated from over 90 percent of their historical range. Least chub currently exist in only a few springs. Special emphasis, including the current development of a conservation strategy and agreement, has been given to this species for several years. Introduction of nonnative fish has been identified as the primary cause for decline.

MOLLUSKS
Endangered Species
Kanab Ambersnail (*Oxyloma haydeni kanabensis*): This is a terrestrial species, but it is associated with soils wetted by springs and seeps at the base of sandstone cliffs. It is closely associated

with semiaquatic plants, such as monkey flower and watercress. Significant declines have been noted in Arizona and it is thought one population in Utah has been extirpated. The significant threat to this species has been identified as loss of habitat due to human development.

Fish Springs Pond Snail (*Stagnicola pilsbryi*): This is a freshwater snail that occurs in isolated groups of springs in a scrub desert environment. It appears to have been closely associated with a locally extinct species, the large ramshorn snail, *Helisoma triblovis subcrenatum*. This species is endemic to the area known as Fish Springs National Wildlife Refuge in Juab County; however, no live specimens have been collected since prior to 1871. It is now thought that the species may be extinct. It appears that overmanagement for the purpose of enhancing duck habitat may have caused the extinction of this species. Further investigations are required.

Utah Valvatasnail (*Valvata utahensis*): Historically, this species was known to occur in Utah Lake. The species has not been documented in Utah in the last 100 years and may be extirpated. However, populations may occur where habitat still exists.

Threatened Species
California Floater (*Anodota californiensis*): This is a freshwater clam that lives in shallow areas of unpolluted perennial waters and which is dependent on host fish during its larval stage. Found in Bear River south of Evanston, Wyoming, and near Randolph under rare conditions; west of Mona Lake; in Otter Creek below the dam; at Callao; and in Redden Spring. Collected historically from Huntington Creek in the San Rafael River drainage. Found historically in Farmington Canyon, Salt Lake City, Provo River, and Utah Lake. Several factors have been identified as causing declines in this species. They include alteration and destruction of habitat, declining water quality, and

competition with and predation by non-native fish and grayfish. Arizona has noted that possible declines may also be linked with reduced populations of native fish that serve as larval hosts. Rare in Nevada, also indicating severe declines from historic times.

Thickshell Pondsnail [Utah Band Snail] (*Stagnicola utahensis*): The species was historically abundant in Utah Lake until the late 19th century. By 1933 it survived only in a few springs along the west side of Utah Lake. No recent collections have been noted. Major threat to this species is habitat loss and degradation.

Species of Special Concern (Declining Populations)

Round Mouth Valvata (*Valvata humeralis*): Historical records are from Lake Bonneville Basin; the Bear River in Wyoming, Utah, and Idaho; Bear Lake; and the Snake River in Idaho. Post-Pleistocene records are from Utah Lake, Bear River in Idaho, and the Snake River. Living populations are now apparently restricted to the Snake River in Idaho.

Species of Special Concern (Due to limited distribution)

Clinton Cave Snail (*Pristiloma [Ogaridiscus] subrupicola*): This species occurs in the north end of the Oquirrh Mountains in Clinton Cave. This species may also occur in Nevada and Oregon but in very restricted populations.

Eureka Mountainsnail (*Oreohelix eurekensis eurekensis*): This is one of a small group of mountain species which occurs principally at high elevations. It is only known to occur in the East Tintic Mountains in Juab and Utah County, at least from Mammoth Peak to Godiva Mountain and on Lime Peak.

Lyrate Mountainsnail (*Oreohelix haydeni haydeni*): One of a conspicuous species having only a few, widely separated colonies, *O.H. haydeni* appears to be restricted to a single population located

in Quarry Cottonwood Canyon west of Devils Slide in Morgan County. Habitat consists of west-facing, xeric slopes. Possible future threats to species include increases in grazing practices or expansion of quarry activities.

Ogden Rocky Mountainsnail (*Oreohelix peripherica wasatchensis*): This subspecies of mountain snail is only known to occur in a small area near the mouth of Ogden Canyon. This subspecies is typically found under leaf litter and among quartzite boulders on open slopes associated with scrub oak clones. Fire appears to be the only current threat to the continued existence of this species.

Wet-rock Physa [Zion Canyon Snail, Zion Tadpole Snail] (*Physella zionis*): It is a primitive species without close living relatives. This is the smallest species within the family Physidae, reaching only 5 millimeters in maximum length. Unlike other physids, all of which are truly aquatic, the natural habitat of *P. zionis* is the subaerially exposed surface of wet cliffs. This species is only known from Zion National Park, Washington County.

Yavapai Mountainsnail (*Oreohelix yavapai*): This species is only known to occur in Utah in the Abajo Mountains in San Juan County. A land snail found in large, stable colonies in very xeric, open rocky areas, this species has a very limited distribution and may be declining due to habitat degradation from livestock grazing.

Species of Special Concern (Declining Populations and Limited Distribution)

Brian Head Mountainsnail (*Oreohelix parowanensis*): This is a rather small mountain snail which occurs at high elevations. It is known only from the type locality near the top of Brian Head, Parowan Mountains, in Iron County. No live specimens have ever been collected. This species may also occur in the LaSal Mountains, Logan Canyon, Beaver Canyon, and Panguitch Creek.

Fat-whorled Pondsnail [Banded Bonneville] (*Stagnicola bonnevillensis*): This is a rather large relict lymnaeid resembling some morphs of the widely distributed *Stagnicola catascopium* (Say). It occupies small spring-fed, well-vegetated ponds, although the presence of this species in Lake Bonneville deposits suggests that it previously lived in a large lake. Shells are widespread in the Bonneville Basin; however, live specimens have only been found near Corinne in Box Elder County. The threats to this species remain unclear.

Utah Physa [Utah Bubble Snail] (*Physella utahensis*): This is a relict freshwater snail of Pleistocene Lake Bonneville. It only exists in six verified sites, four in Utah and two in Colorado. It is a rare species with only two confirmed living populations in Utah, near Utah Lake and Redden Springs in the West Desert. The threats to this species remain unclear.

Uinta Mountainsnail (*Oreohelix eurekensis uinta*): Known only from the type locality from Whiterocks River in the Uinta Mountains. Possible reasons for its decline include range management practices for sheep (e.g. burning).

Desert Spring Snail (*Pyrgulopsis deserta*): This species is known only from springs along the Virgin River in southwestern Utah. Potential threats include water and land development. Currently *Pyrgulopsis* is under study in the Great Basin, which may result in a description of over 50 new species including many throughout the Bonneville Basin.

Fish Lake Physa Snail (*Physella microstriata*): This is a freshwater snail species that has only been found in shallow water along the shore of portions of Fish Lake, Utah. Recent surveys have not observed this species, and it is suspected that it may now be extinct. It is suspected that the decline of this species may be attributed to the management activities of Fish Lake designed to propagate sport fishes and to improve boating (e.g. removal of shoreline vegetation).

Appendix B
Utah Wildlife Species Checklist

This list is courtesy of the Utah Division of Wildlife Resources.

Amphibian
Tiger Salamander, *Ambystoma tigrinum*
Boreal Toad, *Bufo boreas boreas*
Great Plains Toad, *Bufo cognatus*
Southwestern Toad, *Bufo microscaphus*
Red-Spotted Toad, *Bufo punctatus*
Woodhouse's Toad, *Bufo woodhousii*
Canyon Treefrog, *Hyla arenicolor*
Boreal Chorus Frog, *Pseudacris maculata*
Pacific Chorus Frog, *Pseudacris regilla*
Bullfrog, *Rana catesbeiana*
Green Frog, *Rana clamitans*
Columbia Spotted Frog, *Rana luteiventris*
Relict Leopard Frog, *Rana onca*
Northern Leopard Frog, *Rana pipiens*
Lowland or Yavapai Leopard Frog, *Rana yavapaiensis*
Plains Spadefoot, *Spea bombifrons*
Great Basin Spadefoot, *Spea intermontana*
New Mexico Spadefoot, *Spea multiplicata*

Bird
Cooper's Hawk, *Accipiter cooperii*
Northern Goshawk, *Accipiter gentilis*
Sharp-Shinned Hawk, *Accipiter striatus*
Spotted Sandpiper, *Actitis macularia*
Clark's Grebe, *Aechmophorus clarkii*
Western Grebe, *Aechmophorus occidentalis*
Northern Saw-Whet Owl, *Aegolius acadicus*
White-Throated Swift, *Aeronautes saxatalis*
Red-Winged Blackbird, *Agelaius phoeniceus*
Rufous-Crowned Sparrow, *Aimophila ruficeps*
Wood Duck, *Aix sponsa*
Chukar, *Alectoris chukar*
Grasshopper Sparrow, *Ammodramus savannarum*
Sage Sparrow, *Amphispiza belli*
Black-Throated Sparrow, *Amphispiza bilineata*
Northern Pintail, *Anas acuta*
American Wigeon, *Anas americana*
Northern Shoveler, *Anas clypeata*
Green-Winged Teal, *Anas crecca*
Cinnamon Teal, *Anas cyanoptera*
Blue-Winged Teal, *Anas discors*
Mallard, *Anas platyrhynchos*
Gadwall, *Anas strepera*

Greater White-Fronted Goose, *Anser albifrons*
American Pipit, *Anthus rubescens*
Western Scrub-Jay, *Aphelocoma californica*
Golden Eagle, *Aquila chrysaetos*
Black-Chinned Hummingbird, *Archilochus alexandri*
Great Egret, *Ardea alba*
Great Blue Heron, *Ardea herodias*
Ruddy Turnstone, *Arenaria interpres*
Short-Eared Owl, *Asio flammeus*
Long-Eared Owl, *Asio otus*
Burrowing Owl, *Athene cunicularia*
Verdin, *Auriparus flaviceps*
Lesser Scaup, *Aythya affinis*
Redhead, *Aythya americana*
Ring-Necked Duck, *Aythya collaris*
Greater Scaup, *Aythya marila*
Canvasback, *Aythya valisineria*
Juniper Titmouse, *Baeolophus griseus*
Cedar Waxwing, *Bombycilla cedrorum*
Bohemian Waxwing, *Bombycilla garrulus*
Ruffed Grouse, *Bonasa umbellus*
American Bittern, *Botaurus lentiginosus*
Canada Goose, *Branta canadensis*
Great Horned Owl, *Bubo virginianus*
Cattle Egret, *Bubulcus ibis*
Bufflehead, *Bucephala albeola*
Common Goldeneye, *Bucephala clangula*
Barrow's Goldeneye, *Bucephala islandica*
Red-Tailed Hawk, *Buteo jamaicensis*
Rough-Legged Hawk, *Buteo lagopus*
Broad-Winged Hawk, *Buteo platypterus*
Ferruginous Hawk, *Buteo regalis*
Swainson's Hawk, *Buteo swainsoni*
Common Black-Hawk, *Buteogallus anthracinus*
Green Heron, *Butorides virescens*
Lark Bunting, *Calamospiza melanocorys*
Lapland Longspur, *Calcarius lapponicus*
Sanderling, *Calidris alba*
Dunlin, *Calidris alpina*
Baird's Sandpiper, *Calidris bairdii*
Red Knot, *Calidris canutus*
Stilt Sandpiper, *Calidris himantopus*
Western Sandpiper, *Calidris mauri*
Pectoral Sandpiper, *Calidris melanotos*
Least Sandpiper, *Calidris minutilla*
Semipalmated Sandpiper, *Calidris pusilla*
California Quail, *Callipepla californica*
Gambel's Quail, *Callipepla gambelii*

Costa's Hummingbird, *Calypte costae*
Cactus Wren, *Campylorhynchus brunneicapillus*
Common Redpoll, *Carduelis flammea*
Pine Siskin, *Carduelis pinus*
Lesser Goldfinch, *Carduelis psaltria*
American Goldfinch, *Carduelis tristis*
Cassin's Finch, *Carpodacus cassinii*
House Finch, *Carpodacus mexicanus*
Turkey Vulture, *Cathartes aura*
Veery, *Catharus fuscescens*
Hermit Thrush, *Catharus guttatus*
Swainson's Thrush, *Catharus ustulatus*
Canyon Wren, *Catherpes mexicanus*
Willet, *Catoptrophorus semipalmatus*
Gunnison Sage Grouse, *Centrocercus minimus*
Sage Grouse, *Centrocercus urophasianus*
Brown Creeper, *Certhia americana*
Belted Kingfisher, *Ceryle alcyon*
Snowy Plover, *Charadrius alexandrinus*
Mountain Plover, *Charadrius montanus*
Semipalmated Plover, *Charadrius semipalmatus*
Killdeer, *Charadrius vociferus*
Snow Goose, *Chen caerulescens*
Ross's Goose, *Chen rossii*
Black Tern, *Chlidonias niger*
Lark Sparrow, *Chondestes grammacus*
Lesser Nighthawk, *Chordeiles acutipennis*
Common Nighthawk, *Chordeiles minor*
American Dipper, *Cinclus mexicanus*
Northern Harrier, *Circus cyaneus*
Marsh Wren, *Cistothorus palustris*
Oldsquaw, *Clangula hyemalis*
Evening Grosbeak, *Coccothraustes vespertinus*
Yellow-Billed Cuckoo, *Coccyzus americanus*
Northern Flicker, *Colaptes auratus*
Band-Tailed Pigeon, *Columba fasciata*
Rock Dove, *Columba livia*
Inca Dove, *Columbina inca*
Olive-Sided Flycatcher, *Contopus cooperi*
Western Wood-Pewee, *Contopus sordidulus*
American Crow, *Corvus brachyrhynchos*
Common Raven, *Corvus corax*
Blue Jay, *Cyanocitta cristata*
Steller's Jay, *Cyanocitta stelleri*
Trumpeter Swan, *Cygnus buccinator*
Tundra Swan, *Cygnus columbianus*
Black Swift, *Cypseloides niger*
Blue Grouse, *Dendragapus obscurus*
Yellow-Rumped Warbler, *Dendroica coronata*
Grace's Warbler, *Dendroica graciae*
Black-Throated Gray Warbler, *Dendroica nigrescens*
Yellow Warbler, *Dendroica petechia*
Blackpoll Warbler, *Dendroica striata*
Townsend's Warbler, *Dendroica townsendi*

Bobolink, *Dolichonyx oryzivorus*
Gray Catbird, *Dumetella carolinensis*
Passenger Pigeon, *Ectopistes migratorius*
Snowy Egret, *Egretta thula*
Hammond's Flycatcher, *Empidonax hammondii*
Dusky Flycatcher, *Empidonax oberholseri*
Cordilleran Flycatcher, *Empidonax occidentalis*
Willow Flycatcher, *Empidonax traillii*
Southwestern Willow Flycatcher, *Empidonax traillii Extimus*
Gray Flycatcher, *Empidonax wrightii*
Horned Lark, *Eremophila alpestris*
Brewer's Blackbird, *Euphagus cyanocephalus*
Merlin, *Falco columbarius*
Prairie Falcon, *Falco mexicanus*
Peregrine Falcon, *Falco peregrinus*
American Kestrel, *Falco sparverius*
American Coot, *Fulica americana*
Common Snipe, *Gallinago gallinago*
Common Moorhen, *Gallinula chloropus*
Common Loon, *Gavia immer*
Pacific Loon, *Gavia pacifica*
Greater Roadrunner, *Geococcyx californianus*
Common Yellowthroat, *Geothlypis trichas*
Northern Pygmy-Owl, *Glaucidium gnoma*
Whooping Crane, *Grus smericana*
Sandhill Crane, *Grus canadensis*
Blue Grosbeak, *Guiraca caerulea*
California Condor, *Gymnogyps californianus*
Pinyon Jay, *Gymnorhinus cyanocephalus*
Bald Eagle, *Haliaeetus leucocephalus*
Black-Necked Stilt, *Himantopus mexicanus*
Barn Swallow, *Hirundo rustica*
Yellow-Breasted Chat, *Icteria virens*
Bullock's Oriole, *Icterus bullockii*
Hooded Oriole, *Icterus cucullatus*
Scott's Oriole, *Icterus parisorum*
Least Bittern, *Ixobrychus exilis*
Varied Thrush, *Ixoreus naevius*
Dark-Eyed Junco, *Junco hyemalis*
White-Tailed Ptarmigan, *Lagopus leucurus*
Northern Shrike, *Lanius excubitor*
Loggerhead Shrike, *Lanius udovicianus*
Herring Gull, *Larus argentatus*
California Gull, *Larus californicus*
Ring-Billed Gull, *Larus delawarensis*
Glaucous Gull, *Larus hyperboreus*
Bonaparte's Gull, *Larus philadelphia*
Franklin's Gull, *Larus pipixcan*
Thayer's Gull, *Larus thayeri*
Black Rosy-Finch, *Leucosticte atrata*
Gray-Crowned Rosy-Finch, *Leucosticte tephrocotis*
Short-Billed Dowitcher, *Limnodromus griseus*

Long-Billed Dowitcher, *Limnodromus scolopaceus*
Marbled Godwit, *Limosa fedoa*
Hooded Merganser, *Lophodytes cucullatus*
Red Crossbill, *Loxia curvirostra*
Acorn Woodpecker, *Melanerpes formicivorus*
Lewis's Woodpecker, *Melanerpes lewis*
White-Winged Scoter, *Melanitta fusca*
Surf Scoter, *Melanitta perspicillata*
Wild Turkey—Rio Grande, *Meleagris gallopavo intermedia*
Wild Turkey—Merriam's, *Meleagris gallopavo merriami*
Swamp Sparrow, *Melospiza georgiana*
Lincoln's Sparrow, *Melospiza incolnii*
Song Sparrow, *Melospiza melodia*
Common Merganser, *Mergus merganser*
Red-Breasted Merganser, *Mergus serrator*
Northern Mockingbird, *Mimus polyglottos*
Black-and-White Warbler, *Mniotilta varia*
Brown-Headed Cowbird, *Molothrus ater*
Townsend's Solitaire, *Myadestes townsendi*
Ash-Throated Flycatcher, *Myiarchus cinerascens*
Brown-Crested Flycatcher, *Myiarchus tyrannulus*
Painted Redstart, *Myioborus pictus*
Clark's Nutcracker, *Nucifraga columbiana*
Long-Billed Curlew, *Numenius americanus*
Whimbrel, *Numenius phaeopus*
Black-Crowned Night-Heron, *Nycticorax nycticorax*
Macgillivray's Warbler, *Oporornis tolmiei*
Sage Thrasher, *Oreoscoptes montanus*
Flammulated Owl, *Otus flammeolus*
Western Screech-Owl, *Otus kennicottii*
Ruddy Duck, *Oxyura jamaicensis*
Osprey, *Pandion haliaetus*
House Sparrow, *Passer domesticus*
Savannah Sparrow, *Passerculus sandwichensis*
Fox Sparrow, *Passerella iliaca*
Lazuli Bunting, *Passerina amoena*
Indigo Bunting, *Passerina cyanea*
American White Pelican, *Pelecanus erythrorhynchos*
Gray (Hungarian) Partridge, *Perdix perdix*
Gray Jay, *Perisoreus canadensis*
Cliff Swallow, *Petrochelidon pyrrhonota*
Phainopepla, *Phainopepla nitens*
Double-Crested Cormorant, *Phalacrocorax auritus*
Common Poorwill, *Phalaenoptilus nuttallii*
Red-Necked Phalarope, *Phalaropus lobatus*
Wilson's Phalarope, *Phalaropus tricolor*
Ring-Necked Pheasant, *Phasianus colchicus*

Rose-Breasted Grosbeak, *Pheucticus ludovicianus*
Black-Headed Grosbeak, *Pheucticus melanocephalus*
Black-Billed Magpie, *Pica pica*
Downy Woodpecker, *Picoides pubescens*
Ladder-Backed Woodpecker, *Picoides scalaris*
Three-Toed Woodpecker, *Picoides tridactylus*
Hairy Woodpecker, *Picoides villosus*
Pine Grosbeak, *Pinicola enucleator*
Abert's Towhee, *Pipilo aberti*
Green-Tailed Towhee, *Pipilo chlorurus*
Spotted Towhee, *Pipilo maculatus*
Western Tanager, *Piranga ludoviciana*
Summer Tanager, *Piranga rubra*
Snow Bunting, *Plectrophenax nivalis*
White-Faced Ibis, *Plegadis chihi*
American Golden-Plover, *Pluvialis dominica*
Black-Bellied Plover, *Pluvialis squatarola*
Horned Grebe, *Podiceps auritus*
Eared Grebe, *Podiceps nigricollis*
Pied-Billed Grebe, *Podilymbus podiceps*
Black-Capped Chickadee, *Poecile atricapillus*
Mountain Chickadee, *Poecile gambeli*
Blue-Gray Gnatcatcher, *Polioptila caerulea*
Black-Tailed Gnatcatcher, *Polioptila melanura*
Vesper Sparrow, *Pooecetes gramineus*
Sora, *Porzana carolina*
Purple Martin, *Progne subis*
Bushtit, *Psaltriparus minimus*
Vermilion Flycatcher, *Pyrocephalus rubinus*
Great-Tailed Grackle, *Quiscalus mexicanus*
Common Grackle, *Quiscalus quiscula*
Virginia Rail, *Rallus lmicola*
American Avocet, *Recurvirostra americana*
Ruby-Crowned Kinglet, *Regulus calendula*
Golden-Crowned Kinglet, *Regulus satrapa*
Bank Swallow, *Riparia riparia*
Rock Wren, *Salpinctes obsoletus*
Black Phoebe, *Sayornis nigricans*
Say's Phoebe, *Sayornis saya*
Northern Waterthrush, *Seiurus noveboracensis*
Broad-Tailed Hummingbird, *Selasphorus platycercus*
Rufous Hummingbird, *Selasphorus rufus*
American Redstart, *Setophaga ruticilla*
Mountain Bluebird, *Sialia currucoides*
Western Bluebird, *Sialia mexicana*
Red-Breasted Nuthatch, *Sitta canadensis*
White-Breasted Nuthatch, *Sitta carolinensis*
Pygmy Nuthatch, *Sitta pygmaea*
Red-Naped Sapsucker, *Sphyrapicus nuchalis*
Williamson's Sapsucker, *Sphyrapicus thyroideus*
American Tree Sparrow, *Spizella arborea*
Black-Chinned Sparrow, *Spizella atrogularis*

Brewer's Sparrow, *Spizella breweri*
Chipping Sparrow, *Spizella passerina*
Northern Rough-Winged Swallow,
  Stelgidopteryx serripennis
Calliope Hummingbird, *Stellula calliope*
Caspian Tern, *Sterna caspia*
Forster's Tern, *Sterna forsteri*
Common Tern, *Sterna hirundo*
Spotted Owl, *Strix occidentalis*
Western Meadowlark, *Sturnella neglecta*
European Starling, *Sturnus vulgaris*
Tree Swallow, *Tachycineta bicolor*
Violet-Green Swallow, *Tachycineta thalassina*
Bewick's Wren, *Thryomanes bewickii*
Bendire's Thrasher, *Toxostoma bendirei*
Crissal Thrasher, *Toxostoma crissale*
Le Conte's Thrasher, *Toxostoma lecontei*
Brown Thrasher, *Toxostoma rufum*
Lesser Yellowlegs, *Tringa flavipes*
Greater Yellowlegs, *Tringa melanoleuca*
Solitary Sandpiper, *Tringa solitaria*
House Wren, *Troglodytes aedon*
Winter Wren, *Troglodytes troglodytes*
American Robin, *Turdus migratorius*
Sharp-Tailed Grouse, *Tympanuchus phasianellus*
Eastern Kingbird, *Tyrannus tyrannus*
Western Kingbird, *Tyrannus verticalis*
Cassin's Kingbird, *Tyrannus vociferans*
Barn Owl, *Tyto alba*
Orange-Crowned Warbler, *Vermivora celata*
Lucy's Warbler, *Vermivora luciae*
Tennessee Warbler, *Vermivora peregrina*
Nashville Warbler, *Vermivora ruficapilla*
Virginia's Warbler, *Vermivora virginiae*
Bell's Vireo, *Vireo bellii*
Warbling Vireo, *Vireo gilvus*
Red-Eyed Vireo, *Vireo olivaceus*
Plumbeous Vireo, *Vireo plumbeus*
Gray Vireo, *Vireo vicinior*
Wilson's Warbler, *Wilsonia pusilla*
Yellow-Headed Blackbird, *Xanthocephalus
  xanthocephalus*
White-Winged Dove, *Zenaida asiatica*
Mourning Dove, *Zenaida macroura*
White-Throated Sparrow, *Zonotrichia albicollis*
Golden-Crowned Sparrow, *Zonotrichia
  atricapilla*
White-Crowned Sparrow, *Zonotrichia
  leucophrys*
Harris' Sparrow, *Zonotrichia querula*

Fish

Black Bullhead, *Ameiurus melas*
Yellow Bullhead, *Ameiurus natalis*
Sacramento Perch, *Archoplites interruptus*

Goldfish, *Carassius auratus*
Utah Sucker, *Catostomus ardens*
Desert Sucker, *Catostomus clarki*
White Sucker, *Catostomus commersoni*
Bluehead Sucker, *Catostomus discobolus*
Flannelmouth Sucker, *Catostomus latipinnis*
Mountain Sucker, *Catostomus platyrhynchus*
June Sucker, *Chasmistes liorus*
Jaguar Guapote, *Cichlasoma managuense*
Mottled Sculpin, *Cottus bairdi*
Paiute Sculpin, *Cottus beldingi*
Utah Lake Sculpin, *Cottus echinatus*
Bear Lake Sculpin, *Cottus extensus*
Brook Stickleback, *Culaea inconstans*
Red Shiner, *Cyprinella lutrensis*
Common Carp, *Cyprinus carpio*
Gizzard Shad, *Dorosoma cepedianum*
Threadfin Shad, *Dorosoma petenense*
Northern Pike, *Esox lucius*
Tiger Muskie, *Esox lucius X E. masquinongy*
Plains Killifish, *Fundulus zebrinus*
Western Mosquitofish, *Gambusia affinis*
Utah Chub, *Gila atraria*
Leatherside Chub, *Gila copei*
Humpback Chub, *Gila cypha*
Bonytail, *Gila elegans*
Roundtail Chub, *Gila robusta*
Virgin River Chub, *Gila seminuda*
Brassy Minnow, *Hybognathus hankinsoni*
Plains Minnow, *Hybognathus placitus*
Channel Catfish, *Ictalurus punctatus*
Least Chub, *Iotichthys phlegethontis*
Virgin Spinedace, *Lepidomeda mollispinis*
Green Sunfish, *Lepomis cyanellus*
Bluegill, *Lepomis macrochirus*
Rainwater Killifish, *Lucania parva*
Smallmouth Bass, *Micropterus dolomieu*
Largemouth Bass, *Micropterus salmoides*
White Bass, *Morone chrysops*
Wiper, *Morone chrysops X M. saxtilis*
Striped Bass, *Morone saxatilis*
Golden Shiner, *Notemigonus crysoleucas*
Emerald Shiner, *Notropis atherinoides*
Spottail Shiner, *Notropis hudsonius*
Sand Shiner, *Notropis stramineus*
Golden Trout, *Oncorhynchus aguabonita*
Cutthroat Trout, *Oncorhynchus clarki*
Yellowstone Cutthroat Trout, *Oncorhynchus
  clarki bouvieri*
Lahontan Cutthroat Trout, *Oncorhynchus
  clarki henshawi*
Colorado River Cutthroat Trout,
  Oncorhynchus clarki pleuriticus
Bonneville Cutthroat Trout, *Oncorhynchus
  clarki utah*

Rainbow Trout, *Oncorhynchus mykiss*
Sockeye Salmon (Kokanee), *Oncorhynchus nerka*
Yellow Perch, *Perca flavescens*
Logperch, *Percina caprodes*
Trout-Perch, *Percopsis omiscomaycus*
Fathead Minnow, *Pimephales promelas*
Woundfin, *Plagopterus argentissimus*
White Crappie, *Pomoxis annularis*
Black Crappie, *Pomoxis nigromaculatus*
Bear Lake Whitefish, *Prosopium abyssicola*
Bonneville Cisco, *Prosopium gemmifer*
Bonneville Whitefish, *Prosopium spilonotus*
Mountain Whitefish, *Prosopium williamsoni*
Colorado Pikeminnow, *Ptychocheilus lucius*
Longnose Dace, *Rhinichthys cataractae*
Speckled Dace, *Rhinichthys osculus*
Redside Shiner, *Richardsonius balteatus*
Brown Trout, *Salmo trutta*
Tiger Trout, *Salmo trutta X salvelinus fontinalis*
Brook Trout, *Salvelinus fontinalis*
Lake Trout, *Salvelinus namaycush*
Splake, *Salvelinus namaycush X S. fontinalis*
Creek Chub, *Semotilus atromaculatus*
Walleye, *Stizostedion vitreum*
Arctic Grayling, *Thymallus arcticus*
Razorback Sucker, *Xyrauchen texanus*

Mammal
Moose, *Alces alces*
White-Tailed Antelope Squirrel,
    Ammospermophilus leucurus
Pronghorn, *Antilocapra americana*
Pallid Bat, *Antrozous pallidus*
Ringtail, *Bassariscus astutus*
American Bison, *Bos bison*
Pygmy Rabbit, *Brachylagus idahoensis*
Coyote, *Canis latrans*
Gray Wolf, *Canis lupus*
American Beaver, *Castor canadensis*
Elk or Wapiti, *Cervus elaphus*
Long-Tailed Pocket Mouse, *Chaetodipus
    formosus*
Rock Pocket Mouse, *Chaetodipus intermedius*
Desert Pocket Mouse, *Chaetodipus penicillatus*
Southern Red-Backed Vole, *Clethrionomys
    gapperi*
Townsend's Big-Eared Bat, *Corynorhinus
    townsendii*
Gunnison's Prairie Dog, *Cynomys gunnisoni*
White-Tailed Prairie Dog, *Cynomys leucurus*
Utah Prairie Dog, *Cynomys parvidens*
Desert Kangaroo Rat, *Dipodomys deserti*
Merriam's Kangaroo Rat, *Dipodomys merriami*
Chisel-Toothed Kangaroo Rat, *Dipodomys
    microps*

Ord's Kangaroo Rat, *Dipodomys ordii*
Big Brown Bat, *Eptesicus fuscus*
Common Porcupine, *Erethizon dorsatum*
Spotted Bat, *Euderma maculatum*
Mountain Lion or Cougar, *Felis concolor*
Northern Flying Squirrel, *Glaucomys sabrinus*
Wolverine, *Gulo gulo*
Allen's Big-Eared Bat, *Idionycteris phyllotis*
Silver-Haired Bat, *Lasionycteris noctivagans*
Western Red Bat, *Lasiurus blossevillii*
Hoary Bat, *Lasiurus cinereus*
Sagebrush Vole, *Lemmiscus curtatus*
Snowshoe Hare, *Lepus americanus*
Black-Tailed Jackrabbit, *Lepus californicus*
White-Tailed Jackrabbit, *Lepus townsendii*
Northern River Otter, *Lutra canadensis*
Lynx, *Lynx canadensis*
Bobcat, *Lynx rufus*
Yellow-Bellied Marmot, *Marmota flaviventris*
American Marten, *Martes americana*
Fisher, *Martes pennanti*
Striped Skunk, *Mephitis mephitis*
Dark Kangaroo Mouse, *Microdipodops
    megacephalus*
Long-Tailed Vole, *Microtus longicaudus*
Mogollon Vole, *Microtus mogollonensis*
Montane Vole, *Microtus montanus*
Meadow Vole, *Microtus pennsylvanicus*
Water Vole, *Microtus richardsoni*
House Mouse, *Mus musculus*
Ermine, *Mustela erminea*
Long-Tailed Weasel, *Mustela frenata*
Black-Footed Ferret, *Mustela nigripes*
Mink, *Mustela vison*
Nutria, *Myocastor coypus*
California Myotis, *Myotis californicus*
Western Small-Footed Myotis, *Myotis
    ciliolabrum*
Long-Eared Myotis, *Myotis evotis*
Little Brown Myotis, *Myotis lucifugus*
Fringed Myotis, *Myotis thysanodes*
Long-Legged Myotis, *Myotis volans*
Yuma Myotis, *Myotis yumanensis*
White-Throated Woodrat, *Neotoma albigula*
Bushy-Tailed Woodrat, *Neotoma cinerea*
Arizona Woodrat, *Neotoma devia*
Desert Woodrat, *Neotoma lepida*
Mexican Woodrat, *Neotoma mexicana*
Stephens' Woodrat, *Neotoma stephensi*
Desert Shrew, *Notiosorex crawfordi*
Big Free-Tailed Bat, *Nyctinomops macrotis*
American Pika, *Ochotona princeps*
Mule Deer, *Odocoileus hemionus*
White-Tailed Deer, *Odocoileus virginianus*
Muskrat, *Ondatra zibethicus*

Northern Grasshopper Mouse, *Onychomys leucogaster*
Southern Grasshopper Mouse, *Onychomys torridus*
Mountain Goat, *Oreamnos americanus*
California Bighorn Sheep, *Ovis canadensis californiana*
Rocky Mountain Bighorn Sheep, *Ovis canadensis canadensis*
Desert Bighorn Sheep, *Ovis canadensis nelsoni*
Olive-Backed Pocket Mouse, *Perognathus fasciatus*
Plains Pocket Mouse, *Perognathus flavescens*
Silky Pocket Mouse, *Perognathus flavus*
Little Pocket Mouse, *Perognathus longimembris*
Great Basin Pocket Mouse, *Perognathus parvus*
Brush Mouse, *Peromyscus boylii*
Canyon Mouse, *Peromyscus crinitus*
Cactus Mouse, *Peromyscus eremicus*
Deer Mouse, *Peromyscus maniculatus*
Northern Rock Mouse, *Peromyscus nasutus*
Pinyon (Pinon) Mouse, *Peromyscus truei*
Heather Vole, *Phenacomys intermedius*
Western Pipistrelle, *Pipistrellus hesperus*
Raccoon, *Procyon lotor*
Norway Rat, *Rattus norvegicus*
Black Rat, *Rattus rattus*
Western Harvest Mouse, *Reithrodontomys megalotis*
Abert's Squirrel, *Sciurus aberti*
Masked or Cinereous Shrew, *Sorex cinereus*
Merriam's Shrew, *Sorex merriami*
Dusky or Montane Shrew, *Sorex monticolus*
Dwarf Shrew, *Sorex nanus*
Water Shrew, *Sorex palustris*
Preble's Shrew, *Sorex preblei*
Vagrant Shrew, *Sorex vagrans*
Uinta Ground Squirrel, *Spermophilus armatus*
Belding's Ground Squirrel, *Spermophilus beldingi*
Wyoming Ground Squirrel, *Spermophilus elegans*
Golden-Mantled Ground Squirrel, *Spermophilus lateralis*
Great Basin Ground Ground Squirrel, *Spermophilus lateralis*
Spotted Ground Squirrel, *Spermophilus spilosoma*
Thirteen-Lined Ground Squirrel, *Spermophilus tridecemlineatus*
Rock Squirrel, *Spermophilus variegatus*
Western Spotted Skunk, *Spilogale gracilis*
Desert Cottontail, *Sylvilagus audubonii*
Mountain Cottontail, *Sylvilagus nuttallii*
Brazilian Free-Tailed Bat, *Tadarida brasiliensis*

Yellow-Pine Chipmunk, *Tamias amoenus*
Cliff Chipmunk, *Tamias dorsalis*
Least Chipmunk, *Tamias minimus*
Hopi Chipmunk, *Tamias rufus*
Uinta Chipmunk, *Tamias umbrinus*
Red Squirrel, *Tamiasciurus hudsonicus*
Badger, *Taxidea taxus*
Botta's Pocket Gopher, *Thomomys bottae*
Idaho Pocket Gopher, *Thomomys idahoensis*
Northern Pocket Gopher, *Thomomys talpoides*
Common Gray Fox, *Urocyon cinereoargenteus*
Black Bear, *Ursus americanus*
Brown (Grizzly) Bear, *Ursus arctos*
Swift (Kit) Fox, *Vulpes velox*
Red Fox, *Vulpes vulpes*
Western Jumping Mouse, *Zapus princeps*

Reptile

Spiny Softshell, *Apalone spinifera*
Glossy Snake, *Arizona elegans*
Zebra-Tailed Lizard, *Callisaurus draconoides*
Rubber Boa, *Charina bottae*
Snapping Turtle, *Chelydra serpentina*
Painted Turtle, *Chrysemys picta*
Western Whiptail, *Cnemidophorus tigris*
Plateau Striped Whiptail, *Cnemidophorus velox*
Western Banded Gecko, *Coleonyx variegatus*
Racer, *Coluber constrictor*
Mojave Desert Sidewinder, *Crotalus cerastes cerastes*
Speckled Rattlesnake, *Crotalus mitchellii*
Mojave Rattlesnake, *Crotalus scutulatus*
Midget Faded Rattlesnake, *Crotalus viridis concolor*
Great Basin Rattlesnake, *Crotalus viridis lutosus*
Hopi Rattlesnake, *Crotalus viridis nuntius*
Mojave Black-Collared Lizard, *Crotaphytus bicinctores*
Collared Lizard, *Crotaphytus collaris*
Ringneck Snake, *Diadophis punctatus*
Desert Iguana, *Dipsosaurus dorsalis*
Great Plains Rat (Corn) Snake, *Elaphe guttata*
Many-Lined Skink, *Eumeces multivirgatus*
Western Skink, *Eumeces skiltonianus*
Longnose Leopard Lizard, *Gambelia wislizenii*
Desert Tortoise, *Gopherus agassizii*
Banded Gila Monster, *Heloderma suspectumcinctum*
Lesser Earless Lizard, *Holbrookia maculata*
Night Snake, *Hypsiglena torquata*
California Kingsnake, *Lampropeltis getula californiae*
Sonoran Mountain Kingsnake, *Lampropeltis pyromelana*
Milk Snake, *Lampropeltis triangulum*

Western Blind Snake, *Leptotyphlops humilis*
Smooth Green Snake, *Liochlorophis vernalis*
Coachwhip or Red Racer, *Masticophis flagellum*
Striped Whipsnake, *Masticophis aeniatus*
Short-Horned Lizard, *Phrynosoma hernandesi*
Desert Horned Lizard, *Phrynosoma platyrhinos*
Spotted Leaf-Nosed Snake, *Phyllorhynchus decurtatus*
Gopher Snake, *Pituophis catenifer*
Long-Nosed Snake, *Rhinocheilus lecontei*
Mojave Patch-Nosed Snake, *Salvadora hexalepis mojavensis*
Chuckwalla, *Sauromalus obesus*
Sagebrush Lizard, *Sceloporus graciosus*

Desert Spiny Lizard, *Sceloporus magister*
Western Fence Lizard, *Sceloporus occidentalis*
Plateau Lizard, *Sceloporus undulatus*
Ground Snake, *Sonora semiannulata*
Southwestern Black-Headed Snake, *Tantilla hobartsmithi*
Black-Necked Garter Snake, *Tamnosphis cyrtopsis*
Western Terrestrial Garter Snake, *Thamnophis elegans*
Common Garter Snake, *Thamnophis sirtalis*
Lyre Snake, *Trimorphodon biscutatus*
Northern Tree Lizard, *Urosaurus ornatus*
Side-Blotched Lizard, *Uta stansburiana*
Desert Night Lizard, *Xantusia vigilis*

Appendix C
Utah Wildlife Viewing Locations

This list is courtesy of *Utah Wildlife Viewing Guide*, by Jim Coles. For a more complete description of each site, the book is available through Falcon Publishing, 1-800-582-2665 or <www.falcon.com>. Wildlife watching sites are organized by the nine travel regions of Utah. The kinds of animals that frequent each site are in thirteen categories: carnivores, hoofed mammals, small mammals, freshwater mammals, waterfowl, upland birds, songbirds, birds of prey, fish, wildflowers, reptiles and amphibians, shorebirds, and wading birds.

BRIDGERLAND
Woodruff Cooperative Wildlife Management Area
Along east side of highway on Utah 16 north of Evanston, Wyoming.

What you may see: hoofed mammals, upland birds, birds of prey.

Rich County Bottoms
Loop trip from Utah 16 near Randolph to Utah 30 then east to Wyoming Road 220 then south to Crawford Mountain Road, then west to point of beginning.

What you may see: waterfowl, songbirds, birds of prey, shorebirds, wading birds.

Round Valley
Loop trip that begins near intersection of U.S. 89 and Utah 30.

What you may see: hoofed mammals, waterfowl, songbirds, birds of prey, shorebirds, wading birds.

Bear Lake Overlook
On U.S. 89 five miles west of Garden City.

What you may see: hoofed mammals, small mammals, upland birds, songbirds, birds of prey.

Riverside Nature Trail
Trail between Spring Hollow and Malibu-Guinavah Campground approximately six miles east of Logan off U.S. 89.

What you may see: hoofed mammals, small mammals, waterfowl, songbirds, shorebirds.

Rock Creek
U.S. Forest Service Area of Rock Creek west of Randolph.

What you may see: hoofed mammals, small mammals, freshwater mammals, upland birds, songbirds, wildflowers.

Hardware Ranch
At east end of Utah Highway 101.

What you may see: hoofed mammals (elk), birds of prey.

Porcupine Reservoir
Reservoir is southeast of Avon off Utah Highway 165.

What you may see: fish (Kokanee spawning site).

Cutler Marsh
Approximately five miles west of Logan off Utah Highway 30.

What you may see: small mammals, waterfowl, songbirds, birds of prey, shorebirds, wading birds.

Wellsville Wilderness
Deep Canyon Trail west of Mendon off Utah Highway 23.

What you may see: small mammals, birds of prey.

GOLDEN SPIKE
Clear Creek Campground
U.S. Forest Service campground on Utah-Idaho border off Utah Highway 42.

What you may see: hoofed mammals, small mammals, songbirds, birds of prey.

Salt Creek Waterfowl Management Area

At north end of Great Salt Lake west of Corinne off Utah Highway 83.

What you may see: small mammals, waterfowl, birds of prey, shorebirds, wading birds.

Golden Spike National Historic Site

West of Utah Highway 83 near Promontory and Cedar Springs.

What you may see: hoofed mammals, small mammals, waterfowl, upland birds, songbirds, birds of prey, wildflowers.

Willard Bay-Harold Crane Marsh

Walk-in is from south marina of Willard Bay. Exit 354 off I-15.

What you may see: small mammals, waterfowl, upland birds, birds of prey, shorebirds, wading birds.

Ogden Bay Waterfowl Management Area

On east shore of Great Salt Lake west of I-15's Roy exit.

What you may see: waterfowl, upland birds, songbirds, birds of prey, shorebirds, wading birds.

Ogden Nature Center

At 966 12th Street in Ogden.

What you may see: small mammals, waterfowl, upland birds, songbirds, birds of prey, wading birds.

North Fork Park

Near Liberty at north end of Ogden Valley.

What you may see: hoofed mammals, small mammals, birds of prey, upland birds, songbirds.

Middle Fork Wildlife Management Area

East of Huntsville off Utah Highway 39.

What you may see: hoofed mammals, small mammals, upland birds, songbirds, birds of prey.

North Arm

Where the North Fork of the Ogden River dumps into Pineview Reservoir.

What you may see: hoofed mammals, small mammals, waterfowl, songbirds, birds of prey, shorebirds, wading birds.

Beus Park

An Ogden City Park east of the city.

What you may see: small mammals, waterfowl, songbirds, birds of prey, fish, wading birds.

Davis Peaks

Ridgetop drive from Bountiful to Farmington.

What you may see: carnivores, hoofed mammals, small mammals, upland birds, songbirds, birds of prey, wildflowers.

Morgan-Henefer Loop

Off Utah Highway 66, loop from East Canyon Creek to East Canyon State Park and reservoir.

What you may see: hoofed mammals, small mammals, upland birds, birds of prey, fish.

GREAT SALT LAKE COUNTRY
Pioneer Trail State Park

In foothills of Wasatch Mountains on Sunnyside Avenue in Salt Lake City.

What you may see: carnivores, hoofed mammals, small mammals, songbirds, birds of prey.

Hotel Utah

Downtown Salt Lake at Main and South Temple.

What you may see: songbirds, birds of prey.

Lower Jordan River Delta

Near Redwood Road and 2300 North in Salt Lake City.

What you may see: freshwater mammals, waterfowl, songbirds, birds of prey, shorebirds, wading birds.

Great Salt Lake Shore

Exit 104 off Interstate 80.

What you may see: waterfowl, birds of prey, shorebirds, wading birds.

Lake Point

Northwest corner of Oquirrh Mountains, Tooele exit off Interstate 80.

What you may see: hoofed mammals (elk).

Timpie Springs

Near Rowley exit off Interstate 80.

What you may see: waterfowl, birds of prey, shorebirds, wading birds.

Rush Lake

Off Utah Highway 36 near Stockton.

What you may see: waterfowl, songbirds, birds of prey, shorebirds, wading birds.

Vernon

Near town of Vernon on Utah Highway 36.

What you may see: hoofed mammals, small mammals, birds of prey.

Dimple Dell Regional Park

Salt Lake County Park on 9400 South.

What you may see: hoofed mammals, small mammals, upland birds, songbirds, birds of prey, reptiles and amphibians.

Snowbird Mountain Trail

At Snowbird Resort on Utah Highway 210.

What you may see: hoofed mammals, small mammals, songbirds, birds of prey, wildflowers.

White Pine Lake

Up Little Cottonwood Canyon on Utah Highway 210.

What you may see: hoofed mammals, small mammals, songbirds, wildflowers.

MOUNTAINLAND
Mount Timpanogos Wilderness

Timpooneke trailhead off Utah Highway 92.

What you may see: hoofed mammals, small mammals, songbirds, birds of prey.

Cascade Springs

Near Utah 92 at junction of Forest Road 114.

What you may see: small mammals, songbirds, fish, reptiles and amphibians.

Bridal Veil Falls

On U.S. 189 east of Orem.

What you may see: hoofed mammals (mountain goats).

Provo Bay

South of Provo near Exit 263 of I-15.

What you may see: small mammals, waterfowl, birds of prey, shorebirds, wading birds.

Steele Ranch

Near Santaquin exit of I-15.

What you may see: hoofed mammals (elk and mule deer).

Mount Nebo Scenic Loop

Off Utah Highway 132 east of Nephi.

What you may see: hoofed mammals, small mammals, upland birds, songbirds, birds of prey.

Indianola Wildlife Management Area

On U.S. 89 south of U.S. Highway 6 near Sanpete County line.

What you may see: hoofed mammals (elk and mule deer).

Strawberry Valley

Near intersection of U.S. 40 and Forest Road 131.

What you may see: hoofed mammals, small mammals, waterfowl, birds of prey, fish, shorebirds, wading birds.

Rockport State Park

Off U.S. 189 south of Interstate 80.

What you may see: hoofed mammals, small mammals, waterfowl, songbirds, birds of prey, shorebirds, wading birds.

Henefer-Echo Wildlife Management Area

Just north of junction of I-84 and I-80.

What you may see: hoofed mammals, small mammals, upland birds, songbirds, birds of prey.

Hole-in-the-Rock

On the north slope of the Uinta Mountains south of Lone Tree, Wyoming.

What you may see: hoofed mammals, small mammals, songbirds.

Ptarmigan Loop

Hike on Forest Trail 117 on north slope of Uinta Mountains that begins at Henry's Fork trailhead.

What you may see: hoofed mammals, small mammals, upland birds, songbirds.

Whitney Basin

Whitney Reservoir area off Utah Highway 150.

What you may see: hoofed mammals, freshwater mammals, waterfowl, songbirds, birds of prey.

Bald Mountain

Trailhead of Utah Highway 150 in Uinta Mountains.

What you may see: hoofed mammals, small mammals.

DINOSAURLAND
Mirror Lake Nature Trail

At Mirror Lake Campground of Utah Highway 150.

What you may see: hoofed mammals, small mammals, songbirds.

Sheep Creek

Sheep Creek Canyon off Utah Highway 44.

What you may see: hoofed mammals, small mammals, songbirds, birds of prey, fish.

Flaming Gorge Reservoir

Northeastern corner of Utah reached by U.S. 191.

What you may see: hoofed mammals, waterfowl, birds of prey, shorebirds.

Lucerne Peninsula

Peninsula of Flaming Gorge Reservoir reached by Utah Highway 43.

What you may see: hoofed mammals, small mammals, waterfowl, songbirds, birds of prey, wading birds.

East Uinta Mountains Drive

Drive from Manila on Utah Highway 44 to its junction with U.S. Highway 191.

What you may see: hoofed mammals, small mammals, songbirds, birds of prey, wildflowers.

Diamond Mountain

Near Jones Hole Fish Hatchery east of Vernal.

What you may see: hoofed mammals, upland birds.

Ouray National Wildlife Refuge

Off Utah Highway 88 reached via U.S. Highway 191.

What you may see: hoofed mammals, waterfowl, songbirds, birds of prey, shorebirds, wading birds.

Pariette Wetlands

Near Myton on U.S. 40.

What you may see: small mammals, waterfowl, songbirds, birds of prey, shorebirds, wading birds.

Yellowpine Trail

Starts at Yellowpine Campground on Forest Road 134 reached from Mountain Home.

What you may see: hoofed mammals, small mammals, songbirds.

Strawberry River Wildlife Management Area

Southeast of Fruitland reached by U.S. 40.

What you may see: hoofed mammals, small mammals, freshwater mammals, waterfowl, songbirds, birds of prey, fish.

Indian Canyon

Sixteen miles south of Duchesne on U.S. 191.

What you may see: hoofed mammals (elk and mule deer).

CASTLE COUNTRY
North Skyline Drive
Intersects Utah 31 about eight miles east of Fairview.

What you may see: hoofed mammals, small mammals, birds of prey.

Huntington Canyon
Begins on Utah 31, 12 miles west of Huntington.

What you may see: hoofed mammals, small mammals, freshwater mammals, songbirds.

Desert Lake Waterfowl Management Area
South of Elmo reached on Utah Highway 10.

What you may see: freshwater mammals, waterfowl, songbirds, birds of prey, shorebirds, wading birds.

Joes Valley Ski Trail
West side of Joes Valley Reservoir reached by Utah Highway 29.

What you may see: hoofed mammals, small mammals, birds of prey.

PANORAMALAND
Elks Knoll
Off Skyline Drive south of Ephriam Canyon.

What you may see: carnivores, hoofed mammals, small mammals, upland birds, songbirds, birds of prey.

Ferron Reservoir Interpretive Trail
East of Mayfield near National Forest Campground on Ferron Reservoir reached by Forest Road 022.

What you may see: small mammals, songbirds, birds of prey, wildflowers.

Hogan Pass
Northeast of Loa on Utah Highway 72.

What you may see: hoofed mammals, small mammals, birds of prey.

Fish Lake Basin
Near junction of Utah Highways 24 and 25.

What you may see: hoofed mammals, small mammals, waterfowl, songbirds, birds of prey, shorebirds, wading birds.

Chalk Creek
In U.S. Forest Service area east of Fillmore.

What you may see: hoofed mammals, small mammals, songbirds, birds of prey, reptiles and amphibians.

Fish Springs National Wildlife Refuge
Reached by old Pony Express Road 30 miles east of Nevada border.

What you may see: waterfowl, songbirds, birds of prey, shorebirds, wading birds.

Clear Lake Waterfowl Management Area
South of Delta reached by Utah Highway 257.

What you may see: carnivores, waterfowl, songbirds, birds of prey, shorebirds, wading birds.

Fremont Indian State Park
Near exit 15 of I-70.

What you may see: hoofed mammals, small mammals, songbirds, birds of prey, reptiles and amphibians.

Otter Creek Reservoir
East of Circleville off Utah Highway 62.

What you may see: hoofed mammals, small mammals, waterfowl, birds of prey, shorebirds, wading birds.

COLOR COUNTRY
Big Flat
East of Beaver off Utah Highway 153.

What you may see: carnivores, hoofed mammals, small mammals, songbirds, birds of prey.

Parowan Front
I-15 frontage road between Cedar City and Summit.

What you may see: hoofed mammals (mule deer).

Pine Valley

In Dixie National Forest reached via Utah Highway 18 and Forest Road 035.

What you may see: hoofed mammals, small mammals, songbirds, birds of prey.

Snow Canyon State Park

Eleven miles north of St. George on Utah Highway 18.

What you may see: small mammals, songbirds, wildflowers, reptiles and amphibians.

Lytle Ranch Preserve

Southwestern corner of Utah south of Shivwits.

What you may see: carnivores, small mammals, freshwater mammals, songbirds, birds of prey, reptiles and amphibians.

Joshua Tree Natural Area

On border of Arizona reached by I-15 Littlefield exit.

What you may see: carnivores, small mammals, songbirds, reptiles and amphibians.

Zion National Park

On Utah Highway 9 one mile east of Springville.

What you may see: hoofed mammals, small mammals, songbirds, birds of prey, reptiles and amphibians.

Tom Best Loop

Begins at junction of Utah Highway 12 and Utah Highway 22.

What you may see: hoofed mammals, small mammals, songbirds, birds of prey.

Escalante State Park

Two miles west of Escalante on Utah 12.

What you may see: small mammals, waterfowl, songbirds, birds of prey, shorebirds, wading birds.

Aquarius Plateau

North of Escalante reached via Utah Highway 12.

What you may see: hoofed mammals, small mammals, songbirds, birds of prey.

Boulder Mountain

Drive between Boulder and Torrey on Utah Highway 12.

What you may see: hoofed mammals, small mammals, upland birds, songbirds, birds of prey.

Henry Mountains

Southwest of Hanksville reached by Utah Highway 95.

What you may see: carnivores, hoofed mammals, small mammals, songbirds, birds of prey.

CANYONLANDS
Natural Bridges National Monument

West of Blanding off Utah Highway 275.

What you may see: hoofed mammals, small mammals, songbirds, reptiles and amphibians.

San Juan River

Between Sand Wash put-in three miles west of Bluff and Mexican Hat.

What you may see: hoofed mammals, small mammals, waterfowl, songbirds, birds of prey, wading birds.

Elk Ridge

Off South Cottonwood Creek Road southwest of Blanding.

What you may see: carnivores, hoofed mammals, small mammals, upland birds, songbirds, birds of prey.

Devil's Canyon Campground

North of Blanding on Utah Highway 191.

What you may see: hoofed mammals, small mammals, songbirds, reptiles and amphibians.

Canyon Rims Recreation Area

North of Monticello on U.S. 191.

What you may see: hoofed mammals, small mammals, upland birds, songbirds, birds of prey.

Dead Horse Point State Park
West of Moab on Utah Highway 313.
What you may see: hoofed mammals, small mammals, songbirds, birds of prey, reptiles and amphibians.

Old LaSal
On Utah Highway 46 about 16 miles from U.S. 191.
What you may see: hoofed mammals (elk).

LaSal Loop
Southeast of Moab via Utah Highway 128.
What you may see: hoofed mammals, small mammals, upland birds, songbirds, birds of prey, reptiles and amphibians.

Cisco to Moab Drive
Begins two miles north of Moab on Utah Highway 128.
What you may see: hoofed mammals, small mammals, waterfowl, birds of prey, wading birds.

Appendix D
National Wildlife Refuges in the Intermountain Area

UTAH
Bear River Migratory Bird Refuge
58 South 950 West Brigham City, UT 84302
(435) 723-5887, (435) 723-8873 Fax
<r6w_brr@mail.fws.gov>

Fish Springs National Wildlife Refuge
PO Box 568 Dugway, UT 84022
(801) 831-5353, (801) 831-5354 Fax
<r6w_ory@mail.fws.gov>

Ouray National Wildlife Refuge
266 West 100 North, Suite 2 Vernal, UT 84078
(801) 789-0351, (801) 789-4805 Fax
<r6w_ory@mail.fws.gov>

ARIZONA
Bill Williams National Wildlife Refuge
60911 Highway 95 Parker, AZ 85344
(520) 667-4144, (520) 667-4015 Fax
<r2w_bw@mail.fws.gov>

Buenos Aires National Wildlife Refuge
PO Box 109 Sasabe, AZ 85633
(520) 823-4251, (520) 823-4247 Fax
<r2w_bar@mail.fws.gov>
<Wayne_Shifflett@mail.fws.gov>

Cabeza Prieta National Wildlife Refuge
1611 N. Second Ave. Ajo, AZ 85321
(520) 387-6483, (520) 387-5359 Fax
<r2w_cp@fws.gov>

Cibola National Wildlife Refuge
Route 2, Box 138 Cibola, AZ 85328-9801
(520) 857-3253, (520) 857-3420 Fax
<r2w_ci@mail.fws.gov>

Havasu National Wildlife Refuge
PO Box 3009 Needles, CA 92363
(760) 326-3853, (760) 326-5745 Fax
<r2rw_ha@mail.fws.gov>

Imperial National Wildlife Refuge
PO Box 72217 Yuma, AZ 85365
(520) 783-3371, (520) 783-0652 Fax
<r2rw_imp@mail.fws.gov>

Kofa National Wildlife Refuge
356 W. First St. Yuma, AZ 85366-6290
(520) 783-7861, (520) 783-8611
<r2rw_ko@mail.fws.gov>

Leslie Canyon National Wildlife Refuge
c/o San Bernardino National Wildlife Refuge
PO Box 3509 Douglas, AZ 85608
(520) 364-2104, (520) 364-2130 Fax
<r2rw_sb@mail.fws.gov>

San Bernardino National Wildlife Refuge
PO Box 3509 Douglas, AZ 85608
(520) 364-2104, (520) 364-2130 Fax
<r2rw-sb@mail.fws.gov>

IDAHO
Bear Lake National Wildlife Refuge
PO Box 9 Montpelier, ID 83253-1019
(208) 847-1757, (208) 847-1319 Fax
<dick_sjostrom@fws.gov>

Camas National Wildlife Refuge
2150 East 2350 North Hamer, ID 83425-5030
(208) 662-5423, (208) 662-5525 Fax
<gerry_deutscher@fws.gov>

Deer Flat National Wildlife Refuge
13751 Upper Embankment Rd. Nampa, ID 83686-8046

(208) 467-9278, (208) 467-1019 Fax
<elaine_johnson@fws.gov>

Grays Lake National Wildlife Refuge
74 Grays Lake Rd. Wayan, ID 83285-
5006
(208) 574-2755, (208) 574-2756
<mike_fisher@fws.gov>

Kootenai National Wildlife Refuge
HCR 60 Box 283 (Westside Rd.)
Bonners Ferry, ID 83805-9518
(208) 267-3888, (208) 267-5570 Fax
<dan_pennington@fws.gov>

Minidoka National Wildlife Refuge
961 East Minidoka Dam Rupert, ID
83350-9414
(208) 436-3589, (208) 436-1570 Fax
<mike_r_johnson@fws.gov>

Oxford Slough WPA
1246 Yellowstone Ave., Ste. A-4
Pocatello, ID 83201-4372
(208) 237-6616, (208) 237-6617
<terry_gladwin@fws.gov>

NEVADA
Anaho Island National Wldlife Refuge
c/o Stillwater National Wildife Refuge
PO Box 1236 Fallon, NV 89407-1236
(702) 423-5128, (702) 423-0416 Fax
<donna_withers@fws.gov>

Ash Meadows National Wildlife Refuge
HCR 70, Box 610-Z Amargosa Valley,
NV 89020
(775) 372-5435, (775) 372-5436 Fax
<eric_hopson@fws.gov>

Desert National Wildlife Range
c/o Desert Complex 1500 North Decatur
Blvd.
Las Vegas, NV 89108-1218
(702) 646-3401, (702) 646-3812 Fax
<dick_birger@fws.gov>

Fallon National Wildlife Refuge
c/o Stillwater National Wildife Refuge
PO Box 1236 Fallon, NV 89407-1236
(702) 423-5128, (702) 423-0416 Fax
<richard_grimes@fws.gov>

Moapa Valley National Wildlife Refuge
c/o Desert Complex 1500 North Decatur
Blvd.
Las Vegas, NV 89108-1218
(702) 646-3401, (702) 646-3812 Fax
<dick_birger@fws.gov>

Pahranagat National Wildlife Refuge
PB Box 510 Alamo, NV 89001-0510
(775) 725-3417, (775) 725-3389 Fax
<dick_birger@fws.gov>

Ruby Lake National Wildlife Refuge
HC 60 Box 860 Ruby Valley, NV
89833-9802
(775) 779-2237, (775) 779-2370 Fax
<kim_hanson@fws.gov>

Sheldon National Wildlife Refuge
c/o Sheldon/Hart Mountain Complex
PO Box 111 Lakeview, OR 97630-0107
(541) 947-3315, (541) 947-4414 Fax
<mark_strong@fws.gov>

Stillwater National Wildlife Refuge
PO Box 1236 Fallon, NV 89407-1236
(702) 423-5128, (702) 423-0416 Fax
<richard_grimes@fws.gov>

About the author . . .

Mark Gerard Hengesbaugh is a freelance writer who lives in Salt Lake City, Utah. For the past six years Hengesbaugh has been researching and writing articles about the native plants, animals, and landscapes of the Intermountain West. He spends most of his free time tramping the West's backcountry and animal watching with his wife, Jean. His monthly column, "Wild Things," is published in *Utah Outdoors* magazine. He is a contributing editor for *Sports Guide* magazine, as well.

Hengesbaugh's stories usually have a natural history, travel, or local culture component. He frequently writes for *Salt Lake* magazine, has written cover stories for *Salt Lake City Weekly* and *Mountain Times*, and writes feature articles for *The 'Bird* (Snowbird resort's in-room magazine), *Utah Business* magazine, *Catalyst* magazine, and the now-defunct *Network* magazine. Newspapers that have published his articles include the *Austin-American Statesman*, the *Los Angeles Daily News*, and the *Deseret News*.

A former feature editor and feature writer for *Clipper Today* newspaper in Layton, Utah, and a former technical writer and analyst with Dan Jones & Associates in Salt Lake City, Hengesbaugh came to writing from the production end of the publishing process. He spent 25 years designing, composing, and printing magazines, books, newspapers, and brochures. In 1986, he began his own typesetting and graphic design company in Salt Lake City. In 1989 he published his first book, *Typography for Desktop Publishers*, which was published by Dow-Jones Irwin (now McGraw-Hill).

Hengesbaugh was born in Flint, Michigan, in 1951 and has lived in the Intermountain West for 25 years.

About the contributing artists . . .

Steve Dewey has a B.S. in plant science from Utah State University, an M.S. in agronomy from Montana State University, and a Ph.D. in crop science from Oregon State University. He is co-author of *Weeds of the West* and *Utah-Wyoming-Montana Weed Management Handbook*. He was recently appointed to the national Invasive Species Advisory Committee.

Rick Egan studied photography and journalism at Brigham Young University. He has been a staff photographer for the *Salt Lake Tribune* for 16 years. He lives in Layton, Utah, with his wife, Erin, and three children.

Rick A. Fridell has been photographing wildlife for nearly ten years. After receiving a B.S. in wildlife biology from Kansas State University and an M.S. in wildlife ecology from the University of New Hampshire, he joined the Utah Division of Wildlife Resources in 1991. He is the southern region's native aquatic project leader.

Alan Huestis is owner of Fast Focus Productions and Studio 404 in Logan, Utah. Alan has over 25 years of experience behind video and still cameras and covers diverse assignments that take him underwater, up in the air, and around the world.

Photojournalist **Steve Howe** covers remote wilderness journeys. His essays and images have appeared in *National Geographic* books, *Outside, Backpacker, Climbing, Summit,* and *National Parks* magazines. Howe has been editor of *Sports Guide* and a columnist for *Summit, the Mountain Journal.* He is Rocky Mountain field editor for *Backpacker* magazine and a videographer for *Anyplace Wild,* a PBS series.

William H. King is a Salt Lake businessman whose passion is native wild flowers and alpine plants. He is a board member and past president of the Utah Native Plant Society. In addition, King is

program director for the Wasatch Rock Garden Society.

Mitch Mascaro was born and raised in Salt Lake City, Utah, but moved to Logan in 1987 to attend Utah State University, where he graduated in communications. Mitch is chief photographer at Logan's *Herald Journal.*

Dan Miller's photography career began in 1979 at *Utah Holiday* magazine. He has been a staff photographer at the *Salt Lake Tribune,* Logan's *Herald Journal* (as photo editor), and *Lakeside Review.* Currently he is a freelance photographer and book designer. His book credits include *High in Utah; Visions of Antelope Island and Great Salt Lake;* and *Utah! A Family Travel Guide.*

Mark Parchman's photographs have been published in various books and magazines and most depict Colorado, Wyoming, and Utah. You can see more of his images at <www.imagesfromnature.com>. He lives in northwest Colorado.

Brent R. Paull's photographic career began with a trip to Yellowstone in 1985. The adventure led to his photo awakening and to his first travel article, which included four wildlife photos and was printed by the *Deseret News.* Paull was born near San Francisco, California, and went to school at Gavilan College and Brigham Young University.

Karen Riddell is a native Utahn who is self-taught in "art making." Riddell has won many awards for her work in fine art and in illustration, including a 1996 National Resources Defense Council International ECO Award.

Dick Spencer is a freelance nature photographer from Utah's Cache Valley. He photographs smaller creatures for the challenge of getting close. Dick enjoys sharing his experiences with others through his nature slide programs and by displaying his original color photos at art fairs.

Ron Stewart is regional wildlife conservation outreach manager for the Utah Division of Wildlife Resources. He has been a reporter, photographer, and Peace Corps volunteer. He received a biology degree from the University of Utah and received a M.S. in communication from Utah State University.

Bob Sutton is a professional photographer based in the high desert community of Apple Valley, California. He has photographed wildlife throughout the United States and has an extensive image library.

S. John Wilkin grew up in Rochester, New York, and received his M.F.A. in photography and art history from St. Vincent College in Pennsylvania. He began his career at the *Catholic Courier* in Rochester and earned over 20 awards there. In 1997, John moved to Ogden, Utah. Until recently he was a staff photographer for Logan's *Herald Journal*.

Index

Compiled by Jean Houger Hengesbaugh

population density, 11, 13
status, 11, 14
tips for viewing, 11
TreeUtah, conservation organization (UT)
on Jordan River, 107, 108
Trout, Al, Bear River Migratory Bird Refuge Manager
quoted on birds, 77–78
quoted on Nature Conservancy, 140
Trout (fish), natives versus introduced species, 92

Utah Birdline, hotline for sightings, 151
Utah (State of)
animals and plants at risk, 90
bald eagle viewing, 152
best bird watching times, 148
growth of bird watching, 145, 169
rural population density (1940), 1
urban population density (2001), 1, 145, 166

Walters, Bob, Utah Division of Wildlife Resources, Watchable Wildlife Coordinator
as developer of park for watching Burrowing Owls, 30
quoted on Burrowing Owls, 30, 32
quoted on cholera deaths in birds, 23
Weeds
building roads or ski runs, 97, 118–19
defined, 95, 96
habitat loss examples, 95

noxious or dangerous (for animals), 97
rate of spread and means, 96, 97
removal of, 97–98
Whooping Crane. *See* Cranes
Wierenga, Otto, Alta Ski Resort General Manager, quoted, 115
Willey, Dr. David, University of Alaska-Fairbanks, Professor of Biology, quoted on owls, 9, 10–11
Williams, Bob, U.S. Department of Fish and Wildlife, quoted, 135–36
Windham, Dr. Michael, Utah Museum of Natural History, Curator of Garrett Herbarium
quoted on Burke's and Maguire Mustard, 63, 64, 65
quoted on Moss Campion, 60, 61
Wixom, Hartt, wildlife writer, quoted, 128
Wyss, Larene, Salt Lake Birders member, quoted, 149–50

Yellowstone National Park
coyotes breeding, 126
cranes at, 82
elk herds at, 93
gray wolves loss at, 89

Zablan, Marilet, U.S. Fish and Wildlife Service Biologist, quoted on Utah prairie dogs, 29
Zion's National Park (UT), Mexican spotted owls, 7
Zwinger, Ann and Beatrice Willard, authors of *Land Above the Trees*, 62